The Scream of

A Suitable Passion

Copyright © 2017 by Bud Suiter

All rights reserved. No part of this publication may be used or reproduced by any means, graphic, electronic or mechanical, including photocopying, recording, taping or by any information storage retrieval system without the written permission of the publisher except in the case of brief quotations in critical articles.

The information in this book is distributed on an "as is" basis, without warranty. Although every precaution has been taken in the preparation of this work, neither the author nor the publisher shall have any liability to any person or entity with respect to any loss or damage caused or alleged to be caused directly or indirectly by the information contained in this book.

Suiter Publishing books and publications may be ordered when available in Kindle electronic form, and in hard copy through Amazon.com and retail outlets.

Background on author Bud Suiter and Suiter Publishing is found on the Suiter Publishing Facebook Page. Because of the dynamic nature of the Internet, web addresses or links may have changed since publication and may no longer be valid.

ISBN: 978-0-9853806-9-4
Suiter Publishing
Printed by CreateSpace

Foreword

This is a collection of short stories focused on how we become car enthusiasts.

I'm a gearhead. I became one long before the first recorded use of the word. Miriam Webster notes that first occurred in print in 1974. Miriam Webster also describes a gearhead as a person who pursues mechanical or technological interests - as in automobiles. Or computers. Brits use the term petrolheads for gearheads when it comes to cars.

I'll limit gearheads to those with passion for domestic and foreign automobiles living on the west side of the Atlantic.

The popular press often lumps gearheads and fans together as *enthusiasts*, as in *Road & Track* is an *enthusiast's* magazine. In *The Scream of an Engine*, I argue that gearheads are extreme enthusiasts, fans less so.

Fans are different from gearheads: fans love cars; gearheads are passionate about them. Fans aren't as excited about fixing their cars themselves. Having someone else make their cars perfect is OK. That's part of the fan package. Both fans and gearheads are more interested in technical features than the average vehicle buyer who's more turned on by convenience, efficiency, fuel economy and resale value. Or could care less about cars in the first place.

As a gearhead, I love the eagle-like scream of a road-going V-12 at 9,000 RPM, older Formula 1 V-12 engines hitting 18,000 RPM. My gearhead pulse races as a V-12 engine starts.

The Scream of an Engine

I savor a double overhead cam - DOHC - four ripping from 4,000 to 8,000 RPM, like my Alfa race car, or an inline DOHC six Jaguar XK120 accelerating from 2,000 RPM.

And the bull-like burble and roar of a big V-8. Whining, purring superchargers and turbochargers are OK. Tachometers essential. Six or seven speed manual transmissions are better than three, four or five speeds. Synchromesh preferred. Paddles OK.

Sounds are a critical element of the automotive experience for me, on back-country roads or at race tracks. With sounds come smells: of burning oil, a whiff of gasoline and the heady aroma of smoking rubber.

Behind the wheel, I love the feel of a smooth, firm suspension at work in a high-speed S-turn. Colorful trees and shrubs streaming rapidly by in a blur while I'm negotiating the S-turn, with the top down, blue skies above and hair whipping in the wind. Steering that's both quick and sensitive to the road surface, picking up the feel of the undulating pavement. Smooth transitioning from left to right, the car quickly setting up on the opposite side.

Giddy feeling in the chest. Pulse rising.

Alert to wild animals jumping out of the forest on both sides of a mountain road. Grinning when it all comes out just right.

To complete the picture, an elegant exterior design is critical. The Scaglietti bodied Ferrari 250 Testa Rosa, Alfa Romeo T-33, D-Type Jaguar or Ford GT 40 are preferred to others I know.

Fifties American gearheads like me focus on earlier *European* cars – as in my case – particularly Alfa Romeo, Jaguar, Sprite and Mini

The Scream of an Engine

Cooper race cars, sports cars and sports sedans. We also love American versions of European cars like Ford's Sixties Cobras and GT40s.

This list dates me but is accurate if not complete.

But it's not only about the hardware, the steak, but also the race car drivers, the flavorful sauce of motor racing. These individuals especially affected my car culture and I share stories about my top influencers.

Next, follow the stories of the industry personalities that shaped my passion for cars. These men fired my imagination and built my life-long allegiances.

Then the enduring magic of the names and places of the world's road racing: Watkins Glen, Sebring, Elkhart Lake, Andrews Air Force Base, Silverstone, Brands Hatch, Marlboro, Le Mans, Reims, Ramey Air Force Base, Cumberland, Brooklands, Goodwood and more.

The memories of the cars, the drivers, the industry giants and the race courses still excite and inspire me all these years later.

How is an automobile gearhead made? Is it just the scream of an engine? What other factors influence a person to become an enthusiast? What is the turning point? We'll discover the answers to these tough but decipherable questions.

Along the way, we encounter the imminent end of the internal combustion engine. And wonder what becomes of the enthusiast when the scream of an engine is history.

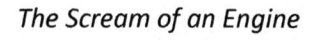

The Scream of an Engine

Acknowledgements

My experience with cars is enriched by many.

For this book, special acknowledgement goes to Fred Puhn, engineer, car builder and racer and Chuck Engberg with forty-nine years of racing experience and an eye for technical detail. They both reviewed the draft manuscript of *The Scream of an Engine*. Their many observations and corrections have enriched the result.

I'm still responsible for what's left.

I want to thank my wife Gaynor whose artistic talents are displayed on the cover and who encouraged me to complete the book.

Several groups of car people enrich this story.

Car owners, friends, race car drivers, car industry personalities, and *journalists.* Many of their stories are told here.

These individuals helped create my suitable passion originally and helped me better understand what that passion is all about today.

Most important of all, I acknowledge my parents, Bud and Dee Suiter, who made my car culture acceptable, clear, interesting and exciting. Yes, I blame them for much of this.

Cover: Tazio Nuvolari's 1934 Alfa Romeo P3, winner of the 1935 German Grand Prix. Author Bud Suiter at the wheel in the photo. Car is pictured at the San Diego Automotive Museum, November 2008, owned by Jon Shirley. Artwork by Gaynor Coller Suiter.

The Scream of an Engine

Table of Contents

Foreword iii

Acknowledgements vii

Table of Contents ix

Chapter One: Cultural Phenomenon 1

Chapter Two: Perspective 7

Chapter Three: Our Culture 15

Chapter Four: My Culture 19

Chapter Five: The Tractor 33

Chapter Six: The Car 43

Chapter Seven: The MG A 45

Chapter Eight: The Alfa Romeo 55

Chapter Nine: Racing 59

Chapter Ten: Race Drivers 87

Chapter Eleven: Characters 143

Chapter Twelve: Race Courses 157

The Scream of an Engine

Chapter Thirteen: Kit Cars 179

Chapter Fourteen: The Sprite 183

Chapter Fifteen: My Turn 189

Chapter Sixteen: The Finish Line 211

Chapter Seventeen: Time for a Maserati 213

Chapter Eighteen: First Ford 221

Chapter Nineteen: The Jaguar 225

Chapter Twenty: Second Ford 235

Chapter Twenty-One: Hail Storm at a Classic Car Show 241

Chapter Twenty-Two: Automotive Design 249

Chapter Twenty-Three: Rally 255

Chapter Twenty-Four: Autocross 261

Chapter Twenty-Five: The Heart of the Matter 265

Chapter Twenty-Six: Epilogue 333

Appendix I. Automotive Revolution 343

Appendix II. Museums 367

Suggested Reading 389

Chapter One: Cultural Phenomenon

Cars are a cultural *phenomenon* with a brief history compared with the human experience. Other cultural characteristics of our species have been as important or more so compared with cars: the evolution of language, the Industrial Revolution, democracy, religion, art, music, the Internet, Johannes Gutenberg or universal education. Many of these have developed over hundreds or thousands of years, the Internet a little quicker.

But no other cultural phenomenon in the human experience has happened as quickly and pervasively as the one for cars, except for one: the Internet. The Internet is arguably a close tie, all things considered. Both cars and the Internet took less than a decade from their beginnings to become global and well-entrenched. Cars from roughly 1900 to 1910, and the Internet from roughly 1994 with the emerging pre-eminence of the World Wide Web, and into the early 2000s.

Cars affect every aspect of the human condition, from jobs to mobility to pollution. The car industry is big, brutal, exciting, mature - even with all the changes coming - and profitable for the survivors. Cars are one of our most important cultural changes.

Cars, like horses before them, are an outlet for our aggression, a natural human trait, and at the same time a way to dissipate tension, anger and unhappiness. To experience adventure. As Steve McQueen so often did simply by going for a ride. A way to re-discover joy in life.

Matteo Giacon says in his recent two-part analysis of the cross-cultural impact of automobile design, *'In my opinion, the automobile changed the world in such a way that all other significant inventions or events are secondary when they are compared with it. With it, we have seen a new way to live, a new way to build things, a new way to market things and services and a new way to consume them; before its introduction, the world had never changed so much in the topography, as well as in the climate and in such a short time, like the last 140 years.'*[1]

High speed mobility for individuals in the early twentieth century with the wherewithal was just too compelling to pass up.

Everyone jumped in: car engineers, manufacturers, buyers, repair garages, after-market parts suppliers, research and development ventures. Horse and buggy and horse-drawn wagons were relegated almost overnight to becoming yesterday's solution for personal transportation and hauling.

Today, about one hundred forty years after the production automobile market officially started with the 1886 German patent issued

---

[1] Daniel Strohl reporting excerpts from Matteo Giacon's *The Italian Influence on American Cars*, Hemmings Daily, February 19, 2017

to Karl Benz, total light Vehicles in Operation (VIO) in the U.S. have reached a record level of more than two hundred fifty million. Nearly twelve million cars are scrapped each year, with an average age of vehicles on the road now above eleven years.[2]

Led by U.S. sales of pickups, sport utility vehicles and crossovers, automakers sold 17.55 million vehicles in 2016 — besting the previous record of 17.47 million set in 2015. And 2015 was the best since 2000, per Autodata Corp.[3] These figures for total vehicles sold are described as including cars, SUVs, crossovers and light trucks, but excluding heavy trucks and motorcycles, golf carts and 4X4s.

This means that the Vehicles In Operation in the U.S. is increasing by roughly five million vehicles a year while owners are keeping cars longer.

In 2016, the number one best-selling vehicle in the U.S. is the Ford F-150 truck series, by a large margin, at 820,799 units sold. This is the basis for the Ford ads which say, 'America's Number One brand.' The number one best-selling car, the Toyota Camry at 388,618, way behind the Ford truck, is down 9.5% this year compared with last, while the number one best-selling SUV, the Toyota RAV4 is up over 11% to 352,139; SUVs, crossovers and light trucks, in total gained in sales over 2015; total sales of cars only are down compared with 2015. There is a massive shift underway in the types of vehicles buyers prefer with SUVs, light trucks and crossovers now accounting for 63% of the U.S. market.[4]

---

[2] 24/7 Wall St., Douglas McIntyre, July 2014
[3] The Detroit News, January 5, 2016
[4] Autodata statistics from the Los Angeles Times at http://www.latimes.com/business/autos/

There's no longer anywhere to park these five million net new cars, SUVs, light trucks and crossovers delivered in the U.S. each year. Garages at home are full, so cars spill out onto driveways and streets, freeways are jammed for four to eight hours a day, and finding a parking spot in today's major metropolises is difficult – and expensive – at best.

And it's not just in the U.S.: China is now the biggest annual market for cars with cities like Beijing suffering the worst pollution in the world, followed by the U.S. market and the western European market.[5]

We're busy building cars for these markets, folks. The top three manufacturers worldwide in 2016 are non-U.S. companies: Volkswagen, Toyota and Hyundai, although General Motors and Ford aren't far behind.[6]

Today we see a drastic change in car culture coming, like the one at the beginning of the twentieth century, only faster. Mobility is still key today for all of us. But private ownership of vehicles has become problematic in the days of city crowding, lack of economic parking, polluted air especially in cities, and freeway traffic jams that have extended commutes from twenty minutes to two hours on the same roads.

The automotive industry has never experienced such rapid changes as those occurring today.

---

[5] Wikipedia, 1-17

[6] Bestsellingcars.com. Sixth through tenth are 6. Nissan, 7. Fiat Chrysler, 8. Honda, 9. Suzuki, 10. Renault. Manufacturing rather than selling by country in 2016: 1. China, 2. U.S., 3. Japan, 4. Germany, 5. India, 6. South Korea per MSN.com 8-17

The internal combustion engine, our bread and butter propulsion system, is on its way out over the next two decades. Autonomous vehicles will take over heavy lifting in the cities even sooner. New car automotive ownership will decline in favor of much less costly solutions such as those provided by autonomous ride-sharing vehicles from Uber, Lyft, Gig and others.

Gasoline and diesel fuels usage will decline sharply as the internal combustion engine phases out. Fewer highway deaths will occur and insurance rates will plummet due to fewer accidents. These incredible, fundamental, imminent changes are detailed in Appendix I, Automobile Revolution.

Chapter Two: Perspective

A history of the car and of enthusiasts - gearheads and fans - provides perspective into where the passion originates.

Most serious enthusiasts today prefer the brands of cars their fathers and even grandfathers before them drooled over or aspired to or owned. Those brands were largely established in the early 1900s. The initial enthusiasts were created then.

In the late 1800s, Western culture began the shift from horse, buggy, wagons and whips to the new model: motorized, self-driven vehicles.

That part of Western culture changed fast. A most dramatic description of that change is presented in the following two photographs

The Scream of an Engine

taken ten years apart on New York City's Fifth Avenue. From 1900 to 1910, horses were removed from their previous role of dominating human transportation and hauling in The City.

*New York City's Fifth Avenue, **1900**: Horses and buggies prevail.* San Diego Automotive Museum

*New York City's Fifth Avenue, **1910**: Cars prevail.* San Diego Automotive Museum

Chapter Two: Perspective

The Scream of an Engine

Today, the advantages of cars over horses for transportation seem obvious. But it wasn't always so. In the early 1900s, many towns required car owners to place a man walking and holding a lantern in front of a car as a safety measure. This reduced the speed advantage of cars but didn't last long, analogous to speed limits being proposed today for autonomous cars by the European Union until Internet bandwidth can handle increased vehicle speeds.

Horses must be fed daily and their manure cleaned up regularly. Manure and urine were a huge problem in large cities like New York during the summers: bad smells and heavy fly infestations resulted. The city's population of 120,000 horses produced nearly 1,320 tons of manure per day, all of which had to be cleaned up and transported for disposal.[7] No easy task, this. No wonder the car caught on fast.

Horses had to go. The scream of an engine had nothing to do with replacing horses. Cars became easier to use and rapidly collected more fans.

For example, early cars were hand cranked to start. If the owner forgot to retard the spark first, a backfire could occur. The resulting pushback on the crank broke the wrist of many an unsuspecting car owner, or worse, an arm or shoulder.

Charles F. Kettering's development of the electric starter was the direct result of a Cadillac breaking the jaw of a close friend of Henry M. Leland, head of Cadillac. Medical complications including pneumonia led to Henry's friend's death.

---

[7] *American Heritage Magazine,* Joel A. Tarr, October 1971

The Scream of an Engine

Upon hearing this news, Henry vowed, "The Cadillac car will kill no more men if we can help it." [8]

Leland made good on his promise by incorporating Kettering's electric starter in all Cadillacs in 1912, the first car company to do so.

From early on, cars were raced. This is where the scream of an engine comes into play. Fans developed an appreciation for the scream and the speed.

In Europe, the Paris to Rouen Race in 1894 is credited with being the first organized automobile speed contest. It was promoted by *Le Petit Journal*. In the U.S., the first race was sponsored by *The Chicago Times-Herald* in 1895. It ran from south Chicago to Evanston and back.

Henry Ford raced one of his early creations in October 1901 in Grosse Point, MI – and beat the favored Alexander Winton. Ford was then able to attract investors to his new car company in 1903.[9] He turned this great promotional tool of racing over to Barney Oldfield. Barney then barnstormed across the country promoting the brand and creating fans. Henry focused on building low price cars in great quantities.

In England, the first purpose-built paved race track in the world was constructed at Brooklands in 1907. More on Brooklands can be found in Appendix II, Museums. While museums were not part of my early car culture, today they've proliferated. Young would-be-enthusiasts can take advantage of what museums offer. Since I've visited many, I tell the story of what I've found in Appendix II.

---

[8]Bernstein, Mark. 1996. *Grand Eccentrics: Turning the Century: Dayton and the Inventing of America*. Wilmington: Orange Frazer Press, p*19*
[9] Motorsport.com

The Scream of an Engine

To supply the rapidly burgeoning demand for cars, car builders proliferated. Over eighteen hundred car manufacturers started operations between the late 1800s and 1930. Only a handful survive today, like Ford, General Motors and Fiat Chrysler. Seventeen manufacturers arose in St. Louis alone between 1905 and 1910. None survive today. But builders surfaced everywhere, especially in and around Detroit, MI, South Bend, IN, Springfield, MA and Auburn, IN.

One of the seventy manufacturers with a name commencing with 'W', like Wasp and Winton, that no longer exist is Willys-Overland. Willys-Overland lasted from 1912 through 1953, when the factory was closed. Yet Willys-Overland was the second largest car producer after Ford between 1912 and 1918 and later won the largest production contract for making their famous Jeeps used during World War II.

There were no guarantees of long term success.

The list of companies whose name started with 'A' alone that failed during the first years of manufacturing is staggering, numbering over one hundred-thirty in the U.S. only.[10] Just a few of the more colorful 'A' company names: ABC, Ace, Aerocar, Albatross, Apollo and Auburn. Many of these were splendid vehicles in their day, like the Auburns built in Auburn, IN.

The Auburn Automobile Company produced vehicles from about 1900 through 1937, just six years before I was born. An Auburn reverse merger with Cord in 1924 and the joining of operations with Duesenberg in 1926 produced iconic American vehicles. The 1935 *Auburn 851 Boattail Speedster,* for example, was powered by a 4.6-liter straight eight that could top 100 MPH. Then there was the supercharger option.

---

[10] Wikipedia, December 2016

The Scream of an Engine

The esteemed automotive designer Gordon Buehrig penned this Auburn Speedster design, as well as the 1929 Stutz Blackhawk Le Mans cars and the 1956 Continental Mark II. Quite a diverse talent, Buehrig.

Buehrig worked for Stutz at the time he drew the Blackhawk. As a sidebar to the Stutz story, the much earlier Stutz Bearcat's low weight, balance, and power made it an excellent racer, winning twenty-five of thirty races in 1912. In 1915, a stock Bearcat was driven by Erwin 'Cannon Ball' Baker from California to New York in eleven days, seven hours, and fifteen minutes, shattering the previous record and inspiring the later Cannonball Run race and film spin-offs.[11]

1935 Auburn 851 Boattail Speedster – one sold for about $650K in early 2017. Note the elegant Buehrig fender treatment. Beaulieu Museum, September 2017

One of my personal favorites from E.L. Cord's wide-ranging offerings is the Duesenberg Model SJ. A 1930 Duesenberg Model J

---

[11] Wikipedia, November 2016

Chapter Two: Perspective

Dual Cowl Phaeton sold for $880,000 at the Barrett-Jackson Auction in Scottsdale, AZ., January 2017. The short wheelbase, 125-inch long, version, now called SSJ, also had a short build run: two cars. One went to actor Gary Cooper, the other on loan to Clark Gable who already owned a Model J. Hollywood buyers carried Duesenberg during the Depression.

Fred and Augie Duesenberg, the brothers who made Duesenberg cars, cut their teeth building racing engines in the 1920s before selling out to Cord. These high-powered double-overhead-cam straight eight engines were then built by another Cord company, Lycoming, in the 1930s, which Cord acquired in 1927. As used in the Duesenberg J series, the engine produced 265 horsepower per the brochure, six times the power of a contemporary Model A Ford.[12] Then there was the supercharged version.

This brief background suggests that the factors creating enthusiasts originated with the beginning of the auto industry. When I came along in the Forties, patterns were well established to create car enthusiasts, fired by the cars of the Thirties and earlier.

As you will see, friend Fred Puhn, like me, was attracted to Thirties cars. He found a Cord in the Fifties for $1,000. But he couldn't raise the cash and settled for a Studebaker.

---

[12] Chris Summers, the Auburn Cord Duesenberg Club's Duesenberg historian, wrote that the Model J Lycoming-built engine produced only around 200 BHP. The result was that the engine had to be rebuilt from the ground up, tuned and tested again to produce the claimed power of 265 BHP, unsupercharged, before being installed in a car. Dennis Simanaitis in a blog 11-15: https://simanaitissays.com/2015/11/06/duesenberg-horsepower-but-which-one/

But the beauty and boldness of these cars – and others like the 1930 Cadillac V-16 Model 452 and the 1934 Packard Twelve LeBaron Runabout Speedster – are never forgotten.

I became aware of the cars described above as part of my cultural immersion. I assembled a 1914 Pierce Arrow Model 48 in red plastic from a kit when I was eight. Why? My Dad told me they were classy cars. Introduced in 1913 with a six-cylinder 38 BHP engine and a 142-inch wheel base, this was an upmarket vehicle accounting for most of Pierce sales from 1913 through 1916.

Founding President of the San Diego Automotive Museum Board of Directors Gil Klecan and his wife Blan own a two-seater 1913 Pierce-Arrow, among an impressive and diverse collection of cars. Gil convinced the Ford Dealers of San Diego to become the founding sponsor of the Museum in 1988.

Let's continue with the building of a gearhead, me.

Chapter Three: Our Culture

We're the product of the culture we're raised in. That culture has now come to include a steaming cup of coffee with a group of enthusiasts who gather to talk about cars.

Cars and Coffee is a term that describes the gathering that takes place one day a month or so. *Cars and Coffee* has become part of the automotive experience.

With the help of a car enthusiast and the auspices of the San Diego Automotive Museum, I started a *Cars and Coffee* in Balboa Park, San Diego, in 2008. There were many obstacles, but we finally prevailed. Early birds showed up to get the best parking spots before the coffee was ready. From the second *Cars and Coffee*, SDAM attracted over one hundred cars to each event, filling to overflow the Balboa Park parking spaces in front of the Museum.

In the broadest sense, we adopt the religions, political views, sports preferences and product preferences of our culture. The cultural sub-group with the most influence is probably the family. Within family, mothers will have the greatest influence on habits of cleanliness, dress, books and study habits. Fathers will have the most influence on sports, beverages and automotive preferences.

Both parents influence religious, racial and political preferences based on what their parents taught them. In most cases, one parent provides the most influence.

Of course, there are exceptions to cultural influence on individuals. Some become aggressively anti-culture: whatever the parents or the society in which they live believe, they choose to believe the opposite.

Cultural influences are local, national and international. In the U.S., regional cultural differences are vivid in religious matters, tolerance of skin color or family country of origin. Acceptance of the outcome of the Civil War, one hundred and fifty years after it ended, is still up for grabs in some southern households.

We are shaped by our culture. Mine allowed British sports cars in before I was ten. Culture affects our preferred design of cars.

A good example of this is a 'modified' car known as the *low rider*.

Aside from a few cars built for racing, the National Historic Vehicle Register has yet to include any modified cars. This omission is being addressed in 2017. Lowriders, customs and hot rods – collectively, modified cars - will be recognized going forward by the Register.

The first – and most colorful – of these three classifications, the low rider, is exemplified by Jesse Valadez's *Gypsy Rose*, the 1964 Chevrolet Impala Sport Coupé. Traditionally, the low rider is a 'chopped' or lowered and otherwise modified American coupé or sedan. Lowriders are a Latin American product, with special roots in Mexico and southern California. Paint jobs on lowriders are artistic miracles. One uniquely low rider trick is to install hydraulic pumps on the suspension at each corner of the low rider. When the feature is activated, each corner of the car rises and falls independently as the car progresses slowly down the street.

Gypsy Rose is fuchsia-colored, adorned with hand-painted, multihued roses. It's hot-pink interior includes swivel seats in the front and a cocktail bar and two small chandelier-like light fixtures in the back. Valadez, founding member and president of the East Los Angeles Imperials Car Club, is credited with establishing the design themes for lowriders. The Petersen Museum in Los Angeles once described his *Gypsy Rose* as the most influential low rider ever built.

Constant cruising along Los Angeles's Whittier Boulevard during the Sixties, along with nationwide exposure in the opening credits to *Chico and the Man*, an NBC sitcom that ran from 1974 to 1978, and in the 1979 movie *Boulevard Nights* helped put the lowrider on the map.

Custom cars abound in car shows and parades throughout America. I met one car owner displaying the ninth Mercury custom he's personally built over the years. This was at the Time Machine Car Show in Surprise, AZ, in March 2017. His latest is purple. A gorgeous purple, chopped and lowered, with many detail modifications like flush door handles to express his individual taste and his mechanical ability.

The Scream of an Engine

The third category of modified cars, *hot rods*, is perhaps best exemplified by Bob McGee's 1932 Ford roadster. Bob's car had just as much influence on hot rods as *Gypsy Rose* on lowriders.

McGee began work on the Ford 'Deuce' in 1947 after returning from World War II, lowering the front end with a drop axle and the rear with a special frame. He added a 237-cu.in. 1934 Ford flathead V-8 from another Deuce roadster he built before the war. The body itself received many modifications, from the three-piece aluminum hood to the concealed door hinges to the 1946 Pontiac taillamps.[13]

Car culture, a key part of the influences on enthusiasts, is divided many ways: geographically, by manufacturer, by type of car – sedan vs sports car, for example - racing, rallying, commuting, drive-ins and drive-throughs, domestic vs imported, over the road long distance trips vs around the block, social vs competition and much more.

I'm the product of my culture. Each of us is the same in that no two are alike in our automotive preferences. An auto fan might be a Chevy fan; almost no way he'll like Fords. An auto fan might prefer NASCAR racing; almost no way he'll also favor Formula 1. Once a Chevy fan, always a Chevy fan.

But only one of these two cars can be called my favorite: Fords.

---

[13] Hemmings Daily, March 21, 2017

Chapter Four: My Culture

If culture is a major contributor to each person's opinions and decisions, as I fervently believe, my culture contributed to my becoming a gearhead and to the cars I like.

Merriam-Webster defines culture as enlightenment and excellence of taste acquired by intellectual and aesthetic training, or acquaintance with and taste in fine arts, humanities and science as distinguished from vocational and technical skills.

I must disagree with Merriam-Webster: in my view, vocational and technical skills are an intimate part of one's culture. There is a many-faceted car culture, including science and engineering. Vocational and technical skills are part of that culture.

Finally, generalized statements such as the U.S. has a culture of materialism are common. Probably misleading as well, since each person, each enthusiast, has his or her own unique culture which runs counter to oft-heard generalized statements.

My parents, family and childhood friends fomented my culture: family focused, from an early age inspired toward learning and a college education, coconut cake with white icing for birthdays, pursuing adventures and especially including cars.

My parents, Bud, Sr. and Dolores Suiter were normal enough until they got behind the wheel of a car. Photo circa 1940

A person's culture can change. Oddly, my car passions haven't changed. My brother, Ron, raised in the same culture I was, never cottoned to cars. He became an airplane gearhead and worked for thirty-two years for McDonnell Douglas and Boeing.

Dad always drove too fast. He told us stories about the family Studebaker. In one of these, he released the brake, without the engine on, and steered and coasted the Studebaker down the hill from their home in Dormont, PA, a suburb of Pittsburgh. He was eight years old at the time in 1919 and took some heat from his father Charles for this downhill escapade. Even after years of racing cars on tracks, he still drove too fast on public streets.

Mom always drove too fast, too. Like the time she and my brother Ron were following Dad and me home on the four-lane highway past Westminster, MD. Mom decided to race us and had the advantage: a new Ford two-door sedan with the Y-block V-8 Police Interceptor engine. The night was cold so the top was up on our 1955 MG A which gave us a few more MPH. As the speedometer needle on the MG crept toward 90 MPH, the engine screaming in top gear, the side curtain flaps were sucked out horizontally by the wind stream.

The MG had automatic windows when driven fast enough.

And Mom accelerated right past us. Of course, the MG speedometer was optimistic, so we probably weren't going 90 MPH. Mom modelled at Walters Academy in Baltimore. She was usually a calm influence in our lives when not racing Dad.

Mom could exhibit a soft touch, too, when driving. Once we were returning home in a snowstorm from Baltimore to our farm west of Westminster. It was already dark. As we came down the slope to cross the reservoir, Mom was driving 40 MPH, well below the speed limit. When she touched the brake to slow down further, the car entered a 360-degree skid from which there was no recovery. Black ice under the snow. As my brother who was in the back-seat recalls, the car stopped about a foot from a telephone pole. Mom never said a word but calmly put the car in first and slowly accelerated up to speed again. We arrived home safely.

We gained our culture from her, too, when she would say things like, 'If you can't say something nice, don't say anything at all.' I still try to abide by that, although if another driver cuts me off, I forget this part of my cultural upbringing.

Mom always supported Dad in his wild schemes, like raising two sons on a Maryland farm or going sports car racing.

Dad liked fishing. For years, he proudly displayed a stuffed marlin over his desk at the office. We always found time for a little fishing. I caught a crab fishing with him in Ocean City, MD when I was six. Later in my forties, I'd take Dad fishing for albacore off San Diego. We caught big fish. That's no fish story.

Dad's father, Charles Spurgeon Suiter, passed away at the age of forty-two in 1925 before Dad's twelfth birthday. The family didn't talk much about the cause, but from tidbits overheard, most likely heart disease. My grandmother, who never remarried, teared up when talking to me about Charles fifty years after Charles passed. Before his demise at an early age, Charles had several careers, including as pharmacist at a Pittsburgh pharmacy, and editor of the *Loch Haven Express*, a local Pittsburgh, PA newspaper, where he increased circulation twenty-five percent during his tenure. He later had a stint in animal husbandry with the U.S. Department of Agriculture.

Dad's family was musical. Every Sunday my grandmother Leola played the piano, Dad played the violin and Charles sang. Leola was self-taught: she never took a lesson. Charles sang in a church choir and with a semi-professional group that was in demand locally to sing for special occasions.

After Charles passed away, the family scrambled for income. Dad produced photographic copies and enlargements from negatives in the family basement dark room which were sold for cash. Leola learned bookkeeping which helped the family remain afloat.

The Scream of an Engine

Because Charles was a Freemason, Dad qualified for the Patton Trade School in Elizabethtown, PA, a Masonic boarding high school for families in their situation. Grandma had one less mouth to feed at home.

At Patton, classes were offered in two trades: brick laying – from the stonemason trade group started in the late 1300s - or tool and die. Dad selected the latter. He also played guard on the Patton football team at the hefty weight of 145 pounds. After graduation, he joined the aircraft industry with Glenn L. Martin Company in Baltimore, MD.

At Glenn L. Martin, Dad earned kudos for solving a previously intractable windshield cracking problem on PBM Mariner airplanes. 1,366 twin engined, Patrol Bomber and Marine PBMs were built to support the U.S. effort in World War II and later as passenger planes. With their ability to land and take off on water, PBMs became the plane of choice for rescuing downed pilots or crews of sunken freighters. PBMs competed with the better known Consolidated PBY and first flew in February 1939.

Dad left Glenn L. Martin to form his own tool and die company, Chase Engineering. During World War II, Chase manufactured mortar aiming tubes in huge quantities for the war effort. There were other war related contracts. The company prospered after the war making children's watches and magnetic tape recorders, in addition to the bread and butter tool and die business.

After the war, Dad became Grand Master of the Baltimore Masonic Lodge. He acquired two airplanes, a used twin-engined Cessna T-50, a light cargo/five passenger, Jacob radial engine airplane developed in 1939, and a new V-tailed single six cylinder opposed engine Beechcraft Bonanza Model 35 developed in 1947. He flew them everywhere. The Cessna, with longer range, was selected to fly on business trips to and from Chicago from Baltimore. Dad hired a professional pilot for these cross-country trips.

Dad told stories about his cars, like the '32 Ford Coupé with the flathead V-8. This new for '32 Ford designed V-8 was 3.6-liters with 65 BHP, in U.S. production in various forms for twenty-one years until replaced by the Y-Block V-8. He said he got all four wheels off the ground going over railroad crossings. Or the 1938 Lincoln Zephyr, top end car of the Ford family in its day. Lincoln wasn't a separate division of Ford until years later in 1955.

We kids flew along on the Sunday airplane rides. On one flight, I rode shotgun in the Bonanza. Dad turned to me and said, 'Go ahead, drive.' I took the second, duplicate wheel in front of the front passenger seat and 'steered' for a few minutes. Scared me silly.

Our family owned a maroon 1941 Mercury two-door coupé in 1947. On a trip one day, Mom turned left onto the alley at the foot of our street. The passenger door popped open. I fell out. The chassis flexed so much turning into the alley that the latch wouldn't hold the door shut. No damage to four-year old me. We were barely moving at the time. But the Mercury disappeared from the family garage.

By the late 1940s, the stories switched to cars Dad didn't own, like the new Jaguar XK 120 which was the fastest production sports car of its day just starting to arrive in America. He attended the newly formed Sports Car Club of America sports car races at Bridgehampton, NY and Watkins Glen, NY and got to know the cars, the drivers and the mystique of post-World War II sports car culture in America.

The Scream of an Engine

A newer version of our Beechcraft Bonanza that I 'steered' at age five in 1948. Google Images

Aston Martin and Jaguar

This story requires telling since it defines my car culture for the next sixty years.

Dad managed to drive both an XK 120 and an Aston Martin DB 2 in the 1951-time frame. He reported that the DB 2 had 'very heavy' steering. He preferred the Jaguar. This simple event affected my car culture: no matter what the facts are, to this day I prefer Jaguar over Aston Martin.

Later, by filling in the details on these two makes, I could better defend my position. And still do today.

Aston Martin commenced its adventures in the car business in 1913, producing its first car in 1915, well before Jaguar. After World War II, industrialist Sir David Brown – knighted by Queen Elizabeth II in 1968 - had the opposite experience from my father: his time behind the wheel of the Aston Martin Atom – a 2-liter, four-cylinder saloon car with tubular space frame and aluminum body - convinced Brown to purchase Aston Martin for the sum of £20,500 in 1947. Remember: this is back in the day when a pound was a pound.

Brown saw the classified advertisement for a 'high class motor business' in London's *The Times* newspaper. Two men, Sutherland and Hill, developers of the Atom in 1939, were retained as employees and instructed to begin development of a new Aston Martin model based on the Atom prototype.

Meanwhile, in 1948 Brown also purchased the British automaker Lagonda for £52,000, believing that its recently developed 2.6-liter inline six-cylinder engine would be a good match for future Aston Martin automobiles. The six was later increased to 3-liters and became an Aston Martin staple through the 1959 Le Mans 24-Hour race win.

The first product to come from the new 'Brown' Aston Martin was the 2-Litre Sports, a two-seat roadster introduced in 1948. Styled by Frank Feeley, it was reminiscent of the Atom yet more conventional in appearance, thanks in part to a traditional grille, and powered by the same 2-liter four added to the Atom in 1944. The model might have been a success, but for the concurrent introduction of the Jaguar XK120, a higher-performance model priced at £500 less than the Aston Martin.[14]

Today, Aston Martin's cars are at the top of the automotive pyramid. But my culture doesn't include them as favorites.

Jaguar's story is different. Jaguar was home-built instead of acquired.

---

[14] Hemmings Daily, February 20, 2017

Sir William Lyons was knighted by Queen Elizabeth II in 1956, twelve years ahead of Brown. In my book, another win for Jaguar. It took a while to get there but by 1956 everyone knew about Jaguar's contributions to the Empire.

Lyons at eighteen owned a Sunbeam 'oil bath' motorcycle. He was then selling Sunbeams for a dealer in Blackpool, England, having just completed an engineering apprenticeship at Crossley Motors in Manchester. The year was 1919.

By age twenty-one, Bill Lyons owned a Norton and bought a Swallow sidecar for it. He admired the cleverly designed 'octagonal shaped' Swallow sidecar that friend William Walmsley was building and selling. Walmsley's garage was just across the street from where Lyons lived with his parents in Blackpool.

Lyons then suggested to Walmsley that the business Walmsley had started could be expanded. Walmsley liked Lyons ideas. With parent financial support, the pair founded the Swallow Sidecar Company in 1922. They secured a larger facility. Soon the changes in the Swallow design, along with production line methods adopted and an increased sales effort led to growing popularity of the Swallow. William Walmsley, ten years Lyon's senior, built the Swallows and Lyons sold them.[15]

With success came more ideas and the pair expanded into automobile building by the mid-1920s. Starting with the Austin engine and chassis, a two-seater painted in two colors - most cars were black or single color at the time – was soon followed by a four-door saloon, or sedan, car.

---

[15] http://www.jag-lovers.org/library/lyons.html, 1995, and Wikipedia, 2017

With production of cars increasing from twelve to fifty a week, Swallow Sidecar Company was moved to the Midlands area of England in 1928. The Foleshill Factory near Coventry brought Coventry's nearby skilled labor supply and industrial resources. The Coventry area would be the manufacturing center of the company for the next seventy years.

Soon, Swallow integrated its own chassis design with the Austin 16 engine, calling the result the S.S. 1 and 2 in 1931. With the Depression well underway, S.S. cars were bargain priced and offered design flair.

S.S. Jaguars then appeared in the lineup in 1935, the first time the Jaguar name was used. William Heynes was hired to run the growing engineering department and Harry Weslake to design the first Jaguar engine.

The result was the very stylish SS 100 Jaguar. Philip Porter put it this way, "The SS 100 was the company's first genuine sports car and to many people it remains the epitome of the stylish pre-war sports car, Lyons at his flamboyant best. The beautiful, flowing feline shape suggested speed and when the new 3.5-liter engine was added to the range, a car of vivid performance was the result".[16]

World War II necessitated a name change to Jaguar Cars, Ltd., since the SS initials brought an unpleasant post-War connotation.

The XK 120 arrived in 1949 with the new William Heynes/Harry Weslake 3.4-liter XK engine and the rest is Jaguar history. And my history, too.

---

[16] Phillip Porter is an automotive writer and publisher of Jaguar books, often quoted in the press. http://www.porterpress.co.uk/

The Scream of an Engine

Just a few years later, 1951 to be exact, I was aware of and passionate about these new Jaguars.

I carved a model Jaguar XK 120 C out of a block of pinewood at age nine. Dad aspired to buying an XK 120 sports car then, talked about it, showed me pictures. The XK 120 C was Jaguar's competition version of the street sports car. The XK 120 C won Le Mans in 1951 and 1953. A kid just doesn't forget that stuff.

I raced my model XK 120 C on the family garage floor against other blocks of wood. The course? I copied the Sarthe, Le Mans, France 8.2-mile-long circuit. I still have this Jag in my extensive model car collection, rubber tires in place, steering wheel and gear shift lever now lost, the original windscreen departed. I raced this car hard.

How fast was the XK 120 C? The *Road & Track* August 1953 road test estimated a top speed of 141 MPH, 0-60 in 6.6 seconds, with a test weight of 2550 pounds and the 3.4-liter motor delivering 210 BHP. My model wasn't that fast.

Jaguar XK 120 C at a modern vintage car race, North Island Naval Air Station, San Diego, CA, October 1999. A similar Ecurie Ecosse Scottish racing team XK 120 C with credentials sold for $13.2 million in 2015

Chapter Four: My Culture

The Scream of an Engine

My Jaguar XK 120 C model race car which I carved out of a single block of pine wood in 1952, now missing parts like the windscreen and steering wheel in this photo taken in 2017, sixty-five years later

The die was cast.

I was an avid reader of *Road and Track* magazine in 1952, first published in June 1947, five years earlier.

Road and Track focused on the new wave of post-World War II European cars and racing, especially in Europe. John Bond became editor and publisher in 1952, about the time I became hooked. Bond is still one of my automotive idols. Circulation today is 607,000 per issue, six issues per year instead of the twelve that had been the rage for years. Monthly magazines are going the way of the fax machine.

Again, cultural bias worked in the magazine field: *Hot Rod* magazine commenced in 1948 and focused on customized U.S. automobiles, drag racing and street performance enhancements.

Motor Trend – *MT* - started publishing in 1949, focusing on the U.S. market with less about racing. For example, *MT* announced Cadillac as their Car of the Year award winner in 1949 for the new overhead valve V-8 engine.

Chapter Four: My Culture

I rarely read *Motor Trend* or Hot Rod due to my cultural bias.

Then along came *Hemmings Motor News*, founded in 1954 by Ernest Hemmings in Quincy IL. *Hemmings* moved to Vermont with then owner Terry Ehrick in the late 1960's. The new ownership by American City Business Journals, Inc. of North Carolina took control in 2002. *Hemmings* capitalizes on nostalgia and connecting gearheads and fans with historic cars, parts and stories, mostly American but including European. I read *Hemmings* every day because it taps into nostalgia more than anything else.

Car and Driver entered the fray in 1955 as *Sports Cars Illustrated*, featuring European small cars, like *Road and Track*. Karl Ludvigsen broadened the content in 1961 to include 'Detroit Iron' and further expanded to include everything *Road and Track* offered, except being first. Loyalty still dictates which one I read.

By 1958, the *Competition Press* newspaper commenced and covered all racing, but especially racing sports cars and modified sports cars. It morphed into *Competition Press & Autoweek* in 1964 when new car reviews and industry news were added. In 1975 the name was shortened to *Autoweek*.[17] I'm an avid reader of their online publications due to my cultural upbringing favoring racing.

On my first trip to England in 1972, my wife Brooke and I rented a Mini, ideally suited to the narrow two-lane roads we traveled. The return suitcase carried English motoring publications like *Motor* and *Autocar*. And more than one specialty magazine about Jaguars. *Motor* was founded in 1903 and lasted through 1988. *Motor* and *Autocar* are or were both excellent enthusiast publications.

---

[17] Wikipedia, December 2016

Top Gear magazine, related to the BBC show of the same name, was first published in 1993 and now is the largest selling car magazine in the UK.

I stuck with *Road and Track* from the beginning and still subscribe today. Even though other magazines quickly became global and do exceptionally well at reporting the automotive news. Like the car business, the magazine business is very competitive and prolific.

But let's proceed to more factors that affected my car culture.

Chapter Five: The Tractor

In April 1951, my family relocated from Baltimore, MD to a one hundred nineteen-acre farm in Carroll County, MD, just forty miles west of Baltimore. I turned eight the week we moved the furniture in. There is nothing quite like starting a new adventure with a birthday party.

The farm is where I met the tractors that contributed to my gearhead trajectory.

Our two-story farmhouse was a five-bedroom older home without central heating or indoor plumbing. But it featured a wide porch across the front and down one side with an unobstructed view of the creek about forty yards away amidst the huge pastures. My brother Ron was five and our parents were somewhat older.

Our farm was nestled in the rolling hills of northern Carroll County, six miles west of Westminster, the county seat. This was just south of the Pennsylvania line - $54^0 40'$ N latitude, the dividing line between North and South in the Civil War - and only a mile or so from Union Mills. Union Mills is a very small town named for the day the Union Army marched through the town on July 2, 1863, traveling from Washington, DC to Gettysburg, PA.

We were surrounded by other farms about the same size as ours. We all entered or exited our farms on dirt roads. The nearest paved road was a three-eighths mile drive north up a hill from our farm to Maryland 140 which connected Westminster to Union Mills, Silver Run and parts west. That dirt road is the one my brother and I walked each day to catch the school bus on Maryland 140. The bus delivered us to Charles Carroll Junior High School. The school name was a misnomer. First through eighth grades were offered.

My Dad had spent summers on a family farm near Pittsburgh, PA, where he grew up. He was the driving force to share that positive experience with his two growing sons. Mom would have preferred to stay in Baltimore. But she was a good sport and went along with the plan. Our move was probably based on nostalgia for the good old days when small family farms were important to the future of the country and to the economy. We participated in the reality of the declining economic importance of small farms with marginal profitability in the best of years.

We also joined the Soil Bank.

The USDA Soil Bank program, Title I of the Agricultural Act of 1956, had multiple purposes: reducing production of basic crops – there was a surplus in the U.S. during those years - maintaining farm income and conserving soil. That's how we and our neighbor farms

The Scream of an Engine

made the most money farming in the 1950's. We thrived by Uncle Sam paying us to not plant crops.

The plan was for my Uncle Charlie, Dad's brother, to run the farm that we'd call Four Lakes Farm – although we built only two over the next six years. Uncle Charlie's two daughters were fun and a year or so younger than we were. My brother Ron and I looked forward to spending more time with them.

Meanwhile, Dad continued his tool and die business in Baltimore, an hour's commute each way from the farm. We soon committed to fifteen Holstein dairy cows. My Uncle Charlie was thereby committed to a seven day a week, ten-hour per day work schedule. There were no breaks or holidays. Uncle Charlie learned to work hard in the U. S. Army, a skill he now put to the test.

The whole scheme worked for about two years. Our new farm held lots of promise.

Like the big red barn complete with silo and separate corn crib, equipment shed and chicken coop, and eighty acres or so on which we could plant crops out of the total of one hundred-nineteen. Twenty acres of woods provided new white oak fencing for the pastures or as a product to sell on the open market.

We soon added two rooms to the back of the house, a brand-new kitchen and a separate bathroom with all the modern amenities. Sears put new white asbestos siding on the outside as we anticipated the coming of winter. This is before anyone knew about asbestos' darker side. The revelation that asbestos killed came from research in the Sixties.

A forced air central heating system replaced the kerosene room heaters after a harsh winter. We filled the equipment shed with two tractors, plough, mower, post hole digger, hay rake, corn planter, spring tooth harrow, and a 'sub-soiler' – an advanced farming device which aerated soil to a depth of thirty inches, allowing moisture and nutrients to penetrate deeply into the earth.

At thirty inches depth, it was difficult to pull that sub-soiler. So, we upgraded the Ferguson TO-20 transmission from four forward speeds to twenty. Wide open in new first gear, the tractor would pull the sub-soiler. However, the speed was so slow that it was easy to step off the tractor while it ran forward, walk around it and get back on the other side. I tried that for the fun of it.

Dad wanted to employ the most advanced farming techniques. After a fire destroyed the original barn and silo in January 1954, and threatened everything else including the farmhouse. Our new barn was equipped with drying fans so that green hay, rather than field dried hay, could be harvested and dried in the barn. This way the alfalfa leaves stayed on the stalk, for example. The cows appreciated that.

This was to be a working farm with all the trimmings: chickens soon filled the coop; milking Holsteins and Shropshire sheep filled the barns. Later, geese, rabbits and a Great Dane or two were added to the mix.

The farmhouse was plenty big enough for four kids and four adults and the arrangement started out on strong footing. Especially when we raised the forty-foot-high TV antenna uphill from the farmhouse using the front loader on one of the tractors. We could then receive signals from all three Baltimore television stations.

Before the new dirt road was bulldozed the three eighths of a mile distance directly to Maryland State Route 140, we drove out the opposite end of the farm on an unpaved single lane road to an unpaved county road that eventually led to the State Route 140.

The Scream of an Engine

This back-end farm road became quickly impassable when it rained or snowed hard.

The way out on this back-end farm road consisted of navigating two dirt tracks with a grass strip down the middle. The design helped hold the road in place and reduce washouts. But when the tracks grew wet, cars sunk into the mud and bottomed on the grass strip. Then tires started to spin, even knobby winter snow tires, until they got hot and smoked.

At that point, Uncle Charlie or Dad would fire up a tractor to pull out whoever's car was stuck in mud or snow. Day or night, no problem. There were lots of stuck cars.

One day that first summer on the farm, Uncle Charlie drove the Ferguson tractor with mowing bar attached into the pastures to cut weeds. The cows and sheep just wouldn't eat everything. Especially thistles. Thistles quickly multiplied, became unsightly and snagged animals and people passing by.

Soon Uncle Charlie returned to the farmhouse on foot.

I was the only person home. He announced that the tractor was stuck in the creek bed and asked me to drive the second tractor to pull the first out. At the tender age of eight, I was to have my first shot at driving a motorized vehicle.

Uncle Charlie drove our used Ford 8N tractor out of the equipment shed. He carried a towing chain across this lap. The Ford 8N was the most popular farm tractor of all time in North America.

I hopped on the back of the tractor. Up the pasture we went. The cows and sheep grazing nearby watched.

The Scream of an Engine

The Ford 8N tractor came new in gray with the engine/transmission painted red: our used 8N was an exception and was painted all-gray just like our brand-new Ferguson TO-20. Over 350,000 Ford 8N tractors were sold, all using the English Ferguson patented three-point implement attachment system at the rear which the Ferguson also carried. They were very similar tractors.

1951 Ferguson Model TO-20 tractor like ours, very similar in appearance to the Ford 8N, but with 20 BHP rather than 16. The 30 BHP Model TO-30 replaced this model in 1952. Over 60,000 TO-20s were sold.
TractorData.com

Soon the Ford was attached to the Ferguson. From my position in the driver's seat on the Ford, Uncle Charlie asked me to hold the clutch down until he signaled. He moved the gear shifter into first, the throttle set to 'just open.' Then he ran back and jumped up on the Ferguson.

'OK,' Uncle Charlie shouts to me over the noise of both motors, 'let the clutch out slowly, and when I say, push it down again.'

The Ferguson pops out of the creek, wheels spinning, mud flying everywhere. I'm instructed to put the clutch down again. I drive about ten feet. My first tractor experience is complete and successful. I'm out of control excited. What an adventure.

Now fully fledged, I drove the Ford back to the equipment shed, following Uncle Charlie down the pasture the way we'd come. Another tractor drive completed, this ride into the shed maybe a quarter of a mile, the second of hundreds to follow over the next six years of living on the farm and driving all the tractors.

Uncle Charlie and his family left the farm in 1953 for health reasons.

We immediately switched from Holstein dairy cattle which were milked twice a day to Herefords. Herefords weren't milked at all but were raised as meat animals. So, the new animal line up became Hereford beef cattle, Shropshire sheep, Rhode Island Red chickens, rabbits, geese and three horses. We purchased the sixteen Herefords at auction, fifteen heifers and a steer which became my 4-H project. I named him Gus.

When the truck arrived to deliver the Herefords from auction, our Great Dane, Pete, was asleep on the farmhouse porch. He missed the action of unloading these young animals off the truck and into our pasture. Pete was a huge fawn colored Dane, then about three. Suddenly, Pete woke up, raced down to the pasture, leaped over the four-foot oak board fence and barked. None of the Herefords had ever seen anything quite like this. They immediately took off running for their lives. When they reached the opposite end of the pasture, they ran right through the wire fence on that end and into the neighboring farm pasture and beyond.

It took us two days to catch the last heifer down near Union Mills and bring her back hooked with a rope to the tractor and resisting every step of the way.

The Scream of an Engine

One day, the Ford tractor needed a new head gasket. Dad asked me to replace it. I said, how do you do that? He said, there's the tool box, figure it out. I did. Parts all over the garage floor. Finally, back together again, it ran.

Dad said, 'What took you so long?'

Many tractor stories still resonate in my mind. Like me racing the neighbor's much larger red Farmall M with our Ferguson TO-20 and winning. The Ferguson had just over half the horsepower of the Farmall. Of course, I was taking advantage of using 20th speed - top gear - in the new transmission we'd installed to pull the sub-soiler. The Farmall M had only five speeds. I was twelve and our neighbor fourteen. Our parents weren't home. I don't think they ever found out.

The Farmall M, the largest of International Harvester's 'Letter Series' of tractors targeted at small to medium sized farms, was made from 1939 to 1954. The Farmall M would pull three 14" bottom plows, compared with the Ferguson's two 12" bottom plows. By the 1970s, small family farms were largely gone, replaced by 100,000 acre and grander farms that required much larger tractors than Farmall M's.[18]

Ford's license of Ferguson's power take-off and hydraulic lift system patents was later disputed by Ferguson. Ferguson won a $22/tractor payment on over 350,000 tractors Ford had sold: a tidy $7.7 million, big bucks in the day.[19]

Harry Ferguson, an Irish born British engineer, secured many patents, including those on over one hundred fifty farm implements. And he fought hard to protect his company.

---

[18] Wikipedia, 1-17
[19] Tractordata.com, 1-17

The Scream of an Engine

Ferguson also developed a four-wheel drive system for the Ferguson P99 Formula 1 car.

I was given a one-acre patch at age twelve to grow my own corn crop. I figured a way to plow right to the road bank at the end of a furrow: pulling up the hydraulic lift with the tractor in motion, which made the front end of the tractor raise up six inches off the ground, then hitting the right rear wheel brake at just the right instant with the front wheels in the air. The tractor swung right ninety degrees, I released the brake and the front end slammed down. Then I could proceed to turn into the next furrow. My Mother said, 'No way!' when she saw me employing this technique in the field one day. My Dad said, 'Don't worry, he can handle it.'

So, I kept right on plowing with my own end-of-furrow technique.

Then we acquired a long-term trial Fordson New Major Diesel, made by Ford in England, a much larger tractor at 5308 lbs. vs. 2760 lbs. for the Ferguson TO-20. This big blue model would pull three 14" bottom plows like the Farmall M, but much faster than the Ferguson could pull two 12" bottom plows. Instead of second gear on the Ferguson, we could pull more plows on the Fordson in third gear.[20] A new thrill had arrived in the equipment shed. Gearhead stuff.

Once coming down a grassy road from a hayfield with a load of haybales behind me, I had the Ferguson in first gear. Because it was late in the day and the grass was getting wet and slippery, the tractor started to slide. I shifted to second to keep ahead of the wagon and to keep from getting pushed sideways and flipped by the much heavier wagon. Next to third gear. Then I used the throttle to keep ahead of the wagon. Soon we're flying down the hill, tractor engine roaring. As the

---

[20] Ibid.

road flattened out, the road surface changed to dirt and the tractor could regain control of the wagon. Heart in my mouth for about twenty seconds there.

We now move on from tractors.

Chapter Six: The Car

I fantasized driving a car long before I earned a license. When I turned nine, Dad said, 'Take the keys and wash the Hudson' – a black 1937 Terraplane – 'in the creek.' This epic event unfolded on our Maryland farm. Driving the car to the creek involved a round trip of about three hundred yards. I secured the sponge and a bucket, put them in the Hudson and drove to the creek, stopping within a few feet of the water.

The trajectory to gearhead continued.

The Terraplane was our third car at that time, the first two were Fords. The Terraplane was black with tan cloth seats. No risk me driving the Hudson because the car was already fourteen years old.

The Scream of an Engine

1937 Hudson Terraplane like the first car I washed in the creek on our Maryland farm. Auctions America

There were 83,436 Terraplane Hudsons made that year of 1937. They were produced in four assorted flavors: Business 6, Business 6 Long Wheelbase, Deluxe 6 and Super 6. We owned the Deluxe 6. Like its brothers, all were powered by a straight-six engine of 212 cubic inches which developed ninety-six horsepower at 3900 RPM. Tires on all Terraplane models were 6.00X16. Weight started at a svelte 2370 pounds for the six models.[21]

By the 1950s, Hudsons had morphed into the admired, feared and fast Hornet. Mighty oaks from little acorns grow. The Hornet won NASCAR races by the truckload in the early to mid-Fifties. Hornets earned my admiration from the simple event of my washing a lowly Terraplane in a creek in 1952.

---

[21] http://www.carnut.com/specs/gen/huds30.html, April 2017

Chapter Seven: The MG A

The last Saturday of every month Dad and I drove north from our farm near Union Mills, MD to Hanover, PA, a trip of twenty minutes each way. Our 1953 Ford station wagon was painted off white with blue trim around the windows and sported a three-speed manual column shift. At 40,000 miles, it rattled a lot but was handy around the farm for tasks like hauling pumpkins to market and useful at Dad's tool and die shop for moving materials.

Cars lasted only forty to fifty thousand miles in those days, especially if you lived on a farm.

Dad had discovered a magazine store in Hanover that carried *Road and Track*. We'd buy a copy and drive home. Dad would tell me stories about why European sports cars were better than American sedans. I think he exaggerated here and there, like the time he said that the suspension on the new Jaguar XK-120 was so rigid that you could drive to the nearest service station on a flat tire and not damage the tire. Right.

Our brand new 1955 MG A arrived when I was twelve. The car was painted in Fifties-popular turquoise with silver wire wheels, Dunlop white wall tires, grey leather seats, grey top and black wool carpets. The metal dashboard was painted body color turquoise.

Dad wanted to race. What better way than an MG in the '50s? He was crazy about sports cars and this was his first. I loved the smell of the leather seats and wool carpeting, so different from the rest of the rubber-floormat family fleet. And the idea of 'Safety Fast' – the MG marketing slogan at the time.

Quickly, I assumed the role of cleaning this car, too, by now using a hose and spring water instead of creek water. Dad brought home carbon tetrachloride from Chase Engineering. The 'shop' as we called it had been relocated to Westminster, MD, from Baltimore by this time, reducing his commute from an hour to about twelve minutes. The company was renamed Magnetic Specialties for the magnetic tape recorders being made and sold.

I used 'carbon tet' to clean the MG's wire wheels with a tooth brush. This was before anyone knew that 'carbon tet' could kill you if it touched your skin. The fumes which I liked were also toxic.

I was hooked on MGs.

When Dad travelled on business, he asked me to drive the MG around the farm 'to keep the batteries charged.' That was tough duty. MG A's came with two six-volt batteries located behind the seats in those days. Once he left for the airport to go to Florida on business and would be gone for a week. I waited until his departing dust settled on

The Scream of an Engine

the new dirt road to the main highway. I then jumped into the MG and flew up the hill after him, intending to turn around and come back down before reaching the main highway. The main highway was off limits.

Suddenly, a cloud of dust erupts just ahead: its Dad coming back home. Seems he'd forgotten his plane tickets. I was mortified at having been caught out minutes after he left.

He thought it was funny that I couldn't wait to drive that MG. And of course, charge the batteries.

Then Dad signed up for his first Sports Car Club of America – SCCA - driver's school. Apparently, different SCCA regions approached driver training differently in those days. For example, long time racer Chuck Engberg didn't participate in one before or during his first race in 1959 in Santa Barbara, CA.

After all, Dad had been to the races at Bridgehampton, NY in 1951 and Watkins Glen, NY in 1951, 1953 and 1955, and Andrews Air Force Base in 1954, by this point. That I knew about. He was ready to race.

Dad acquired the mandatory driver's helmet, soaked his Sears-bought Oshkosh coveralls in flame retardant – 20 Mule Team Borax, or sodium borate - and installed a military aircraft style quick release seat belt on the MG. He also fabricated a 'straight through' exhaust pipe, eliminating the muffler.

The SCCA Driver's School was held in Upper Marlboro, MD, between Baltimore and Washington, in Prince Georges County, MD, about an hour and twenty minutes from the farm. Marlboro was an intriguing sports car racing facility. After a two-year period as a dirt track, what became known as the Marlboro Motor Raceway was paved in 1954.

The Scream of an Engine

I was invited to ride shotgun on the way to this barely year-old race track. Hard to turn that one down. The sound of the straight-through exhaust still resonates in my ears. I was crew for Dad's first driver's school.

The Marlboro track was 1.9-miles long with several straights – one of which provided a real high-speed run, many twisties and a NASCAR-like bowl, in the center of which were located the pits. That's where I stood taking in the sights, sounds and smells of motor racing.

The driver's school and regional races attracted budding SCCA participants like Duncan Black, Jr., son of the Black & Decker founder Duncan Black. Son Duncan later won many SCCA races in a Daimler SP 250,[22] a 4.9-liter Ferrari and other cars.

Bob Holbert, a Warrington, PA Porsche dealer, like Duncan and most others, started slowly but soon was to win four national championships in Porsches. Other names becoming recognized and racing at Marlboro included Jaguar, Porsche and Corvette driver Dr. Dick Thompson; racer, race car builder and auto entrepreneur Roger Penske, who first raced at Marlboro in 1958; and the Lavender Hill Mob founders who were also present at Marlboro for races if not the driver's schools. Holbert sold Penske Roger's first race car in 1958.

The Lavender Hill Mob, founded by Washington, DC SCCA club members, talked the SCCA into holding a national race on the Marlboro course in 1957. The Mob crammed eleven races into the one-day national SCCA program. The race track was used for fifteen years and closed permanently in 1969.[23]

---

[22] Marlboro Race Track, video of racing in color with voice over in late 1959 or early 1960: http://www.racing-sp250.co.uk/Duncan-Black.html, the sights and sounds of the day

[23] http://www.si.com/vault/1957/07/29/603115/the-lavender-mob

The Scream of an Engine

Before closing, Marlboro sponsored a 12-Hour race in August 1966. The under 2-liter class was won by an Alfa Romeo GTA driven by Sam Posey and Harry Theodoracopulos, beating all the Porsches in the process.

It will become obvious why that's important to me.

At the Marlboro track in fall 1955, we removed the MG's windshield, installed a small Plexiglas windscreen that Dad made himself, taped the headlights and went racing. On Dunlop bias ply, whitewall street tires. Those tires didn't last long. Since our family was tight on budget due partly to the 1955 recession, the worn-out Dunlop's were replaced by low cost Montgomery Ward blackwalls for subsequent outings. These are the tires in the MG A photo below.

Dad was assigned an instructor who knew MGs. Dad said that his instructor scared him silly when he gave Dad the lesson on how to drive fast. Dad said he'd no idea that the MG would do what the instructor proved it could.

After several trips to Marlboro, his logbook showed he'd achieved the mandatory track time. Dad was awarded an SCCA driver's license.

Dad was quick but liked to start from the back of the pack for driver's school races: then he would try to catch everybody in front of him. He invariably did, with one or two exceptions. One exception was a slightly newer MG A that had higher compression pistons and 72 BHP instead of the 68 BHP our engine made. Both were 1498cc.

Our MG was always right on this faster MG's bumper by the end of a lap but would lose three lengths down the main straight. In one race, the 72 BHP MG came off the bowl a little too hot, went into the next turn a little too hot, and did a slow roll over. Since this MG A was a convertible without roll bar – almost none of the cars had roll bars then - this was a big deal. Dad had seen it coming and immediately stopped. I watched from the edge of the bowl not one hundred yards away. Several other drivers stopped to help Dad and three corner workers gather around and right the flipped MG. The driver was fine. The race was restarted, and Dad beat this now wrinkled competitor with slightly more horsepower.

MG A fan, age twelve, on a victory lap at Le Mans, but really at parade rest on a Maryland farm. Original whitewall tires had been replaced with blackwalls at this point. The fan taped the numbers. Spring 1956

The other exception was a 1300cc Porsche 356 Super coupé. He never did catch that Bob Holbert-driven Porsche, which of course leads to the reason for this part of the story: the MG as stepping stone to Alfa Romeo.

But first, the Cumberland, MD SCCA National race arrived in May of 1956 and our MG was entered. Racing was conducted here from 1952 through the mid-Sixties on this short 1.6- mile course which favored smaller cars because the straights were short.

The Scream of an Engine

I attended the Cumberland race by the skin of my teeth: I was supposed to play my first piano recital in Westminster, MD that same Saturday. But I hadn't practiced my piece, anticipating the race, and finally talked my way into going to Cumberland. I was so traumatized by almost having to play a concert piece never practiced that I refused taking piano lessons ever afterward.

During practice at the Cumberland track, I was so excited I couldn't sit still. From the hill above the course, the racetrack spread out before us. The ground we sat on was covered with black cinders, most likely remnants of the coal mining industry here. A clear view presented itself for watching the cars all the way around the track. After a warm up practice with what must have numbered forty MG As, Dad pulled our MG pulled into the pits. I ran down the hill to see what was up. Mechanics were gathered around the MG, listening. The consensus was that our MG needed new rod bearings. We wouldn't be able to race this weekend. This was a common MG complaint but an immense disappointment for me.

For consolation, our family watched Jack McAfee in a Porsche 550 pass each of the three Briggs Cunningham Team long nose white D-Type Jaguars during the main event. McAfee finished second to Walt Hansgen in a British racing green short nose D-Type Jaguar, the one without the Le Mans tail fin. I loved that Hansgen won.

But as far as the MG was concerned, the die was cast: Dad decided we needed a faster, more robust car to race, one that would catch Porsches.

The MG with new rod bearings was traded in on a brand-new Alfa Romeo 'Super Spyder' Veloce. The deal to buy the Alfa was struck at Manhattan Auto in Washington, DC. I must admit that the name of this car, which I vividly remember from the dealer and sales rep talk, isn't backed up by Alfa documentation, which called it a

The Scream of an Engine

Giulietta Spider Veloce. I prefer my memory for purposes of this discussion.

This model is now known by the shorthand factory identification as a 750F: 1290cc all aluminum engine with twin Weber carburetors and dual overhead camshafts, all synchromesh four speed transmission, windup windows, and big Alfin finned aluminum drum brakes all around.

Our MG, by contrast, employed an overhead valve cast iron engine, twin SU carburetors, a four-speed transmission with synchromesh only on the top three gears, cast iron drum brakes albeit with competition brake linings, and removable plastic window side curtains instead of windup glass windows.

Technically, the Alfa was a design light year ahead of the MG A in the fall of 1956. It made 105 BHP vs 68 for our MG; although to be fair, the Alfa Owners Handbook says 90 BHP for the Sprint Veloce, the coupé version of the Spider. Maybe the Spider version got a few more horsepower. The Alfa engine was a smaller displacement than the MG's 1498ccs. Of course, the Alfa cost twice the MG. The Alfa would do 0-60 MPH in 10.6 seconds, top speed 109 MPH, the MG 0-60 MPH in 15.0 seconds with a top speed of 98 MPH - which I think required a tail wind.

But the 1955 recession took its toll on Magnetic Specialties and the company was merged with Downing Crystal Company in Westminster, MD. That didn't work out, so Dad left to find a job. This put racing the new Alfa on hold. Our race team was on a tight budget then: my brother and I raided our piggy banks so our family could bowl in nearby Westminster on Friday nights. Duck pins, of course.

Dad was selected by Proctor Silex, headquartered in Mt. Airy, MD, to manage their manufacturing plant outside San Juan, Puerto

Rico. The plant was producing 200,000 Mary Proctor steam irons a year. Over the next three years, Dad built production to one million steam irons each year. I've always wondered how one million steam irons are sold. Every year.

And he started racing the Alfa right away.

The Scream of an Engine

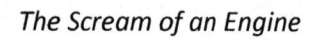

Chapter Eight: The Alfa Romeo

How is an Alfa Romeo fan created?

Perhaps its reading how Tazio Nuvolari came from way behind and won the July 28, 1935 German Grand Prix in a P3 Tipo B Alfa, beating the larger engined, faster Auto Union and Mercedes teams in the process. Or reading about Juan Manuel Fangio winning his first of five World Championships in the beautiful Alfa Tipo 158/159 in 1951. Or more recently in 2009, seeing Sophia Loren and Daniel Day-Lewis driving the streets of Rome, Italy in an Alfa Spider that looks suspiciously like the one we owned in the 1950s, for the movie *Nine*. The movie received four Academy Award nominations.

But just maybe its driving a new 1957 750F 'Super Spyder' at age fourteen like I did. In my case, I had lots of help becoming an Alfa fan.

The Scream of an Engine

These events made me into a fan. Eventually a gearhead.

Sophia Loren and Daniel Day Lewis in the 1290cc Alfa Spider for the movie, Nine

On the road, this new Italian 8000 RPM Alfa motor could be heard long before the car appeared. To say this Alfa was loud with the stock mufflers in place was an understatement.

Gary Stonesifer, my best friend at the time, said the first time he experienced the Alfa fly by his house on Maryland 140 he thought it was a fire engine. But before the new Alfa could be track tested, Dad took the job in San Juan, Puerto Rico. The Alfa was already an integral part of the family, so Dad had a friend drive the car to New York City and load her on a plane to San Juan.

Along with our Great Dane, Pete. And a Guernsey heifer that had been given to my brother to raise, then pass the first offspring to another young farmer. Dad insisted we meet that commitment, so the heifer went with us. We lived on a fourteen-acre farm south of San Juan with fruit trees and a pasture. So, we met the commitment and a calf was soon presented to another little boy on a nearby farm.

The Scream of an Engine

Soon after our arrival in Puerto Rico in October, a race was scheduled in November 1957 at Ramey Air Force Base.

General Curtis LeMay headed the Strategic Air Command. To entertain the troops, he joined with the Sports Car Club of America to sponsor sports car races on airfields across the U.S., one of which was Ramey AFB at the northwest end of Puerto Rico.

Ramey AFB was an hour and a half drive from San Juan on good roads, past Vega Baja and Arecibo. I couldn't wait to see how our Alfa stacked up in its first race. I rode to Ramey with Dad. Mom and younger brother Ron followed along in the family 1956 Ford sedan, the one with the V-8 engine with attitude.

The windshield came off the Alfa, the new Plexiglas screen went on and the headlights taped. The MG's seatbelts were now in the Alfa.

There were twenty MGs and two white Alfa Romeo 'Super Spyders' in the ten-lap race on the airport runways. The course was minimally marked with orange traffic cones. At the start, our Alfa left from the pole position and streaked into the lead. But when they came around on the first lap, Dad was last. Seems he'd missed the cones for turn one and it took him a whole lap just to catch up to the back of the pack. In a few short laps, our Alfa was solidly in first place again and won by a huge margin. This was a race car. Bring on the Porsches!

I was hooked on Alfas.

Since Dad had to fly back to Maryland often for business, it was now my job to charge the batteries on the Alfa. At age fourteen, I was experienced at this task. And our driveway was a twisty half mile long paved, single lane macadam ribbon. Unlike the Maryland farm road, there was no dust.

The Scream of an Engine

Sure enough, the one time I followed Dad down the hill on his way to the airport, he'd had to come back for something, and I was caught charging batteries again.

Pete, our Great Dane, checking the Alfa 'Super Spyder' out before a battery charging run. March 1958

Business precluded racing over the next few years, so the Alfa - Dad's daily driver - was sold as a one race winner. The car was hugely popular in San Juan and sold for nearly what we'd paid for it in Washington three years earlier. Car fans know.

Chapter Nine: Racing

Cars have always been raced. For me, following favored cars and drivers on legendary race tracks was hugely exciting. Most of my induction came before the teen years. Racing became a major part of my personal culture even before the MG A and the Alfa 'Spyder' became part of our family.

I was raised in a culture friendly to the idea of sports car racing. The organizing body for sports car racing is the Sports Car Club of America and has been from its founding in 1944. It was built on the ashes of the pre-war Automobile Racing Club of America founded by Miles and Sam Collier in 1933.

From the simple idea that the Sports Car Club of America – SCCA - directs European sports car and sedan racing in America on an amateur basis with no prize money for winners, SCCA has expanded to include American sedans – the Trans American series – open wheel racing like Formula Ford and other 'sports racing' classes that brought American V-8 power to the SCCA in a big way, including the exciting and short-lived Canadian American series from 1966 through the early Seventies.

The SCCA still conducts a national championship of its own in twenty-four different classes each year building from the first championship race in 1951. And the SCCA is not limited to imported cars and has offered professional series – with prize money – since 1962.

Today, the organizations and series that promote racing have proliferated with the arrival of more big-time professional sponsorships.

By now you've guessed I've a special passion for Jaguar, Alfa Romeo and Ford. Cultural bias. One of the reasons is that these marques are raced, often successfully.

Along the way to these becoming my favorites – most of which occurred in the Fifties, less in the Sixties, there were important side events that built my car culture. The Brits, our allies in World War II, designed and constructed exciting small sports cars in small quantities after the war and brought them to the U.S., like MGs, Austin Healeys, Ace Bristols, Aston Martins and Jaguars. British Formula 1 cars, like the Vanwall, the first English car to win a major Grand Prix – the 1957 British Grand Prix with Stirling Moss and Tony Brooks – since Henry Seagrave's win in a Sunbeam at Tours in 1923, sharpened my interest in seeing English cars on top.

This is the story about how Jaguars, Alfas and Fords raced into my life. Jaguars came first.

The Scream of an Engine

Jaguar Racing

In the early 1950s and ever after, I've rooted for Jaguars to win races. This worked for me because Alfa Romeo and Ford almost never competed directly with Jaguar, with exceptions as noted.

Those that dared to compete directly with Jaguar, like Aston Martin, Mercedes, Porsche or Ferrari were automatically enemy combatants.

Old stories from the Thirties and Forties carried forward into my indoctrination in the Fifties. Bear with me on the details as I try to recapture the thrills I discovered in racing.

William Lyons, founder of Jaguar, got in on the racing fun with the SS cars which dated from 1935. Lyons won his first and only ever race in the SS Car Club's May 1938 meeting at Donington. Lyons drove the SS 100, with Sammy Newsome a close second and Bill Heynes, Jaguar's engineering Director, third, both also in SS 100s. Lyons also set the fastest lap of the day even ahead of regular SS 100 racing drivers.[24]

Dave Garroway was the television pioneer and host who introduced NBC's 'Today' show and ran it for many years. In 1948, Garroway bought a 1938 SS 100 with the 3.5-liter engine. According to the Jaguar Heritage Museum, one-hundred eighteen of these were built. Dave then raced the car at Bridgehampton, Elkhart Lake and Watkins Glen. My Dad said he witnessed Garroway in action at Bridgehampton in 1951, but on that occasion, Garroway didn't finish. Garroway also competed in hill climbs like Giant's Despair and Mt. Equinox.

---

[24] Op.cit., Skilleter, page 32

The Scream of an Engine

Garroway's friend Walter Cronkite said that Garroway, 'like many of us, was a dilettante racer.' Garroway also worked on the SS 100 in his own garage, though, qualifying him as a gearhead. He kept the car for thirty years, saying at one time, it was his favorite possession. That's an indication this was a good car. Garroway also owned a Rolls Royce.[25]

Garroway's car was offered at Gooding and Co. auction in Scottsdale, AZ, January 2017 but not sold. The average price of other 1938 SS 100s sold recently is $385,000.[26]

The first prototype XK 120 sports car, which replaced the pre-war SS 100, was completed for the October 27-November 6, 1948 London Motor Show at Earl's Court. This was the first London Motor Show since 1938 and 563,000 attended.[27] The XK 120 was the hit of the show. Jaguar committed to build two hundred forty-eight cars with aluminum bodies and ash wood frames based on the show response.

Racing takes all forms. A big day that Jag fans recite is the measured mile that the new Jaguar XK 120, introduced just a few months earlier, achieved. On May 30, 1949 with test driver Ron 'Soapy' Sutton at the wheel the car achieved a two-way average of 132.596 MPH. Soapy was so nicknamed because he often arrived at work with shaving cream still on his face. Soapy noted the only problem in setting this record was the speedometer: it only read to 120. This record lasted until another Jaguar XK 120, most likely highly modified, did it again October 23, 1953 at 172.416 MPH.

Eventually, 12,055 Jaguar XK 120s would be built through 1954, almost all steel-bodied after the first two hundred forty-eight.

---

[25] Wikipedia, April 2017
[26] http://www.conceptcarz.com/valuation/9298/Jaguar-SS-100.aspx
[27] Wikipedia, April 2017

The Scream of an Engine

Then in August 1949 three XK 120s – aluminum bodied and possibly the only three in existence at the time - lined up for their first production car race at Silverstone. The XK 120 received the first Heynes/Weslake overhead cam XK engine, which produced a strong 160 BHP.

The three Silverstone race cars were painted red, white and blue respectively. The rear wheel covers – known as spats in England – were left on for the race. Lofty England was asked to find drivers who could win. England selected 'B. Bira,' Prince of Siam – now Thailand – to be lead driver. Bira, a pseudonym, was the first and last Thai to race in Formula 1. Bira was experienced with earlier Maserati and ERA Grand Prix cars. But Englishmen Leslie Johnson and Peter Walker finished first and second in the race. Bira led the race at the seventeen-lap mark – the race was one hour long, so this would be toward the end. His blue Jag with yellow wheels then blew a tire and spun off backwards into the hay bales at Woodcote. When Bira tried to change the tire, the jack sunk into the dirt and Bira couldn't finish the race.

These stories built my car culture.

The Jaguar factory decided to make a go at Le Mans in June 1950 with three aluminum-bodied XK 120s. Phil Weaver, Jaguar's London-based service representative, came in to oversee preparation at the factory. The three cars were privately entered with 'factory assistance.' A turbine-like brake cooling device was installed on the cars. William Heynes, the chief engineer, knew the brakes were the weak point. After all, the cars weighed 3360 pounds with twenty-four gallons of fuel and the required tools and spare parts.

Leslie Johnson, the hare on the team, was in third place overall against Ferrari and Talbot-Lago competition when the clutch center failed at the halfway point of the race. The drivers used the clutch and

The Scream of an Engine

gearbox to slow down, saving the weak brakes. The other two cars finished 12th and 15th.

Heynes realized then that a tube framed, purpose built race car could meet the competition. The XK 120 C was born in time for the 1951 Le Mans race. Malcolm Sayer, with inevitable consultation from Lyons, designed the magnificent, sleeker, lightweight body. The car was designed with one purpose: win at the high speed, billiard table smooth Le Mans course. It did and set the lap record in the process. The XK 120 C brought Jaguar international recognition for the first time.

In the 1951 Le Mans event, the competition was expected to be the 4.5-liter French Talbot-Lagos, which won in 1950 but were now faster, the American 5.4-liter Cunninghams, the 4.1-liter Ferraris and even the Aston Martins with smaller 2.6-liter engines.

Le Mans start positions were determined by engine size then, so the smaller 3.4-liter Jaguars were down at the start to a quarter of the competitors. The Saturday, June 23rd weather was wet and overcast. By the end of the second lap, Stirling Moss' Jaguar was pushing Froilán González in the lead Talbot-Lago. Moss passed the Argentinian by the fifth lap for the lead. Moss then set the race lap record at 105.2 MPH.

When an overwhelming Jaguar victory seemed possible with XK 120 Cs in the first three positions, Biondetti lost oil pressure and was retired since the damage couldn't be repaired with parts and tools carried in the car, the rule at the time. Then Moss in the lead car suffered the same fate, the problem traced to bad welds on the oil feed pipe. With hours left to go, the team instructed the remaining and now leading car, Peter Walker/Peter Whitehead in No.20, to keep the RPMs down to reduce vibration and hope the weld held.

Chapter Nine: Racing

It did. Jaguar won the race by forty-five minutes over the second-place Talbot-Lago of Pierre Mayrat and Guy Mairesse, followed a lap further behind by the Aston Martin DB 2 of Lance Macklin and Eric Thompson.

In addition to international fame, the win was hugely popular with the Jaguar employees who welcomed the race cars back with a big celebration. After all, this was the first time the proud English had won Le Mans since Lagonda pulled it off in 1935.

Even people like eight-year-old me in Maryland, USA, noticed.

Stirling Moss, who'd won the September 1950 Tourist Trophy Race in Dundrod, Northern Ireland driving an XK 120, returned in September 1951 to win driving the factory XK 120 C, No. 7. Moss was followed home by Peter Walker in XK 120 C, No. 8. Wins for the XK 120 C now poured in from all over the world, especially in America with drivers like Phil Hill, Walt Hansgen and Masten Gregory.

A new streamlined body adopted in 1952 for the Le Mans race cooked the Jaguar teams' engines and hopes in short order. Lack of testing time under warmer conditions did the team in and Mercedes won with their new 300 SL coupés. The French, not fond of the Germans either, almost disqualified the Mercedes team before the start because of the new gull wing doors.

No one would ever say racing is easy.

But Jaguar returned in 1953 with the standard bodied XK 120 C, adding Weber carburetors for more horsepower, now up to 220 BHP, and disk brakes, winning a stunning 1-2-4, the sweep broken up by the Phil Walters/John Fitch Cunningham C5 R in third. Jaguar is credited for first winning with disk brakes on an XK 120 C at Goodwood in 1952.

The Scream of an Engine

I was glued to Dad's short-wave radio that could pick up English broadcasts of the race. It took forever to get the *Road and Track* reports.

In the 1953 Le Mans race, drama for Jaguar continued before the start. The Rolt/Hamilton car was disqualified for running the same number in practice as was on another car. Lofty England somehow talked the scrutineers into reversing themselves to let the boys start the race on time. By which time, Tony Rolt and Duncan Hamilton had been to a bar to celebrate their experience and were in no condition to drive the race. They later denied this was the case.

After the Jaguar win, John Wyer, the Aston Martin racing team manager, is quoted as saying, 'I think it was unfair to Jaguar to say they won Le Mans in 1953 because they went there with disk brakes. They won because they had a hell of a good motor car.'[28]

By 1954, it was clear that Jaguar needed to be faster than the XK 120 C. The D-Type was introduced with one purpose: win Le Mans again. Now the XK 120 C was referred to as the C-Type. The E-Type sports car of 1961 and the S-Type of 1964 cemented the use of 'Type' as designator of Jaguar sports cars and sedans. This continues today with the F-Type sports cars and soon to arrive I-Type electric vehicles.

Testing at Le Mans in May 1954, the new car broke the existing lap record by five seconds, an auspicious start. *Road & Track* – now written this way, although earlier written as *Road and Track* – later tested Pearce Woods' D-Type in May 1956. How fast? 162 MPH timed, not estimated, 0-60 in 4.7 seconds, with a test weight of 2460 pounds and the 3.4-liter DOHC six now producing 250 BHP.

---

[28] Ibid., Skilleter, page 93

These *Road & Track* test series are a must purchase for any gearhead. For cars of that gearhead's interest, of course.

Le Mans 1954 was to be a battle for the ages, according to period publications, pitting power in the form of the 4.9-liter Ferrari 375 Plus against aerodynamics of the wind tunnel-tested Jaguar D-type. Weather played a role in the 1954 24-Hours of Le Mans as well, and the race's conclusion was the closest finish recorded since 1933.

In the race, the Rolt/Hamilton Jaguar came second to José Froilán González' Ferrari, Frenchman Maurice Trintignant co-driving. The Jag was just 2.5 miles – about one fourth a lap - behind. The 3.4-liter English car acquitted itself admirably after twenty-four hours of hard racing in the rain. This included forced pit stops by too-tall Tony Rolt because he couldn't see through the windscreen. He took rain in the face, covering his goggles. Duncan Hamilton took over driving and was gaining at the end – it's not recorded whether he could see or not.

What was it like to drive a D-Type? In 1956, Paul Frère crashed a D-Type at the Nürburgring and is quoted as describing the primitive solid rear axle D-Type as 'just like a frightening, ferocious beast on the bumpy, twisting 'Ring.' It was not a good rough road racer.

Mike Salmon, a privateer racer, had this to say about the D-Type: "The D was lovely to drive on the road, very rigid and all of a piece, not the usual loose, rattling thing that most competition cars were, especially the Ferrari GTO. It was a beautiful handling car, too: you could drive it on the throttle, slide it around."

Mike also had critical comments about the Plessy brake master cylinder which failed at times, like for Moss at Le Mans 1954 at 170

The Scream of an Engine

MPH during the race. Moss refused to drive the car again even after repairs in the pits.[29]

This set the stage for the 1955 Le Mans race. The pre-race hype built this to be a classic Mercedes-Jaguar race with Ferrari given a distant chance to win. The prognosticators were correct: in the early going, Juan Fangio in the 300 SLR roadster and Mike Hawthorn in the long nose, tail finned D-Type exchanged the lead many times, with Hawthorn finally getting the race lap record. Rumors had the Hawthorne D-Type clocked at 191 MPH on the Mulsanne Straight. Eugenio Castellotti in the big 4.9-liter Ferrari V-12 was mixed into the middle of the fray for a time.

Then the horrid accident struck two and a half hours into the race. The highly-experienced French driver Pierre Levegh crashed his Mercedes into the crowd opposite the pits on the pit straight. Hawthorn had passed Lance Macklin, then braked to enter the pits as the experienced Macklin was accelerating his Austin Healey out of the pits. When Macklin swerved to avoid Hawthorn, Levegh was coming through at high speed and hit Macklin. That touch catapulted the Mercedes over the earthen barrier between the race course and the crowd, hitting a concrete barrier head on. The resulting disintegration and fire from Levegh's wreck killed eighty-two spectators plus Levegh, the worst racing accident in history.

Many races were delayed, changed or discontinued as the result of this event.

This accident – as the race stewards later ruled it to be – would affect racing for years to come. The stewards blamed the accident on

---

[29]http://www.motorsportmagazine.com/archive/article/june-2004/50/d-type-cast

The Scream of an Engine

the thirty-year old race course design not keeping up with the speed of the cars. Races were cancelled immediately, like the Reims 12-Hour the following month. Calls for spectator safety improvements were a major topic of discussion. Slowing the cars down with fuel consumption and engine size reductions at Le Mans came as early as the following year.

Mercedes withdrew their two remaining cars from the race the following morning while leading. Jaguar decided to soldier on, winning the race with Hawthorn/Bueb finishing 1st in the factory car, followed by the Peter Collins/Paul Frère Aston Martin DB3 S five laps down and the Ecurie Francorchamps privately-entered short nose D-Type in third.

The 1955 Le Mans racing accident was the second time during this same event that Jaguar made the decision to continue in the face of devastating adversity. Before the race, William Lyons' son John was killed in his Mark VII in a crash on French roads on the way to Le Mans. Lyons finally decided John would've wanted the team to continue with the plan. They did.

One race not cancelled was the September 1955 Tourist Trophy Race at Dundrod, Northern Ireland. This turned into another Fangio/Hawthorn and Mercedes/Jaguar battle. Hawthorn again set the race lap record. However, toward the end with the Moss/Fitch Mercedes now leading in a downpour, Hawthorn's car broke a crankshaft on the last lap, an unusual failure, and denied Hawthorn second place. Mercedes earned a 1-2-3 sweep. The enemy won. I was crushed.

To lighten a dark period in racing, Duncan Hamilton blew a tire as he crossed the finish line at Snetterton, England on September 9, 1955 in his D-Type, spun and crossed the finish line pointed backwards. He won the race.

Finishing my culturally formative Fifties with Jaguar, my heroes won Le Mans again in 1956 and 1957. Whatever else happened didn't matter: Le Mans was it for me.

For 1956, fuel consumption limits were placed on all Le Mans entrants. Thirty-four laps must be covered before taking on another one hundred twenty liters of fuel. The 10.9 MPG that resulted from this rule could just be achieved by de-tuning the XK engine. The Reims 12-Hour race was a fuel consumption test for Jaguar in which the cars also finished 1-2-3. Duncan Hamilton won but was sacked immediately by Lofty England for disobeying team orders and passing Frère for the win.

Jaguar had produced fifty D-Types by this time, so qualified in 1956 under the old prototype rules allowing engines over three liters. No changes had to be made to the engine, other than the experimental fuel injection to meet the fuel consumption targets. Track safety changes delayed the race start about a month.

In the 1956 Le Mans race, accidents eliminated Frère and Fairman's factory Jaguars, and Hawthorn/Bueb suffered a split and leaking injection tube. It was up to Ecurie Ecosse, the private Scottish team, to carry the honors for Jaguar. Frère felt so bad about causing his accident on a very slippery wet track that he later said, 'Through my fault, Jaguar were going to be deprived of a victory which would have been theirs for the taking, and on which they depended to sell thousands of cars all over the world.'[30]

Ninian Sanderson and Ron Flockhart pulled the win with Ecurie Ecosse's Jaguar. The Aston Martin DB3S of Stirling Moss and Peter Collins came second, a lap down. Fourth went to another private Jaguar entry, Equipe Nationale Belge, with Jacques Swaters and Freddy

---

[30] Ibid., Skilleter, page 124

The Scream of an Engine

Rousselle driving. Hawthorn and Bueb fought back to sixth place in the fuel injected factory car after spending hours in the pits for repairs, still twenty laps behind the winner. One report said they were having fun and not complaining about the incessant rain.

The final Jaguar win of the Fifties at Le Mans, cementing my cultural attachment to the track, the drivers and to Jaguar, came the following year, 1957. The new E1A successor to the D-Type was running but couldn't be completed for the race in June, so Jaguar relied on private entrants again, with factory support, of it's now 'obsolete' race cars.

The first new 3.8-liter engine was tested at Sebring in March with fuel injection, finishing third in the hands of Hawthorn and Bueb in a Jaguar North America-entered D-Type. They finished behind two durable Maseratis, the 4.5-liter 450S of Jean Behra and Juan Fangio winning, followed by Stirling Moss and Harry Schell in a 3-liter 300S. The Jag suffered brake problems resulting in the rear brakes being sealed off and carrying on with only the front brakes working. That's a tough assignment at Sebring.

Le Mans 1957 was the complete blowout for Jaguar: winning first through fourth and sixth places. All Jaguars that started the race finished. The 1951-win set Jaguar on the way to stardom, but 1957 was thick icing on a delicious cake. Three of the cars were prepared at the factory plus all five engines. The two Ecurie Ecosse cars and the Duncan Hamilton car were long-nose versions just purchased from the factory by these two privateers.

The very fast Ferrari 335 4.1-liter V-12s of Mike Hawthorn/Luigi Musso – Hawthorn again set the lap record - and Phil Hill/Peter Collins, and Maserati 4.5-liter 450Ss with Stirling Moss/Harry Schell and Jean Behra/André Simon all dropped out in the first few hours. Ecurie Ecosse then grabbed the lead in the third hour,

Ron Flockhart and Ivor Bueb driving. They were never again headed. Their run was flawless, the pair spending a total of only thirteen minutes nine seconds in the pits over the entire distance, including an unscheduled stop to replace a light bulb.[31] And fun, too: the pair finished in formation with the second Ecurie Ecosse car which was eight laps down at the end.

This race has sealed my Jaguar loyalty to this day. Who knows exactly why this can happen to a person? Loyalty is a factor; being 'part' of a group or team of enthusiasts; being close to an interesting part of automotive history; excitement; risk; nostalgia; memories of what was going on in my personal life at the time; love of adventure and sport. Passion for the shape of these racing Jaguars.

Yet almost none of the individuals involved in the Fifties Jaguar Le Mans story are still alive. None of the factory workers then are still there building cars today. The F-Type sports cars today don't even look like the Jaguar racing cars of the Fifties.

Yes, the passion and the loyalty flowing from this youthful allegiance to Jaguar is indeed a strange and enduring phenomenon.

Alfa Romeo Racing

My passion for Alfas came after Jaguars because I was exposed to Jaguars first. My Dad was to blame. Then a 1957 Alfa 'Super Spyder' joined the family in 1957 and I was toast. Dad was to blame for that, too. Alfas have been raced since the first one was built in 1910 and raced in 1911. By 1925, Alfa won the first 'World Championship.'

---

[31]https://en.wikipedia.org/wiki/1957_24_Hours_of_Le_Mans#Official_results, April 2017

The Scream of an Engine

That winning Alfa was the eight-cylinder, 1987cc, DOHC 'P2,' very successful in 1924-1925 racing with Count Brilli-Peri at the wheel. The P2 was designed by Vittorio Jano, a legend in Alfa history. In 1924, the P2 won the Italian Grand Prix, and in 1925 won at Spa, Montlhéry and Monza, enough to take the World Championship. After 1925 until 1930, the P2 competed for top honors with the first Maserati, a 1.5-liter DOHC design, and the Bugatti Type 35, also a supercharged straight eight without overhead cams but with 1990cc in engine capacity.[32]

By the 1930s, Alfa was winning Le Mans four times, 1931 through 1934, with the 8C 2300 sports car, the engine now 2300cc. To me, it's amazing what those straight eight engines would do in a lightweight sports car chassis.

Also in the Thirties, there were many Alfa Grand Prix wins with the hugely successful P3. Like many cars in that day, only thirteen were built because – like today - it was a costly proposition. Buyers were few and far between and this was the Depression.

My favorite Alfa Grand Prix win was Tazio Nuvolari's defeat of Auto Union and Mercedes at the German Grand Prix in 1935 in the outclassed P3. Today this P3 is fully restored and winning races again in the U.S. under the ownership and driving talents of Jon Shirley since 2000. Shirley's car is a Series II P3 Tipo B, Serial Number 50005, completed in 1934.[33]

---

[32] Historic Motor Racing, Anthony Pritchard, Grosset & Dunlap, New York, 1969, pages 11-12
[33] http://www.finecars.cc/en/editorial/article/news/alfa-romeo-tipo-b-p3/index.html

The Scream of an Engine

'The design features' – of the P3 – 'included cylinder head and block cast as one piece, with no head gasket. It used two of these blocks, four pistons in each, along with a two-piece crankshaft, literally making the engine two engines of four-cylinders each in tandem. A straight-cut gear drive sat between them, sending torque outside the engine and to the left, where it powered two superchargers, one for each block.

'This construction helped torsional stiffness – of the crankshaft - which helped the engine stay in one piece. Because the result was Italian, it was also achingly beautiful. And strong. In early, 2.7-liter form, Vittorio Jano's engine made a reliable 80 BHP per liter. This provided more than 280 BHP in a 1550-pound car the body width of a lawn tractor. By 1935, chasing the Germans, it was a 6000-rpm 3.2-liter powerplant with 89 BHP per liter.

'The rest of the P3 was relatively straightforward. Mechanical brakes, later replaced by hydraulic, at a time when Ettore Bugatti refused to trust fluid for stopping. Leaf springs. Friction dampers and a solid rear axle. A rigid front axle, later changed to independent. And coolest of all, a split rear driveline—a small aluminum-cased differential, the size of a handbag, in the cockpit, under the driver's thighs. Two torque tubes angled out of it, one for each wheel. A ring and pinion sat at each hub.

'The idea, one observer said, 'was to prevent wheel spin . . . to make ratio changing . . . relatively easy, and to drop the driver's seat low down, between the shafts. Ha!

'But when Jano tells our drivers what he plans, Nuvolari snorts through his nose and says, "No! I don't want to be down in the basement like that, I wanna be up on top of the job! I want to see where I am

Chapter Nine: Racing

going in road racing!" And the original idea was changed, narrowed, and we ended up sitting high on top.' [34]

World War II slowed everyone up a bit but soon Giuseppe Farina, son of the founder of the Farina coachbuilding company, won the new Formula 1 driver's championship in 1950 in the Alfa Romeo 158. Farina had previously won the Italian Championship in 1937, 1938 and 1939.

Farina the coachbuilder designed many Alfas including the 1957 'Super Spyder' we owned.

The post-World War II Grand Prix world saw the introduction of the new Formula 1 rules for cars agreed upon in 1947, replacing all those that came before. Actual Formula 1 race cars built to the new rules came later. The first Formula 1 Driver's Championship was staged in 1950.

This new Grand Prix 'Formula 1' rule package included two groups: 1.5-liter supercharged or 4.5-liter un-supercharged, you pick.

The straight eight, 1.5-liter supercharged Alfa motor was producing 350 BHP at 8500 RPM in 1938, which is where they started again in 1950. The heavily finned 158 brake drums almost filled the wheels. A swing rear axle system was combined with a transverse leaf spring.

Ferrari introduced their 125 F1, their first Formula 1 car, in 1948 with a single overhead cam-per-bank 1.5-liter V-12 and torsion bar rear suspension. The car wasn't competitive, so was upgraded to

---

[34] Sam Smith, March-April 2016 issue of *Road & Track* magazine

The Scream of an Engine

two camshafts per bank, DOHC, or four cams in total, and a de Dion tube rear suspension in 1949. That still wasn't enough.

The Alfas were undefeated in 1950. The Alfa Quadrifoglio was prominently displayed on the side of the scuttle on the 158. The distinctive grille was shown on the front pages of many motoring publications of the day.

In parallel, Ferrari was also developing a 4.5-liter unsupercharged car by the new chief designer, Aurelio Lampredi, who replaced Gioacchino Columbo. The first result, the 275 F1 in 1950, was 3.3-liters. This car was followed in short order by the 340 F1 – 4.1-liters – and finally the 375 F1 – 4.5-liters. The 375 became competitive with the 159 by the middle of 1951 but didn't win a race until Silverstone in July 1951. José Froilán González in the 375 beat Fangio in the race by a convincing fifty-one seconds. González also won the pole position.

Columbo returned to Alfa to further develop the 158 into the 159 after Lampredi took over engine design at Ferrari. The 159 developed an extra twenty BHP due to Columbo's efforts and now turned 9500 RPM.

The 1951 Formula 1 car championship with drivers Juan Fangio, Giuseppe Farina and Luigi Fagioli was awarded to the Alfa team which again won most of the marbles. Fangio won his first Driver's Championship.

I was eight when Fangio's and Alfa Romeo's championship milestones were achieved.

In the Sixties, Alfa won two European Touring Car Championships, a Trans American Championship in 1966 with the

The Scream of an Engine

GTA, and numerous SCCA National Championships. These were the stories I grew up with. They helped lead me to racing an Alfa, too.

Al Leake gets a special mention. Al was a passionate Alfa fan, restoration shop owner in Boulder Creek, CA, and amateur U.S race driver, running for trophies, not money. He won twenty-six SCCA national championships driving Sophia, his G Production Alfa Spider. Since this car was the Solex carburetor version of the Weber-carb 1957 1290cc Alfa 'Super Spyder' we owned, Leake's performance gained my attention. Leake's Alfas – he owned twenty-seven at one point – were winners.

Al also raced SCCA Class F production. He said it took too long to change over between races, so he just ran the G production version of the car in the F production class and won that class, too. SCCA gave tow money for those that qualified for the nationals in Atlanta. Al was impressed that he received two towing checks for the same Alfa in one year to the same race weekend.[35]

In the Seventies and Eighties, Alfa won many championships in Europe, including seven in 1983 alone.[36] Only fans and gearheads in the U.S. were even aware this was going on in Europe.

Each Alfa win reinforces my choice for driving my 1750 Spider, my collector's car, on the streets and roads of America for forty-two years.

But the clinching moves by Alfa were in the Sixties, starting with the TZ and TZ2 in the early to mid-Sixties, the GTA and GTAM in the mid-to-late Sixties and early 1970s, and the stunning T33 race

---

[35] *Alfa Owner*, Casey Annis interview of Al Leake, February 2007
[36] *Quadrifoglio* a new Alfa publication in summer 1984

cars. All you had to do was listen to the shriek of the early T33's 2-liter V-8 or savor the sight of that sleek aluminum body.

Al Leake's beloved Alfa 750 F, Sophia, winner of twenty-six national championships. Photo taken at North Island Naval Air Station Historic Car Races, San Diego, CA, October 2003

I knew I had to race an Alfa.

Ford Racing

Ford beat both Alfa Romeo and Jaguar to the track by many years, almost a decade ahead of Alfa, three decades ahead of Jaguar. As is noted in the 'Characters' chapter, Henry Ford himself raced his own creation in October 1901. He then turned the wheel over to professional racer Barney Oldfield.

Then came decades of other racing stories, not the least of which is the Ford story in NASCAR, even though overall Ford has been trounced soundly by Chevy cumulatively in that series. The summary

The Scream of an Engine

of NASCAR Championships through 2016: Chevy – 39, Ford – 15, Hudson Hornet – 3, and Dodge/Plymouth – 3.[37]

My special interest in Ford racing was during the Fifties and Sixties. Ford racing was primarily NASCAR in the Fifties and NASCAR and USAC, including Indy, plus the Cobra and GT 40, in the Sixties.

In the Sixties, Ford re-entered the battle to win Indianapolis. And did: 1965 with Jim Clark, 1966 with Graham Hill and 1967 with A. J. Foyt, breaking the Offenhauser win-string dating back to 1947.

My primary interest in Ford racing in the Sixties was the development of the new Cobra and GT 40 cars. Carroll Hall Shelby led the charge.

In 1961, Shelby was casting around for something new and exciting. He'd been taking nitroglycerin pills for his heart to be able to race cars but decided it wasn't worth his life to continue operating this way. He retired from racing. He wanted to build his own car. After asking Chevrolet for engines, stoutly resisted by Zora Arkus-Duntov and other Chevrolet executives who already had a sports car called the Corvette, he turned to Ford. Of course, that kind of press was just what President Lee Iacocca had in mind. Ford bankrolled the Shelby effort and installed some of its own engineering talent to make sure development went smoothly.

Shelby had certainly by this time seen the English AC Cars Ltd.'s Ace 'Bristol' – the name which identifies the Bristol Cars Ltd. sourced, BMW-328-based engine. Bristol Cars Ltd. had been a division of the Bristol Aeroplane Company, now spun off, and obtained the

---

[37] Wikipedia, May 2017

The Scream of an Engine

rights to the BMW 328 engine design as an outcome of World War II. This Ace Bristol combination was winning class races everywhere in the Fifties.

The roadster version was known officially as the AC Ace and the coupé version the AC Aceca. Car people everywhere respected the clean lines of the body and the BMW-derived six-cylinder motor of this 2-liter beauty. Shelby won the Le Mans race in 1959 for Aston Martin and the AC Ace 'Bristol' won the Grand Touring under 2-liter class at Le Mans the same year, finishing seventh overall and driven by Ted Whiteaway and John Turner.

The major thing the AC Ace brought to the party was light weight. Topped up with gas, oil and water it weighed just a roast beef sandwich or two more than 2,000 pounds. The Corvette of the era weighed about one thousand pounds more, so, with similar horsepower on tap, it wasn't hard to figure which car would prevail on the race track. The fact that the Cobra was equipped with huge 12-inch disc brakes and rack-and-pinion steering in later models, while the Corvette had drums and recirculating ball steering, just tilted the playing field that much more.

The Cobra story and the GT 40 story are closely intertwined with the goal of Goodyear Tire and Rubber Co. to break the Firestone hold on the Indy 500 race. This led indirectly to the formation of Dan Gurney's All American Racers.

In the 1964 Indy 500, the rear engined Lotus-Fords were fastest. But Colin Chapman elected to run Lotus on Dunlop tires, an unproven supplier for Indy conditions. During the race, Jim Clark in one of the Lotus-Fords experienced vibrations. Finally, the left rear suspension collapsed, fortunately on the straight. Clark's race came to an end and it was soon discovered that the tires had chunked which caused the vibrations that tore the rear suspension apart.

Chapter Nine: Racing

The Scream of an Engine

Dan Gurney, in the second Lotus-Ford, was called in and retired by Chapman for safety reasons over the suspect tires. Gurney departed the Lotus program unhappy, perhaps the seminal event leading him to form All American Racers in 1965 and decisions to build his own Indy and Formula 1 cars, with Goodyear's help.

Prior to that point, Dan had a small shop in neighboring Costa Mesa, which was integrated into the new venture. While the two founders were still looking for an appropriate name for their new company, the then-president of Goodyear, ex-basketball champion Victor Holt, suggested All American Racers - AAR.

Goodyear was commencing their upgraded involvement in auto racing on both the Formula 1 circuit - Dan was the first driver to race a Grand Prix car equipped with Goodyear tires - and the Indianapolis 500, which up to that point was mostly a Firestone arena. The cars AAR was designing and building were called Grand Prix and Indy Eagles, one of the many distinguishing features being a 'beak' at the front of the cars. Roger McCluskey became the first driver to achieve a victory in a Gurney Eagle at Langhorne, Pennsylvania in 1966.[38]

In the aftermath of the 1964 Indy 500 race, Ford President Lee Iacocca personally ordered the company's racing executives to take control of future tire selection, pointedly wondering what kind of payment Colin Chapman had received to use Dunlop's.

Goodyear at this point decided to go for the win in 1965 on its Indy 500 program. Testing commenced immediately. The company also turned to Carroll Shelby and poured fifty million dollars into the coffers of its longtime ally, targeted at winning Indy. Shelby, already consumed with running Ford's Le Mans GT 40 and Cobra programs, agreed that his friend Dan Gurney should lead the Indianapolis effort.

---

[38] All American Racers website

Chapter Nine: Racing

Shelby benefited from the Goodyear funding to complete the Cobra series and develop the GT 40s, Marks I, II and IV.

To finish the Goodyear story, Foyt again led the Goodyear contingent at Indy in 1965 and this time he delivered, qualifying on the pole with a new track record. Twelve Goodyear cars in all made the race. But '65 belonged to Clark and his Lotus-Ford now running on Firestones. Goodyear was foiled again.

The tire war accelerated. Firestone matched Goodyear nearly dollar-for-dollar with costs rapidly escalating. The two companies vied for drivers to represent their brand and invested heavily in technology – and not just tire technology. Tire dollars helped fuel the developments in supercharging and turbocharging and even revived the Offenhauser engine, once left for dead.

In 1966, the field was nearly split equally between the two tire companies. A first-lap accident damaged eleven cars, including those of Goodyear's top drivers, Foyt and Gurney. Gurney was now racing his own very promising All American Racers Eagle-Ford.

Graham Hill was the '66 Indy winner, again on Firestones and in a Lola-Ford. Ford was very strong at Indianapolis and in USAC races at this point.

It appeared to be more of the same in 1967 as Parnelli Jones dominated practice and the race in Andy Granatelli's STP gas turbine car with all-wheel drive and Firestone tires. But a bearing in Jones's gear box failed four laps from the finish, allowing A.J. Foyt on Goodyear's to finally reach Victory Lane, the first Goodyear win since 1919.[39]

---

[39] Art Garner's *Black Noon: The Year They Stopped the Indy 500*, available on Amazon

Cobras were by then securely embedded in automotive history. The first Cobra chassis, adapted by AC Cars in England to run the new Ford Windsor 221 cubic-inch V-8 was delivered to Shelby on February 2, 1962. That was the only Cobra to employ the 221-engine. All the Mark II Cobras introduced in 1963 with MG B rack and pinion steering used the 289-engine. But until then, Cobras were delivered with the 260-engine, an upgrade from the first 221-powered car.

At Riverside in late 1962, a Cobra was being tested while Santee Automobiles, Inc. was testing its Santee Super Sports – SS - roadster. Fred Puhn was chief engineer for this very pretty car. John McCann was driving. This Santee was the second serial number of the Santee production, built with a modern tubular space frame and the new small block aluminum Olds V-8 engine.

'On the track that day', John Raifsnider, president of Santee Automobiles, Inc. wrote for *Automobile Quarterly*, 'the Santee looked faster than the Cobra.'[40]

Santee Automobiles, Inc. discovered what Shelby had discovered a year earlier: GM already had a sports car and wasn't about to fund another, albeit this time with an Olds engine. There were only three Santee cars built.

The Cobra legend is based on building very few 260/289/427cars: just nine hundred ninety-eight were assembled from 1961 until 1968, six hundred fifty-five leaf-spring 260/289 Cobras and three hundred forty-three coil-spring 427 Cobras. These numbers include street cars, competition cars and semi-competition roadsters.[41]

---

[40] *Automobile Quarterly* April 1963. John Raifsnider was president of Santee Automobiles, Inc. at the time. Fred Puhn says there were no stop watches involved

[41] *Hemmings Motor News*, May 2012

The Scream of an Engine

The Mark III 427 Cobras, introduced in 1965 and built through 1967, could also be ordered with the 289-engine. But they were winning all kinds of races: Bob Holbert and Dave Macdonald drove a Shelby Cobra Daytona Coupé to fourth overall and first in GT Class in the 1964 Sebring 12-Hour, behind three Ferrari prototypes in the first three positions. Dan Gurney and Bob Bondurant repeated the GT win at Le Mans in 1964, also in the Shelby Cobra Daytona Coupé, also finishing fourth overall behind three Ferrari prototypes.

Original Shelby Cobras were all aluminum bodied. Fiberglass bodies show up today on the original Cobras because fiberglass replacements were cheaper than making new aluminum bodies from scratch after accidents.

Of course, then the knock-offs and replicars started to arrive, expanding the number of Cobras seen on the streets and in the ads of motor magazines. These may have ended up numbering over 20,000 through 2016.[42]

Meanwhile, Shelby enjoyed a halo effect, his reputation carrying over to modifying popular Mustangs and Chryslers, starting with Mustangs in 1965. Even today, gearheads are modifying older Mustangs into Shelby GT 350s to satisfy ancient cravings. Like Lynn Hitson in Phoenix, AZ.

Meanwhile, the GT 40 developments continued unabated. The GT 40 design and original construction was done by Lola in England for Ford, Shelby Automotive in charge, using the Lola T6 as a take-off point. The Mark Is and IIs were built in England. The Mark IVs were designed and built in the U.S.

---

[42] Wikipedia, April 2017

The Scream of an Engine

Race wins in the opening year of 1964 for the new cars were hard to achieve. The engines in the first cars were 260 cubic inch Fords, later upgraded to 289s, just like the Cobras. The GT 40s with world class drivers didn't finish a 1964 race, including Nürburgring in May, Le Mans in June, Reims in July, and Nassau, Bahamas in November and December.

The first GT 40/289 win came after Shelby American took over the program from Ford which occurred at the Daytona 24-Hour race in February 1965. Then the drought continued until July and August of 1965 when Ford of France won two minor races. All six 289-cars entered didn't finish Le Mans in June 1965.

The big wins started again with the Shelby prepared 427-cubic inch Mark IIs at Daytona 1966 in February, Ken Miles and Lloyd Ruby driving. The duo won again at Sebring in March 1966, and then came the huge win at Le Mans in June 1966, the first three places going to 427 Mark IIs. The victory went to Chris Amon and Bruce McLaren when Henry Ford II decreed that all three cars would finish abreast. Ken Miles and Denny Hulme had been leading, but since Amon/McLaren started further back on the grid – so much for Miles/Hulme being faster in qualifying – the French race scrutineers ruled that Amon/McLaren had traveled further during the race, hence won.

The rules changed after 1967 to slow the cars down. Ferrari refused to enter Le Mans 1968 because his P4s were illegal, as were the Ford Mark IVs and Mark IIs with the 427-cubic inch engine.

Later Le Mans wins after 1967 by Ford – a total of four in a row from '66 through '69 – were by the private entrant John Wyer (J.W.) Automotive Engineering, Ltd., team in 1968 and 1969, in the same chassis number 289 Mark II with JWA 'Mirage' modifications. Pedro Rodriguez and Lucien Bianchi drove the 1968 winner and the pair were joined in the 1969 winner's circle with Jackie Ickx.

The Scream of an Engine

The Ford wins in the late Sixties were beyond my culture-forming window, but noted and reaffirmed my notion that Ford was OK.

The J-Car replacement for the Mark II, finally renamed the Mark IV, was developed for Le Mans 1967. Dan Gurney and AJ Foyt won the '67 Le Mans race in Mark IV No. 6 in the series, introduced spraying the crowd around the podium with champagne and set a record still unbeaten: the only victory for an all-American team, car and both drivers, at the Circuit de la Sarthe.

This is the only race No. 6 ever competed in as a 'works' car. The Mark IV/Gurney-Foyt combination soundly trounced the second and third place Ferrari P4s by four laps and eleven laps respectively. Henry Ford II was quite pleased.

The Mark IV No. 4, built by Holman & Moody – not Shelby - was entered in and won the Sebring 12-Hour race in March 1967, Mario Andretti and Bruce McLaren driving. It was then retired. Mark IV No. 5 was built, delivered to Shelby Automotive, Inc., and tested extensively March 21-25, 1967 by Andretti, running over one thousand miles at Daytona. This car finished fourth at Le Mans '67, driven by Bruce McLaren and Mark Donahue. The car was eventually given to A. J. Foyt by Ford. [43]

---

[43] The story on the individual Mark IVs at Le Mans '67 is from *GT 40, An Individual History and Race Record*, Ronnie Spain, Motorbooks International, 2003

Chapter Ten: Race Drivers

My Dad got me started. His inspiration and racing were my launch key. Later, I became a serious fan of many race drivers. Some retired before I was born. Each racing enthusiast will have unique choices of favorite drivers. These are mine with the most influential in forming my passion first. Italy, Argentina, the Brits, then the Americans.

At the Top of the Podium

Tazio Georgio Nuvolari, known as the Flying Mantuan because he was born in the town of Mantua, Italy, captured my imagination as a kid. He was preceded and followed by many outstanding drivers, but we must choose our favorites. Tazio is mine even though he was less influential in forming my culture than say, Juan Fangio or Mike Hawthorn.

The Scream of an Engine

He's also Murray Walker's favorite. Walker is a Grand Prix sports broadcaster with encyclopedic knowledge of Grand Prix racing. His father Graham was a successful motorcycle racer and motorcycle race broadcaster after his retirement from fifteen years of racing. Murray tried racing motorcycles but quickly retired to a budding advertising career, then becoming a BBC commentator. His enthusiastic live commentaries on radio and TV have thrilled racing fans for over fifty years.

In his book, *Murray Walker's Formula 1 Heroes* published in 2000, he has this to say about Nuvolari: '*For me, the fire, the style, the charisma, the all-around brilliance and the sheer ability to win races against overwhelming odds puts Tazio Nuvolari above all others...*' [44]

Tazio Nuvolari in the cockpit. San Diego Automotive Museum

---

[44] Murray Walker's Formula 1 Heroes, Virgin Publishing Ltd, London, 2000, page 13

The Scream of an Engine

Murray's thinking may have been energized by standing beside Nuvolari – and Bernd Rosemeyer, Rudolph Caracciola, Hermann Lang and Manfred von Brauchitsch – at the Donington, England, Grand Prix which Nuvolari won in 1938 in the huge Auto Union.

Unlike Murray, I never stood beside Nuvolari.

Mind you, Murray singles Nuvolari out in his book on Formula 1 heroes, yet Nuvolari was starring and winning races before World War II. Nuvolari raced Grand Prix, but not under Formula 1 rules. Formula 1 rules were developed in 1947, and the cars weren't fully built to those rules until 1950. And I didn't read Murray's book until 2006, long after I'd made up my mind about Nuvolari.

This might sound Biblical, but I thought of Nuvolari as the David of motor racing against the Goliaths of his time. I savor that many – but certainly not all - of his most famous wins were driving Alfa Romeos. I tightly couple my favorite drivers with my favorite cars.

Nuvolari got his start on motorcycles with a racing license at age fifteen.

World War I interrupted his motorcycle activities. At twenty-three, he worked as a driver for the Italian army during the war. Tazio piloted everything from staff cars to ambulances. Once with his ambulance filled with injured soldiers, Nuvolari drove so fast he lost control and crashed into a ditch. He was immediately relieved of his role and told by an officer to 'forget driving.' Nuvolari wasn't 'cut out for the job.'[45]

---

[45] Alex Lloyd, Road & Track, May 23, 2016

When Tazio resumed life with motorcycles after the war, he started racing again and winning. Much like John Surtees in the 1950s and 1960s, Nuvolari excelled in winning two-wheel races before doing the same on four wheels. Unlike Surtees, Nuvolari raced on two and four wheels at the same time as his skills and luck improved in cars. By 1925, Nuvolari won the European Championship in the 350cc motorcycle class for Bianchi.

Nuvolari's epic motorcycle racing story occurred in 1925. He'd been invited to test an Alfa Romeo P2 at Monza, but he crashed the Alfa and broke ribs and one leg. Heavily bandaged, he was lifted next day onto his Bianchi for the Grand Prix of Nations motorcycle race and won in a driving rainstorm.

Nuvolari wasn't invited to join the Alfa team.

Tazio won many motorcycle races such as the Nations Race four times from 1925 through 1928 and the Lario Circuit Race five times from 1925 through 1929 all for Bianchi, all in the 350cc class.[46]

While the budding race driver Nuvolari was honing his skills, he married Carolina Perina Together they produced two fine sons, Giorgio in 1918 and Alberto in 1928 Sadly, Giorgio passed away at nineteen in 1937 from myocarditis, then Alberto passed away from nephritis in 1946. Our life heroes have their challenges.

But Nuvolari was a colorful dude through all of this. His racing outfit consisted of a red leather skull cap – helmets came in much later – blue trousers and yellow jersey. Tazio was short, wiry and emotional:

---

[46] Wikipedia, April 2017

The Scream of an Engine

four-wheel drifts were his specialty, beating his fist on the side of the car to make it go faster, screaming and grinning like a fiery little Italian devil as he did it. His strong jaw line projected determination. Long eye lashes and bushy eye brows added to his classic Italian good looks.

In April 1930, Tazio — wearing his yellow jersey and blue pants — battled arch rival Achille Varzi in the classic Mille Miglia motor race, both in Alfas. Varzi, a fellow Italian, had been told repeatedly at each control point that he was comfortably in the lead. The dark of night still encompassed the Italian countryside, but with morning fast approaching, Varzi knew the race was his. After all, there were no headlights visible from behind. He was out front, all alone.

Until he wasn't.

Nuvolari was catching Varzi. He'd switched off his headlights. Tazio tore through the public roads near Bologna at speeds over 90 MPH, reeling his rival in with every passing mile, despite the perils of darkness. Manhandling an Alfa Romeo 6C 1750 GS Spider Zagato in the pitch black of night, sleep deprived and coated in oil and bugs, would be distressing for any driver. But not so for the Flying Mantuan. With two miles to go in a one-thousand-mile race, Tazio passed Varzi for the lead on the road. Since Tazio was already ahead of Varzi on time, due to the offsets at the start, this was like rubbing salt in the wound. They became lifelong enemies on the track afterward.

Nuvolari led four Alfa 6C 1750s home in the first four positions.

Driving for the Alfa factory in 1932, Tazio started seven races aboard a Tipo B P3. He set fastest lap in all of them, scoring four victories, two seconds and a third in the process. He won the first race the P3 ran, the Italian Grand Prix in June. Nuvolari was annoyed when Alfa Romeo promptly withdrew from racing for 1933 and locked its sensational cars away. The Depression was in full swing. Then Enzo

The Scream of an Engine

Ferrari negotiated taking over the 1932 Alfa team cars and racing them under his own banner, Scuderia Ferrari.

But Tazio's most famous win came in the 1935 German Grand Prix at the Nürburgring. The German High Command and over 300,000 spectators cheered for the Mercedes and Auto Union teams to win with their much larger engined cars. The German government heavily financed both German teams.

Nuvolari drove the outdated, Vittorio Jano designed, 3.2-liter twin Roots supercharged Alfa Romeo P3 Tipo B weighing only 1545 pounds dry. The engine power was reported to be 330 BHP.

The supercharged 4-liter Mercedes was tweaked mid-season with a stroke increase, resulting in 4.3-liters and 395 BHP; the Ferdinand Porsche 5.0-liter Auto Unions, resisting calls to eliminate the rear engine design, were estimated to produce 375 BHP.[47]

Mercedes was constantly fiddling with the engines, naming the changes for 1935 the 'B' version of the W25. But further changes were made mid-season 1935. Reports disagree on how many horsepower they achieved.[48]

Nuvolari's 1935 German Grand Prix Alfa P3 is shown on the cover of this book.

For two days, the approach roads around the Nürburgring race track, some say the finest road-racing circuit in the world, was jammed with traffic heading for the event. The weather was suspect: the day

---

[47] *Historic Motor Racing*, Anthony Pritchard, Grosset and Dunlap, NY, 1969, page 40
[48] Wikipedia, May 2017

The Scream of an Engine

dawned with a fine drizzle and mist cloaked the pine-clad mountains in which the course waited. Patches of light shown upon the distant hilltops, but the track was wet and glistening. Hundreds of flags added color to the scene as they floated above the pits and grandstands.

For the race, Mercedes Benz entered five cars, driven by Caracciola, von Brauchitsch, Fagioli, Geier and Lang. The V-16 4.9-liter 375 BHP Auto Unions were piloted by Stuck, Rosemeyer, Pietsch and Varzi, Nuvolari's earlier friend and now nemesis. Both the German Mercedes and Auto Union cars could exceed 175 MPH.

The Alfa drivers for the Enzo Ferrari-managed team were Nuvolari, Chiron and Dreyfus. The rest of the field for this epic race were there to fill out the grid and hope for the best. These consisted of three Maseratis of the Scuderia Subalpina - Zehender, Etancelin and Siena driving, Balestrero with a private Alfa Romeo, Taruffi with a 3.3 Bugatti, Ruesch, Hartmann and Soffieti with independent Maseratis and Ernst von Delius and Raymond Mays on 2-liter English E.R.A.s.

Six nations and six makes were represented on the starting grid.

In those days, grid positions weren't based on practice times but were random. That's how Nuvolari ended up on the front row which also included Hans Stuck's Auto Union and Balestrero's Alfa.

The start of the race was dramatic with the signal light red, then amber and finally green. The cars roared away, all except two of the Auto Unions, which stalled on the grid.

By the ninth lap on the 14.8-mile circuit, Tazio was lying second behind the Mercedes of Rudy Caracciola. His impressive drive to that point was then undone by a disastrous two-minute pitstop on the twelfth lap due to a broken handle on the refueling pump. This dropped him down to sixth place. The race was that close.

The Scream of an Engine

What happened next is beyond legendary.

By lap twelve, Manfred von Brauchitsch held a lead of a little over a minute over the second-place car, with Nuvolari now dropped back to sixth due to the extended pit stop. The German von Brauchitsch then proceeded to extend the gap.

Storming out of the pits, in one lap Tazio passed Hans Stuck, Rudy Caracciola, Luigi Fagliolo and Bernd Rosemeyer - whose Auto Union was pit-bound - to reclaim second place. The steady rain helped reduce the power advantage of the German cars. The Mercedes tires were known to wear out faster than those on the less powerful Alfa, but von Brauchitsch still pressed and set the race lap record with Nuvolari in pursuit. On the last lap of the twenty-two-lap, three hundred twelve-mile race, Manfred's Mercedes W25B's left rear tire blew as von Brauchitsch headed into the Karussell for the final time.

Nuvolari's Alfa, now close behind in second, swept by to claim a most incredible upset victory, one many sources say was the best of all time. Nuvolari was followed home two minutes and fourteen seconds later by Hans Stuck in the Auto Union B, then Caracciola in the Mercedes W25B another minute back and Rosemeyer's Auto Union B, a further minute back.[49]

Manfred's Mercedes still finished fifth on a flat tire.

At the finish, the Nazi officials were confounded by the lack of a recording of the Italian anthem to play over the loudspeakers. Only

---

[49]This version of the story is mostly from the archives of Motor Sport Magazine:
http://www.motorsportmagazine.com/archive/article/october-2011/53/1935-german-grand-prix

Chapter Ten: Race Drivers

The Scream of an Engine

Deutschland Uber Alles had been ready for the inevitable German triumph. Nuvolari himself righted the situation with his own record of the Italian *Marcia Reale* which he always carried to races as a good luck charm.

Nuvolari beat the Germans in his diminutive red Alfa three more times in 1936 in Hungary, Spain and Italy, lesser 'non-championship' races. Then Auto Union lured him away in 1937. Nuvolari had joined the enemy.

Nuvolari's career effectively ended when World War II broke out. He did return post war, but health issues meant that his performances suffered. He was still a hot item: William Lyons seated him in the new XK 120 in 1949 for publicity photos.

Nuvolari said publicly he wanted to die at the wheel of a race car, such was the man. Having spent his life dancing with death, what sealed his fate was a stroke in 1952. He was partly paralyzed. The following year, 1953, he passed away in bed. I recall stories at the time that he also suffered from asthma and coughed up blood in one of his last races. But that story doesn't appear in the official reports on his death.

Juan Manuel Fangio Déramo

Right up there on my imaginary podium for biggest effect on my car culture with Nuvolari is Juan Manuel Fangio. Fangio won his first World Championship when I was eight. The year was 1951 and he won in the Alfa Romeo 158/159, a vehicle based on the pre-war P3s that Nuvolari used so successfully to beat the Auto Union and Mercedes teams in epic pre-war races.

The Scream of an Engine

I probably felt closer to Fangio, since I spent my high school years in Puerto Rico, which like Fangio's birthplace Argentina, is a Spanish speaking country.

Fangio was born June 24, 1911. He grew up short and stocky and was nick-named *El Maestro,* The Master, for his skills behind the wheel. Like Nuvolari, he drove race cars faster than anyone. Fangio came to dominate the first decade of the new post World War II Formula 1 competition.

From childhood, he abandoned his studies to pursue auto mechanics. In 1938, he debuted in *Turismo Carretera* competing in a Ford V8. In 1940, he competed with Chevrolet – alright, no one is perfect - winning the Grand Prix International Championship and devoted his time to the Argentine *Turismo Carretera* becoming its champion, a title he successfully defended a year later. Fangio then moved to Europe, competing there for two years between 1947 and 1949, building his resume. He was already in his late thirties.

The result? Winning the World Championship of Drivers five times—a record which stood for forty-six years until beaten by Michael Schumacher's sixth win in 2003. Schumacher won his seventh and last in 2004, racking up ninety-one wins in three hundred six starts, for a win ratio of 30%. Fangio raced with four different teams, Alfa Romeo, Ferrari, Mercedes-Benz and Maserati. He signed one-year contracts to give him flexibility to move to the car with the best chance.

Fangio holds the highest winning percentage in Formula 1 – 46% – winning twenty-four of fifty-two Formula 1 races he entered. Fangio is the only Argentine driver to have won the Argentine Grand Prix, having won it four times in his career—the most wins of all drivers.

The Scream of an Engine

After retirement, Fangio presided as the honorary president of Mercedes-Benz Argentina from 1987, a year after the inauguration of his own museum, until his peaceful death on 17 July 1995 at age 84.

Many of his contemporary racing competitors died young in racing accidents.

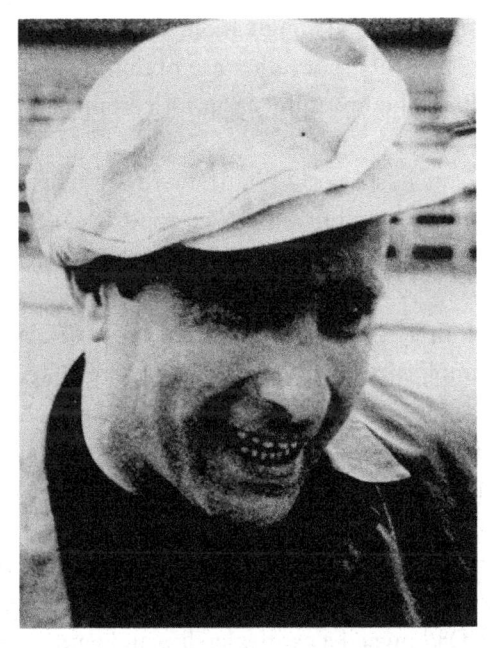

Juan Manuel Fangio pictured in a display at Brooklands, September 2017

I witnessed Fangio in action at Laguna Seca, CA in 1978, driving the mighty Mercedes 300 SLR in a demonstration versus Stirling Moss in a D-Type Jaguar. They exchanged the lead every lap. Just like they did racing against each other in the mid-Fifties until Moss joined Fangio on the Mercedes factory team. If you can't lick 'em, join 'em.

The British Contingent

John Michael Hawthorn

Mike Hawthorn is on my imaginary podium, just below Nuvolari and Fangio, all three favorites and influencers. But Mike's closely followed by half a dozen other drivers who were strong influencers on my childhood imagination. These half dozen drivers may not be 'best' or 'favorite', but rather are big influencers on developing my own car culture and my enthusiasm for certain cars and for racing.

A few years post-World War II, there was a bias in car reporting that favored the English, our allies, as opposed to the Germans and Italians. I succumbed to that, I'm sure. Hawthorn was part of that.

When I first followed him, Mike was officially 'J. Michael Hawthorn' to emphasize that he liked to go by 'Mike.' Tow headed, big grin, tall for a race car driver, I thought Mike cut a charismatic figure on the track. He drove Jaguars. And Ferraris. And Maseratis. And the Cooper-Bristol, Riley TT, BRM, Vanwall, and Lotus-Climax cars.

Mike often raced wearing a dress shirt and bow tie. Classy.

Mike's Dad owned a car dealership and garage, Tourist Trophy Garage, in Farnham, England, which sold Jaguars, Rileys, Fiats and Ferraris. Farnham is a two-hour drive south from Coventry and halfway between London and Southampton, next to the beautiful South Downs National Park in Surrey, the newest of England's National Parks.

Mike's Dad also raced motorcycles. When his Dad died in a motorcycle road accident in 1954, Mike inherited the business. Who wouldn't want to be selling Jaguars and Ferraris?

The Scream of an Engine

Mike won many victories in sports cars and British saloon cars, like winning the Sebring 12-Hour Endurance race for Briggs Cunningham in a D-Type Jaguar and the 24-Hours of Le Mans in the same model for the Jaguar factory, both in 1955. He won the Reims 12-Hour Endurance Race in 1956 with the automotive writer Paul Frère in a D-Type Jaguar.

In saloon cars, Mike won the 1956 Daily Express International Trophy at Silverstone in a Jaguar Mk VII four door sedan. This was a big car. Not sure how anyone made it go this fast. Then in 1957, Mike won the Daily Express International Trophy again at Silverstone, this

6'3" tall Mike Hawthorn raced in a white shirt and bow tie. Wikipedia

time in a 3.4 Jaguar saloon car, one like his personal road car. This smaller, nimbler sedan was a more likely race winner than the larger Mk VII given that they both used the same engine.

At Le Mans in June 1955, Hawthorn and Fangio in the Mercedes 300 SLR battled for the lead for three hours, with Hawthorn eventually setting the lap record at 122.388 MPH. The September 1955 issue of *Road & Track* featured the story of this epic battle. The race details took that long to report in those days. An enduring memory for this gearhead.

You could count on Hawthorn to set the lap record.

The 1955 Le Mans win occurred after the accident during the race with Pierre Levegh's Mercedes that took place in front of the pits and is described earlier.

This image is seared into my memory: the leaders trading places in the early hours of Le Mans 1955. Mike Hawthorn in the 3.4-liter No. 6 Jaguar D-Type followed by Castellotti's 4.4-liter Ferrari and the 3-liter Mercedes 300 SLR of Juan Fangio. Google Images

Mike Hawthorn and Ivor Bueb carried on after the horrendous accident, winning Le Mans 1955 by a five-lap margin over the factory Aston Martin of Peter Collins and Paul Frère. Officially, Hawthorn was exonerated from blame, the final ruling being 'racing accident.' The blame was placed on the track itself for changes not keeping up with the higher speed of the cars. The track was completely redesigned to avoid the speed differentials at the pits. Like most race tracks today, a wall at

The Scream of an Engine

Le Mans separates the track from the pits, resulting in a pit road separate from the racing surface.

But Mike was haunted by the experience until his death nearly three years later. Some say guilt seeks punishment which may explain Mike's own accident later.

Hawthorn was driving Formula 1 cars from early in his racing days. In 1953 and 1954 he competed largely for Ferrari. He won the World Championship in 1958, the first Englishman to do so. This was accomplished as a Ferrari team driver in a Ferrari 246 V-6. Following Hawthorn's death in a road accident, a perpetual trophy was established in his memory in 1959, awarded to the Englishman who wins the Formula 1 Driver's Championship. The most recent to win is Lewis Hamilton who won in 2015 and 2017 for Mercedes.

Mike Hawthorn never married, but fathered a son, Arnaud Michael Delaunay, by a young girl he met in Reims after winning the French Grand Prix in 1953 for Ferrari. In that race, he beat Fangio in a Maserati, González in a Maserati and three other Ferraris driven by Ascari, Farina and Villoresi. Fast company. After the race, Mike was feeling his oats.

Mike was engaged at the time of his death in 1958 to the fashion model Jean Howarth, who later married another racing driver, Innes Ireland.[50]

At the time of Mike's fatal accident, he was driving his hopped up 3.4-liter Jag sedan. The story I remember was that Hawthorn was driving very fast on a narrow, wet road near Onslow Village, Surrey, England. He crested a blind hill when a lorry – truck – pulled out in front of him.

---

[50] Wikipedia, April 2017

The Scream of an Engine

Later, the story turns out to be more complicated. Mike was probably racing Rob Walker, a friend and racing team owner, who was driving his Mercedes 300 SL. Mike had just passed Rob, then entered a right turn, hit a curb and sideswiped a truck coming the other way. This spun Mike off the road and into a tree. He died on impact. But he may have blacked out first from a terminal kidney infection he'd been suffering, another theory. The coroner's report was inconclusive.

He left this world doing what he loved best. Racing. Mike was just twenty-nine.

Peter John Collins

Most of my favorites are British, like Mike Hawthorn. This is cultural bias at work. I guess I'd be classified an Anglophile then, as now. My wife, Gaynor, was born in northern England.

Collins and Hawthorn were good friends inside and outside of racing. They competed intensely with the Italian driving ace, Luigi Musso.

Peter Collins, gentleman driver. Google Images

Fiamma Breschi, Luigi Musso's girlfriend at the time of his death, revealed the nature of Musso's rivalry with Hawthorn and Collins in a television documentary, *The Secret Life of Enzo Ferrari*. Breschi during the interview recalled that the antagonism between Musso and the two English drivers encouraged all three to take more risks: 'The Englishmen - Hawthorn and Collins - had an agreement', she says. 'Whichever of them won, they would share the winnings equally. It was the two of them against Luigi, who was not part of the agreement. Strength comes in numbers, and they were united against him."[51]

In the day, I never heard a whisper of such an arrangement.

In January 1957, Collins married American actress Louise King, daughter of the executive assistant to UN Secretary General Dag Hammarskjold, and the couple took up residence on a yacht in Monaco harbor. Enzo Ferrari figured Collins was partying too hard and dropped him from the team. Enraged, Hawthorn flew to Italy, is alleged to have broken down a door to get to Enzo, and demanded his teammate Collins be reinstated. Enzo relented.

Collins death in 1958 at age twenty-six occurred in the German Grand Prix at Nürburgring. He got wide on a turn, hit a ditch, flipped and was thrown clear. But he then hit a tree and died from head injuries. This was just two months before Hawthorn won the 1958 World Championship for Ferrari. Partly because of his friend's death, Hawthorn retired from racing immediately upon winning the Championship.

Collins was racing at age seventeen, impressing in Formula 3 races. He finished third in the 1951 Autosport National Formula 3 Championship at age 20. Like Hawthorn, he was the son of a car garage owner.

---

[51] Ibid., April 2017

The Scream of an Engine

Collins raced Formula cars for HWM, Vanwall, Maserati and Ferrari. I first noticed him when he raced for Vanwall, an exciting British entrant into Formula 1 racing in 1954. Collins was on the HWM Formula 2 team with Stirling Moss, and moved into a Formula 1 seat with HWM when Moss left the team. He also drove sports cars for Aston Martin, winning the Goodwood 9-Hour Endurance race in 1952, the 1953 RAC Tourist Trophy at Dundrod in a DB3S, and second places at Le Mans in 1955 and 1956 in the DB3S to Jaguar, with Paul Frere and Stirling Moss, respectively, co-driving.

With all this going on, Collins co-drove with Stirling Moss in the 300SLR Mercedes to win the 1955 Targa Florio, an historic win for Mercedes. Then Collins was tapped by Enzo Ferrari to drive in Formula 1, after Mercedes retired from racing. For Ferrari, Collins got second at Monaco in 1956 and won the Grand Prix of Belgium and the Grand Prix of France.

At the time, Enzo Ferrari had just lost his son, Dino, and Collins filled some of the void for the patron, being treated as a member of the family for a time.

Collins was on the verge of becoming Britain's first Formula 1 World Champion when he handed his Lancia-Ferrari D50 over to team leader Juan Manuel Fangio. Fangio had suffered a steering-arm failure toward the end of the Gran Premio d'Italia at the Autodromo Nazionale Monza. Collins eventually finished second, but the advantage handed to Moss, and the extra points gained by Fangio's finish, demoted Collins to third place in the championship. Collins's selfless act gained him respect from Enzo Ferrari and high praise from Fangio who said: '*I was moved almost to tears by the gesture... Peter was one of the finest and greatest gentlemen I ever met in my racing career.*'

Finally, in 1958 Collins won the early-in-the-year 1000 km of Buenos Aires and the 12-Hours of Sebring in a Ferrari 250 TR with Phil Hill. His last World Sports Car Championship podium was another second place at Nürburgring with Mike Hawthorn.

Chapter Ten: Race Drivers

The Scream of an Engine

Peter Collins, a favorite even though he raced mostly Ferraris and Aston Martins. Go figure my logic. But I admired him most for the assessment of his contemporaries: Collins was a gentleman on the race track.

Anthony Peter Roylance Rolt

Tony Rolt was an engineer and a war hero. Powerful combination. He was one of the last pre-war winners remaining to drive when racing recommenced in 1946. Tony won the 1939 British Empire Trophy at age 20. His racing career began in 1935 when he was sixteen and driving a 3-wheeler Morgan in speed trials.

Much later, Rolt won the 1953 24 Hours of Le Mans in the No. 18 C-Type Jaguar with Duncan Hamilton, Stirling Moss finishing second with Peter Walker in the No. 17 C-Type Jag after being slowed by mechanical issues. Rolt also participated in three Formula 1 World Championship Grands Prix.

Rolt was a key engineer developing the Ferguson P99 all-wheel drive Formula 1 car. In 1950, Harry Ferguson – the inventor of the modern tractor in 1935 - was intrigued by Rolt's work in the engineering lab on four-wheel drive, so Tony Rolt, Freddie Dixon and Harry Ferguson founded Ferguson Research Ltd. to pursue the ideas. By the early 1960s, Rolt – without Harry who passed away in 1960 - decided to build a 4WD racing car to demonstrate the value of four-wheel drive technology. Rolt helped design and test the Ferguson P99.

Although Rolt was more than capable of driving the car fast enough for test purposes, Jack Fairman was called in to race it in the 1961 British Empire Trophy and 1961 RAC British Grand Prix at Aintree, proving without doubt the four-wheel drive allied to the Dunlop Maxaret braking system was substantially superior in the wet.

The P99 was run under the banner of Rob Walker Racing and became the only 4WD car to win a Formula One race. In the hands of Stirling Moss, the P99 won the 1961 Oulton Park Gold Cup. The car was also the last front-engined car ever to win a Formula 1 race, albeit a non-championship one. Phil Hill gets the nod for last winner in a front-engined car in a championship Formula 1 race.

Tony Rolt in sunglasses, Duncan Hamilton driving, after winning Le Mans 1953. Getty Images, Klemantaski Collection

The Jensen FF Interceptor four-wheel drive car was developed from Rolt's work in the mid-Sixties.

In 1971, Tony Rolt incorporated a new firm, FF Developments, Ltd., to pursue opportunities in four-wheel drive technology. FF was an abbreviation for Ferguson Formula, a tribute to Tony's mentor, Harry Ferguson. According to Ward's Auto World, the influence that FF Developments had on all wheel drive transcended its size. Just some of the vehicles that have come out of this company, through licensing, are the Ford RS 200 in 1985; the AWD system used on the 1988 Jaguar XJ220 220 mph supercar prototype; the AWD system used on 1990 Chevrolet Astro/GMC Safari vans; and on the 2012 Ferrari FF. A first for a Ferrari model, this new four-wheel drive system weighs 50% less than a conventional four-wheel drive system and maintains an ideal weight distribution with 53% on the rear axle.

Tony Rolt's son succeeded him as president of FF Developments, LTD in 1986.[52]

James Duncan Hamilton

After fighting in and surviving World War II, Hamilton vowed to live life to the fullest and took up motor sport. Although adept in single-seaters, sports cars were where he enjoyed most success, winning the 1953 24 Hours of Le Mans, two Coupé de Paris events, and the 12-Hour International race at Reims, France race in 1956. Hamilton was an outgoing man, full of energy.

The story of the 1953 Le Mans victory is a typical Hamilton tale. Hamilton famously won the race shared with Tony Rolt. Initially, the pair was disqualified for practicing in a Jaguar that had the same racing number as another on the circuit at the same time. But they were reinstated in time to start the race.

When Jaguar team manager Lofty England persuaded the organizers to let them race, both drivers were already drunk in a local bar in the nearby town of Le Mans. England said: 'Of course I would never have let them race under the influence. I had enough trouble when they were sober!'

With the race underway, the team tried to sober Hamilton up by giving him coffee during the pit stops. But he refused it, saying it made his arms twitch; instead he was given brandy. The alcohol must have helped when he was struck by a bird in the face at 130 mph and broke his nose. It's a wonder how the pair managed to drive at all. But more wondrous still is that the pair won, recording the first 100 MPH average speed in the history of the race. Both England and Rolt have denied that they were drunk.[53] Hamilton stayed mum.

---

[52] http://www.offroadvehicle.ru/Jeep%20Comfort/FF%20Developments.html
[53] Wikipedia, April 2017

The Scream of an Engine

Duncan Hamilton leaping from the pit wall to take over from Tony Rolt on the Le Mans 1953 winning Jaguar XK 120 C. Getty Images

Duncan retired from racing in 1958 to operate a garage in Byfleet, Surrey, south-south west of London, a stone's throw from Brooklands. This is a wealthy part of England. He pursued this career until he succumbed to lung cancer in 1994 at the age of 71.

Ivor Bueb

This Englishman always nailed it, often in Jaguars, which counted a lot with me. He came up on my radar when he won the 1955 Le Mans event with Mike Hawthorn in the factory D-Type Jag, followed by another Le Mans win in 1957 with Ron Flockhart in the ex-works Ecurie Ecosse D-Type Jag. But Bueb also raced Lister-Jaguars for Brian Lister and showed up winning firsts at English tracks like Crystal Palace and Goodwood in 1958 and 1959.

The Scream of an Engine

He also excelled in Formula cars, from Formula 3 to Formula 2 to Formula 1 Coopers, and finished second in the British Championship in 1955. In 1966, when I bought a used Morris Cooper 1071S, this same Cooper name was on my mind, along with the history of Coopers and Bueb on English race tracks. For a gearhead, this ties together. Bueb also drove English Connaughts – I thought this car was gorgeous - and Maserati Formula 1 cars.

Like so many of my inspirational favorites, Bueb died from a racing accident at the Charade circuit near Clermont-Ferrand: he crashed at a double apex turn called Gravenoire at the far end of the course and was thrown out of his Formula 2 Cooper-Borgward. He passed away in the hospital six days later, August 1, 1959, age 36.

Bueb's death had unintended consequences. Brian Lister closed his race car business after losing his good friend Bueb as well as his friend Archie Scott-Brown who died at Spa a year earlier. Both raced successfully for Lister.

The Fifties and Sixties took so many lives of outstanding drivers. Jackie Stewart later campaigned for safety improvements which would have saved many of my Fifties favorites had they been in place earlier.

Peter Nield Whitehead

Post-World War II, we Yanks were very pro-British and anti-German, for obvious reasons. This affected my passions: given a choice, I always took the British car or driver in any race or discussion about relative values. Italians were down a peg or two, then you got to the Germans. I can't apologize for this. We humans are wired this way.

Peter won the 24-Hours of Le Mans in 1951 driving an XK 120 C. I was eight. This was a big deal for me. But probably a lot bigger deal for Jaguar, as this was the first of five Le Mans wins for Jaguar in the Fifties. Whitehead also won the first two of the modern series of the 12-Hours of Reims in a C-Type in 1953 with Stirling Moss and in 1954 with Ken Wharton in a D-Type. The modern series at Reims was conducted most years between 1953 and 1967.

Peter Whitehead, born November 12, 1914, died on September 21, 1958, the result of a racing accident at LaSalle, France in the Tour de France. His Jaguar slid off a bridge and into a ravine. His death in 1958 at age forty-four ended a busy racing career that started in 1935, twenty-three years earlier. Stirling Moss called Whitehead one of life's good guys.[54]

Peter Douglas Conyers Walker

Peter Walker was one of a handful of drivers who inspired me to race a C-Type Jaguar carved from a block of wood on our Maryland garage floor in 1952. The reason? With Peter Whitehead, Walker won the 1951 Le Mans 24 Hour Race. He continued racing for many years after that, winning the Goodwood Nine-Hours in 1955 – also in a Jag – but retired from racing in 1956 due to injuries suffered in a crash.

Walker was born in Huby, Yorkshire in 1912 and passed away in Newtown, Worcestershire in 1984 at the ripe age of 71 from dementia. Most of his contemporaries didn't get that far. He proved a strong driver in most disciplines, but was most adept in sports cars.

Peter enjoyed success in both circuit racing and hill climbs driving an ERA prior to World War II, with victories at Brooklands and Donington Park. Throughout this period, he could be found racing Peter Whitehead's ERAs.

---

[54] The details of Peter Walker's life are from Wikipedia, July 2017

The Scream of an Engine

Peter entered the world of up and coming Jaguar cars after the War and finished second in the 1949 Silverstone International, a race which he won the following year also driving an XK 120. In 1951, in addition to winning at Le Mans with his close friend Peter Whitehead, Walker placed second to Stirling Moss in the RAC Tourist Trophy race, again driving the XK 120 C.

Walker then raced Formula 1 cars with less success. His stint with the fledgling BRM company's supercharged 1.5-litre V16 BRM Type 15 was typical. He finished seventh in the 1951 British Grand Prix Formula 1 race held on 14 July 1951 at the Silverstone Circuit in Northamptonshire, England. Most races for these BRMs ended 'Did Not Finish.'

Peter then finished third in the RAC Tourist Trophy in 1953 in the XK 120 C, and in the same car winning the 1954 Silverstone International race. In 1955, Walker switched to Aston Martin and won the Goodwood 9-Hour in a DB3S, his last significant outing before the crash that ended his racing career in 1956.

Stirling Craufurd Moss, OBE

Moss has been described as 'the greatest driver never to win the World Championship.'

But in a seven-year span between 1955 and 1961, Moss finished as World Championship runner-up four times and was third the other three. Many of the wins of other World Champions were by a point or two, and like the win by Phil Hill, dependent on events outside their control. There is a bit of luck in a World Championship. The chips just didn't favor Moss.

Make no mistake: Moss was quick.

The Scream of an Engine

In the Foreword to Chris Harvey's *Jaguars in Competition* written by Moss, Moss' speed becomes clear. When Moss was twenty, he approached car manufacturers for an opportunity to drive for them.

Moss says they turned him down because 'they felt I was driving a bit too quickly and would have an accident.'

Tommy Wisdom gave Moss his first opportunity to race a big manufacturer's car. Wisdom owned a brand new, factory-prepared XK 120 and entered it in the Tourist Trophy at Dundrod, Northern Ireland: the date was September 16, 1950. Conditions for the race were the worst: torrential rain, howling gale and deep mud throughout the pits and washing out onto the course everywhere. But the race commenced anyway.

Moss won the class and came first overall. The next day he turned twenty-one and 'Bill' Lyons called Moss up and asked him to lead the works Jaguar team the following season.

Moss went on to win this Tourist Trophy race six more times, including the 1951 event in an XK 120C; later in the Mercedes 300 SLR, two in the Aston Martin DBR1 and two in the Ferrari 250 GT.

Moss isn't as high on my influential list as you might suspect. Can I just not forgive him for going to Mercedes in 1955? My brand loyalty must be especially difficult to break. After all Moss was knighted by the Queen of England on March 21, 2000, so she clearly got over it.

In 1954, Moss became the first non-American to win the 12-Hours of Sebring overall, sharing the Cunningham team's beautiful but diminutive 1.5-liter Italian O.S.C.A. MT4 with American Bill Lloyd.

Moss's first Formula 1 victory was in the 1955 British Grand Prix at Aintree, a race he was also the first British driver to win. Leading a 1–2–3–4 finish for Mercedes, it was the first time he beat Fangio, his teammate and arch rival, who was also his friend and mentor. It has been

The Scream of an Engine

suggested that Fangio sportingly allowed Moss to win in front of his home crowd. Moss himself asked Fangio repeatedly, and Fangio always replied: 'No. You were just better than me that day.' The same year, Moss also won the RAC Tourist Trophy, the Targa Florio, sharing the drive with Peter Collins, and the 1955 Mille Miglia.

Moss won Italy's thousand-mile Mille Miglia road race, an achievement Doug Nye – journalist and author of seventy motor racing books - described as the 'most iconic single day's drive in motor racing history.' *Motor Trend* headlined it as, 'The Most Epic Drive. Ever.' Still brings chills thinking about it, and of course, smiles from all Mercedes owners around the world.

Stirling Moss. Grand Prix History

Moss, then twenty-five years old, drove one of four factory-entered Mercedes-Benz 300 SLR sports-racing cars. Based on the W196 Grand Prix car, they had spaceframe chassis, magnesium-alloy bodies and modified W196 engines. The team's main race rivals were the factory-entered Ferraris of Piero Taruffi, Eugenio Castellotti, Umberto Maglioli, and Paolo Marzotto.

The Scream of an Engine

Journalist Denis Jenkinson was Moss's navigator. Jenkinson had intended to go with John Fitch, whose idea it had been to take a navigator, but when Mercedes assigned a 300 SL to Fitch, the American agreed to Jenkinson riding with Moss in the faster SLR. Jenkinson had come up with the idea of pace notes in the form of a roller map of the route on which he had noted its hazards—an innovation that helped Moss compete against drivers with greater local knowledge. Jenkinson used hand signals to tell Moss about the road ahead. Radio communication had proved ineffective when they tried it, because when Moss was fully concentrated on his driving he was oblivious to Jenkinson's voice.

John Fitch engineered and built the map device that Jenkinson used for the race.

Fangio, who regarded the race as too dangerous for passengers, drove his SLR alone, as did Karl Kling. Hans Herrmann drove the fourth car with mechanic Herman Eger as passenger.[55]

Moss was said to like racing the C-Type Jaguars, but not the D-Types, and in the day, I never heard the reason why. In my opinion, the turning point for Moss was when he lost the brakes on a D-Type at Le Mans in 1954 at 170 MPH. After a pitstop to repair the brakes, he refused to drive the car again. My own reason would be that my feet are too big to fit in the footwell of either of these cars. So that can't be Moss' reason, because the footwell is about the same size on both C-Types and D-Types. I've tried to drive both these race cars.

Moss mentored Steve McQueen at Brands Hatch in 1961, although McQueen had raced cars since his win in a Porsche 356 at Santa Barbara in May 1959, his first race.

In 1962, on April 23, Moss tried to pass Graham Hill's BRM V-8 on the outside of the high-speed Fordwater Bend in a Formula 1 race at Goodwood. Moss' Lotus-Climax V-8 slid off on the grass at an

---

[55] Wikipedia, April 2017

Chapter Ten: Race Drivers

The Scream of an Engine

estimated 130 MPH and hit a bank designed to protect the spectators on the other side. Moss was rushed to the hospital with head injuries, lacerations and a damaged leg. He was in a coma for a month. Moss was two laps down to Hill at the time, trying to un-lap himself, although there was no way he could catch Hill so late in the race. Moss was always intensely competitive.

And Moss was no stranger to crashing. While practicing for the Belgian Grand Prix at Spa in June 1960, less than two years earlier, Moss crashed at 145 MPH, broke both legs and injured his back.

Goodwood was the end of Moss' racing career for eighteen years - until 1980 when he joined a two car Audi coupé racing team which wasn't competitive.[56] Moss was lucky. He walked away from the sport. Moss test drove for Lotus after retiring and often made demonstration runs on race courses in Europe and North America, like the one I watched with Fangio at Laguna Seca in 1978. He continued doing that up until age 85 two years ago. He's still going strong, though, as this is written.

Norman Graham Hill, OBE

Graham Hill fascinated me with his moustache, calm manner and Englishman's demeanor. Hill was born in 1929 and twice became Formula 1 World Champion. He is the only driver ever to win what's known as the Triple Crown of Motorsport—the 24 Hours of Le Mans, Indianapolis 500 and either the Monaco Grand Prix or the Formula One World Drivers' Championship. Hill won the Monaco Grand Prix five times including driving a BRM P261 to first place in 1964.

After serving his country in the Royal Navy, Hill landed a job with Colin Chapman at Lotus. He continued to badger Chapman until he got to race a Lotus. He won many races while getting his career

---

[56] https://www.theguardian.com/sport/2015/apr/24/stirling-moss-crash-goodwood-1962-archive

The Scream of an Engine

underway. Later in 1967, he returned to Lotus to race the Lotus Cortina successfully.

I stood ten feet from Graham Hill in the pits at the September 1961 U.S. Grand Prix at Watkins Glen, NY. This was the first of twenty Formula 1 races held at the Glen. Nearby, Stirling Moss, Masten Gregory, Walt Hansgen and Jim Clark were preparing to race. But Hill resonated with me, especially his moustache. So did his BRM car, powered by an engine with headers that exhausted straight up, as I recall. Sources today say that engine was a four-cylinder Coventry Climax, so I may be wrong about the headers on the 1961 car. I doubt it! The 'Stackpipe' configuration continued with the BRM V-8 engined P 57 in which he won the 1962 World Championship. I loved the sound of that engine.

On this day, Innes Ireland won for Lotus, Dan Gurney finished second in a Porsche 718, Graham Hill came fifth and Jim Clark seventh. Roger Penske, later a huge figure in U.S. racing, finished eighth.

Hill's Jaguar racing, important for me, came in England in 3.4 and 3.8-liter sedans which were so successful in the late Fifties and early Sixties. He also won in the E-Type debut in 1961 at Oulton Park, England, driving for Ecurie Endeavor. Mike Hawthorn raced Jaguar saloon cars, including the Mark VIIs, 3.4s and 3.8s, to many wins. Walt Hansgen showed up from America to race a 3.4 in England in 1958.

They're all three on my favorites/most influential list.

Graham and his son Damon were the first father and son pair to have both won the Formula One World Championship. Hill's grandson Josh, Damon's son, also raced his way through the ranks until he retired from Formula 3 in 2013 at the age of twenty-two.

The Scream of an Engine

Graham Hill, 1962 and 1968 World Champion. *Hill won the Watkins Glen Formula 1 race three times during the Sixties.* Google Images

Toward the end of his career, Hill formed his own Formula 1 team, Embassy-Hill, which raced Lolas and Shadows.

Hill died at age forty-six when the twin-engine six-seat Piper Aztec airplane he was piloting crashed and burned in foggy conditions at night near Arkley golf course in North London. Hill, Tony Brise and four other members of Hill's racing team were returning from car testing at Circuit Paul Ricard in France and were due to land at Elstree Airfield. All six friends were killed.

Kenneth Henry Miles

I first encountered Ken Miles in 1953, through *Road & Track*, when Miles moved from his native England to the Los Angeles, California area. That year, he won fourteen straight victories in SCCA racing in an MG-based special of his own design and construction. While this is before our family owned an MG A, at this point anything English was good for me, almost anything German or Italian, bad. That would change a bit but not much.

I've always thought of Miles as American, but obviously we can't claim what isn't ours.

In March 1955 driving his second MG Special, dubbed 'The Flying Shingle', Miles won the Palm Springs, CA SCCA race but was disqualified later for having 'fenders too wide.' I've always been concerned about wide fenders. Apparently, the inscrutable SCCA scrutineers agreed with me. Miles had beaten Cy Yedor, also in an MG Special, and an up and coming actor named James Dean in a Porsche 356. With Miles disqualified, the other two moved up in the finishing order.

But Ken was rewarded when the Flying Shingle made the front cover of *Road & Track* in May 1955.

I learned that Ken raced motorcycles before WW II, became a British tank commander during the war and stood six feet four inches tall. Tall people could race, too, I now knew. After the war Miles raced Alfas, Bugattis and Alvises in England.

In 1956, he hooked up with Johnny von Neumann to race von Neumann's Porsche 550 Spyder in west coast races. Then he put his engineering hat on again and shoe horned a Porsche engine into a lightweight Cooper chassis, the result being called a 'Pooper.' Pete Lovely also built his own 'Pooper.' Miles dominated SCCA racing on the west coast with his Pooper in 1957 and 1958.

Now well known, Miles racing career accelerated. He hooked up with Carroll Shelby in the early Sixties where his friends called him 'Teddy Tea Bag' or 'Side Bite' because he drank tea and talked out of the side of his mouth.[57]

---

[57] Wikipedia, April 2017

The Scream of an Engine

Ken Miles winner in a GT 40 at Daytona, FL, 2000KM race in 1965. Won again in 1966 in a GT 40 Mark II, first Daytona Race at 24-Hours. Flick River

With Shelby, who had the development contract with Ford for the GT 40 cars, Ken was test driver. The cars now under Shelby's organization became quickly competitive and Miles as race driver won many events. In the Sebring 12-Hour race, always one of my favorites, Miles won twice in 1965 driving a 289 GT 40 with Bruce McLaren and again in 1966 driving a 427 GT 40 Mark II with Lloyd Ruby.

I mention elsewhere that I witnessed six or so hours of the 1966 race in person.

Miles also won the Daytona 24-Hour race in February 1966 with Lloyd Ruby in the 427 Mark II. Ken was also leading the Le Mans 24-Hour Race in June 1966 when Henry Ford II made the decision to finish the cars three abreast. As mentioned, that decision cost Miles the win.

In what was called the Ford J-Car at the time, but later was renamed the GT 40 Mark IV, Miles was testing at Riverside in August 1966 when the car flipped at high speed, breaking up and killing Ken instantly. Miles was 47.

Speculation centered on the aerodynamic lift at the back of the car's Kamm-design rear end that caused the flip. The new aircraft honeycomb construction wasn't up to the punishment that followed.

The car completely disintegrated. After losing Hansgen at Le Mans in April in a Mark II, and now Miles, Ford insisted on adding a complete NASCAR-style roll cage to the J-car's design. This change probably saved Mario Andretti's life during a bad Mark IV crash at Le Mans in 1967, the race won by Dan Gurney and A. J. Foyt in another Mark IV.

Miles was a British gearhead, we might properly say petrol head, but a gentleman and a popular race driver among his friends and teammates. He's one that seemed a huge loss to me.

The American Contingent

This group of drivers isn't better or worse than the preceding group: mostly just a year or two later in my culture building.

Daniel Sexton Gurney

Dan Gurney is personable, knowledgeable and a perfect gentleman. He's not English. But at 6'4" with broad shoulders, is not a typical small race car driver, either. Dan should have been given a weight handicap. But he didn't need one. Dan has all-American good looks to boot and his popularity was so great during his racing years that *Car and Driver* Editor-in-Chief David E. Davis, Jr. seriously promoted Dan to run for President of the United States in May 1964.

Gurney is noted for many achievements in motor racing and car construction. One I like best is his spritzing the crowd with a jeroboam of champagne after his 1967 Le Mans win with A. J. Foyt. He now displays this jeroboam in a glass case in his Santa Ana, CA conference room.

Dan gave me and Bob Swanson, Director of the San Diego Automotive Museum, each a copy of the drawing celebrating this historic event. Dan autographed them while we visited with him in 2008, preparing for the Museum's 20th Anniversary celebration. Dan agreed to be the Guest of Honor at this event.

I've framed the Le Mans champagne event and the result is featured in my living room to this day. Dan started the champagne tradition that continues at almost every racing event around the world.

Gurney somehow fit into Porsche's only Formula 1 car for the 1961-1962 seasons, winning Porsche's only Formula 1 victory ever at the 1962 French Grand Prix.

The French Grand Prix of 1962 was staged at the Rouen-Les-Essarts street circuit near Rouen, France. The street circuit - which ran on public roads - had a few medium straights, a cobbled hairpin turn called Nouveau Monde and a few blind corners through a wooded hillside. The track was also known as a bumpy, harsh circuit with an especially fearsome downhill section consisting of quick sweepers leading directly into a slow hairpin.

That kind of tough work is Dan's meat and potatoes.

For 1961, Porsche heavily modified the 718 sports car, which had been raced from 1957 to 1962 as the RSK, into a Formula 1 vehicle. It wasn't competitive. But for 1962, Porsche finished the purpose built

The Scream of an Engine

804, which used the same flat eight, 180 BHP, four overhead cam-engine from the last 718s. Porsche was now prepared. So was Dan.

As always, Porsche engineered reliability into the 804. It could take the punishment of the Rouen-Les-Essarts course. At the time, the 804 was down on power compared with BRM's V-8 and behind on technology to the Lotus 25. Dan overcame all that and grabbed the lead with thirteen laps remaining, beating Richie Ginther, Bruce McLaren, and John Surtees in the process.

A few years after the Porsche experience, it's more understandable that Dan would fit into the Eagle Formula 1 car his own company designed and built in Santa Ana, CA. He then won the Spa-Francorchamps Formula 1 race in 1967 in that All American Racers Eagle. Dan was the first American to win a Grand Prix in an American-built car since Jimmy Murphy won the French Grand Prix in 1921 - although Murphy didn't build the Duesenberg. Dan was the first American driver to win in an American car under the Formula 1 Grand Prix rules established in the late Forties.

Then in 1968 at the German Grand Prix, he's credited with wearing the first full face shield racing helmet. Dan was very safety conscious and stayed on the cutting edge of safety design throughout his career, following the vociferous efforts of Jackie Stewart, John Fitch and others in reducing the number of racing deaths.

Dan's also one aggressive and skilled driver, often sent out to be 'rabbit' and lead his team early in long distance races to try to lure the competitors into breakdowns. An indication of how he could pull that rabbit out of the hat is that he won forty-two career pole positions and appeared on the front row of race grids another fifty-eight times.

His All American Racers team has built beautiful, fast, race winning Eagle cars for different race series, like Formula 1, the

Chapter Ten: Race Drivers

The Scream of an Engine

International Motor Sports Association series founded in 1969, and U.S. championship auto racing, centered around cars built to win the Indianapolis 500 and known as IndyCar since 2011.

Dan designed and built the innovative Alligator motor cycle with a low center of gravity. Dan crashed the prototype. The most serious injuries were to his feet. But he found that Croc shoes minimized the pain during recovery. He wore a pair of black Crocs to the Twentieth Anniversary Gala Celebration of the San Diego Automotive Museum, a black-tie affair.

The morning following the Gala, I was on a plane at 7 AM to New Zealand to participate in a wedding. We'd been up until 2 AM taking cars back from the hotel to the Museum. On the plane, I realized that I'd forgotten my wedding shoes. In Auckland, I found a Crocs store and bought a pair of black Crocs for the wedding. Good enough for Dan, good enough for me.

Dan relayed a story during our 2008 meeting in his Costa Mesa, CA conference room when asked about the difference between the 1957 Ferrari Testa Rossa and the 1958 version.

'Not much' he said, 'just a bolt in the front suspension.' I asked him how he remembered all those details. In his self-effacing manner, he just laughed and said he really didn't, except in this one case. Right.

While at Porsche racing in Formula 1, Dan met Evi who was then working at Porsche. They were later married. Evi, bubbly, enthusiastic and knowledgeable, conducted our tour of All American's facilities.

In a fifteen year stretch before retiring to build race cars, Dan won in Formula 1, finished second at the Indianapolis 500, won at Le

The Scream of an Engine

Mans, and won in NASCAR, CAN AM and TRANS AM - everywhere he showed up.

No. 18 Ferrari Testa Rossa, like one Dan Gurney raced in Europe in 1957 and 1958, 1962 GTO in near background, San Diego Automotive Museum, November 2008

Dan and Evi Gurney at the San Diego Automotive Museum 20th Anniversary Gala with Gaynor and Bud Suiter, November 2008

The Scream of an Engine

Dan Gurney and the beautiful 1966 AAR Eagle Indy Car. AAR photo

Walter Edwin Hansgen

I first saw Walt Hansgen race at Watkins Glen in September 1953 when I was ten. Our four-member family had driven up from our Maryland farm with an apprentice tool maker from Dad's tool and die business. Gordon Davis, the apprentice, owned a 1953 Austin Healey 100 with Laycock de Normanville overdrive. He was way cool and joined us for this adventure. We camped out in tents on the back stretch of the new, purpose built 4.6-mile long race course which replaced racing on the 6.6-mile street course the prior five years.

This was my first ever real race. I was out-of-control excited to the point that Dad had to tell me to shut up when I kept asking tons of questions. Like, do you think a C-Jag will be there? Who will be driving it? Can it beat the Ferraris? Will the Cunninghams be there?

At the Glen, Walt was racing a Jaguar XK 120 Special. His Bedminster, NJ car dealership sponsored the Special. George Harris' Allard led off the line at the start of the Glen Grand Prix race, as I recall the announcer screaming, but Dr. M. R. J. Wylie in his XK 120 was in the mix, too, as was Walt. One of the reasons for my excitement: there were sixteen XK 120s in the race, although three would DNF. Four more failed to start the race.

The Scream of an Engine

The progress of the cars around the course was broadcast over the loudspeaker system in front of our position along the back straight. Walt appeared first over the rise. Close behind was Harris' Chrysler-Allard, a class up in B Production. As the race progressed, Harris was so close that one mistake and Hansgen would be history. But the pair maintained their 1-2 positions to the end.

Walt won the race by one second. And my undying enthusiasm for Walt. Always and forever.

The hairpin-turn to the right at the bottom of the hill provided entertainment. Cars slid off onto the dirt coming out of the hairpin turn. Huge clouds of dust resulted. Since the cars had to slow down from very high speed as they went past us, the brakes took a real beating here. The worst offenders seemed to me to be a quartet of XK 120 Jags dicing in the race. Later, I found out that XK 120s suffered brake fade, especially later in the race, and just couldn't slow down enough for the turn. The stopping distance for them was, let's say, uncertain.

Hansgen didn't have that problem. It was exciting to watch his Jag accelerate out of the hairpin, passing cars being lapped as they disappeared into the trees surrounding the track, the Allard close behind.

As mentioned in the MG chapter, we later watched Walt Hansgen run away from the field at the Cumberland, MD SCCA National race in May 1955, this time in a green D-Type Jag. Which was his favored ride at this point of his career: Walt won four SCCA Class C - Modified National Championships from 1956 through 1959, the first three in the D-Type, the fourth in a Lister Jag. Another 'special,' but this special made by Brian Lister in England instead of in New Jersey at the Hansgen dealership.

The Lister-Jag bears further mention.

The Scream of an Engine

Walt Hansgen had become a convert to the Lister-Jaguar from his preceding Cunningham D-Type Jaguar experiences. Briggs Cunningham bought the first two Lister-Jaguar 'Knobblies' directly from the Lister factory in early 1958.

According to Mike Argetsinger's Hansgen biography, Hansgen wrote in April 1958, *"The Lister goes through the 'S' turns and over bumpy parts of the circuit far better than the 'D' Type. I believe this is due to several factors. The rear un-sprung weight is very much lower and the weight distribution is better for braking. The two hundred pounds less in total weight as compared with the 'D' is a considerable asset when approaching a corner.* However, had I spent six hours driving the Lister – at the 1958 Sebring 12-Hour where he quickly DNFed due to the 3.0-liter Jaguar engine failure – *"I suspect that I'd still be in Florida recuperating."*[58]

These two Cunningham team Lister-Jaguars were re-engined immediately after Sebring with full 3.8-litre power units enlarged and perfected by the Momo Corporation. They achieved almost total domination of that year's – 1958 - SCCA National Championship race series. Walt led the charge.

Beginning at Marlboro on April 20, 1958, Walt Hansgen won handsomely in the prototype Cunningham Lister-Jag, and on May 4 at Danville, Virginia, teammate Ed Crawford won in his Lister-Jag with Hansgen second. In a second race at Danville, the Cunningham team pair again finished 1-2, this time Hansgen winning from Crawford.[59]

---

[58] David Bull Publishing, 2006

[59] http://www.bonhams.com/auctions/19289/lot/258/ for the occasion of selling serial no. 1

Chapter Ten: Race Drivers

The Scream of an Engine

Walt also won the Formula Junior race at Sebring, FL, during the inaugural 1959 U.S. Grand Prix, driving an Italian Stanguellini.

Hansgen was offered more rides in other owners' cars. He achieved an interesting foray into Formula 1 in 1961 at Watkins Glen in a Cooper-Climax entered by Al Momo's Momo Corporation. I was in the pits for that race. Walt retired, recording a DNF in his first Formula 1 outing. He was back in 1964 driving a Lotus 33 with a Climax V-8 for Team Lotus. Walt had reached the pinnacle sought by every driver who aspired to race Formula 1 at the time: a seat in a Lotus team car. This time Walt finished fifth, earning two points toward the World Championship.

Also in 1964, Walt raced the MG Liquid Suspension Special, with an Offenhauser engine, for Kjell Qvale at the Indianapolis 500. He finished thirteenth and returned the next year to finish 14th, the year that Jim Clark won the race in a Lotus 49 Ford V-8, spelling the end of domination at the Brickyard by front engined, Offenhauser powered race cars.

Walt was on the wrong side of the power curve at Indianapolis.

Hansgen also gets credit for bringing Mark Donahue into motorsports. In 1966, they had raced together at the Daytona 24 Hour in February and Sebring 12 Hour in March, finishing third and second overall respectively in the Ford GT 40 Mark II. When he got to Le Mans in April, Walt was no stranger to the GT 40.

Like so many of my favorite inspirational drivers, Walt died doing what he loved best. He was racing a Ford GT 40 Mk II for the Holman-Moody team in practice at Le Mans in April 1966. Walt was to race the car with Mark Donahue. The Ford GT 40s now featured the famed Ford 427 side oiler motor, a big step up in power and speed from the 289s of the prior year. The track was wet. Walt hit standing water at speed, the big racing tires aquaplaned, and Walt lost control. He tried to go up the escape road, but a barrier had been put up 'to protect spectators.' The resulting crash broke almost every bone in his body.

Walt passed away five days later at the U.S. Military Hospital in Orléans, a two-hour drive from Le Mans. His wife Beatrice and two teenaged kids were at his side. He was 46.

In March 1973, I stood in the muddy pits at Mid-America Raceway outside St. Louis. It was cold and gray, threatening rain. The temperature was 40^0 F and with the wind blowing, felt like 32^0. As I stood there shivering, listening to the Driver's School Instructor drone on, I remembered Walt specifically that day in 1953 at Watkins Glen, when he inspired me to race. I thought about how he ended. What was I doing out here? What was racing all about that I'd do this after what happened to my heroes?

All I can conclude is that passion overwhelms clear thinking.

From my extended list of inspirational drivers, those that helped build my own culture and led to me standing in the mud at Mid-America Raceway, twelve died behind the wheel including Hansgen: nearly half of them. They, like me at Mid America Raceway, were doing what they wanted to do.

Briggs Swift Cunningham II

Briggs, an American and a Yale graduate, inspired me and many others who also became my heroes, to race cars. I think his middle name suited a man with a passion for driving fast cars and racing fast sailboats. His place of residence as entrant in many car races in the

The Scream of an Engine

1950s and for the America's Cup race in 1958 was noted to be 'Green Farms, CT.'

Cunningham was racing sailboats in 1931. This culminated in building and skippering an America's Cup boat named Columbia in 1958 – the first America's Cup Race after World War II - and winning the Aulde Mug. One of Briggs' many sailing achievements is invention of the 'cunningham', a rig that allows fine tuning the shape of the mainsail from below the tack and near the foot of the mast.

Cunningham joined founders and college buddies Miles and Sam Collier in the Automobile Racing Club of America - ARCA - in 1933, which Cunningham helped become the Sports Car Club of America in 1944. This ARCA was not related to the modern ARCA founded in 1953 for racing American stock cars.

Briggs first raced a car, a Buick-Mercedes of his own design, at Watkins Glen in 1949. He later built a line of Cunningham race and road cars, culminating in a third-place finish at Le Mans in 1953 by Fitch and Spear in a Cunningham C5-R with a 5.5-liter Chrysler V-8.

Briggs signature achievement for me was driving a Cunningham C2-R for nearly twenty of the twenty-four hours at the 1952 Le Mans race with Bill Spear his co-driver. For which he earned the title Ironman. Pierre Levegh, the French race driver, was also attempting to go the distance in 1952 in his Talbot Lago, but missed a shift late in the race while leading and DNFed. Cunningham and Bill Spear ended fourth in the C2-R in 1952, with poor Spear at the wheel for a little over four hours. Long way to come for a short drive.

I was introduced to the Cunningham car collection at the Costa Mesa, CA Museum in 1976. This was the first opportunity I had to see it after moving from St. Louis to San Diego in 1976. John Bishop, who ran the Museum, gave me the tour and said, 'Mr. Cunningham insists that each car in the collection be driven each week.' Tough job, John.

Briggs Cunningham was the son of a Cincinnati financier and businessman who funded the start-up of Proctor & Gamble. A fortune was generated from that investment.

At Le Mans again in 1953, Briggs achieved a seventh-place finish, just nine laps behind the Fitch/Walters Cunningham C5-R which ended third, behind the winning Jaguar C-Types. The Jags were the first race cars to use disk brakes that year, which made a difference in slowing from the high-speed straights. The third Cunningham, a C4-RK, came tenth driven by Moran and Bennett. The C5-R was timed as the fastest car down the straights with its huge 5.35-liter Chrysler V-8: 154.7 MPH. And was equipped with seventeen-inch diameter drum brakes, front and rear, which were still not enough.

Only one C5-R was ever built – in 1953. John Fitch did an end over end crash in the car at the Reims 12-Hour following the fine showing at Le Mans. The car was repaired and later won races in the States. Cunningham went back to the C4-R for Le Mans 1954 with fifteen more horsepower than the C5-R.

Briggs was featured on the April 26, 1954 cover of *Time* magazine, with three of his Cunningham racing cars. The caption reads: Road Racer Briggs Cunningham: Horsepower, Endurance, Sportsmanship. He became an early member of the Road Racing Drivers Club, the famed RRDC, an invitation-only club formed to honor notable road racing drivers.

Briggs Cunningham. Google Images

At Le Mans again in June 1954, the Bill Spear/Sherwood Johnston C4-R finished third with Briggs Cunningham and John Gordon Bennett finishing fifth in another C4-R.

The C6-R competed in the 1955 Le Mans race, powered by a 3-liter Offenhauser engine which expired early in the race with a burned piston, the last year Briggs Cunningham competed in his own cars.

The IRS effectively closed Cunningham's car production lines down due to the hobby rule: in the five years allowed, Cunningham had yet to make a profit. His tax-exempt status was over. After that, Briggs raced D-Type Jaguars and Lister Jaguars, his team winning Sebring in 1955 with Mike Hawthorn and Phil Walters driving the D-Type.

Briggs Cunningham, gearhead, his own man doing things his own way. He passed away in July 2003 at age 96 in Las Vegas, NV.

Philip Toll Hill, Jr.

Phil Hill appeared in one of the first *Road and Track* magazines I read and often thereafter. Phil raced his own MG TC, winning at Carrell Speedway in 1949; the Jaguar XK 120 he owned with which he won at Pebble Beach, CA in 1950; and the Alfa 2900B he owned winning at Carrell Speedway and Pebble Beach in 1951.

What a start to a stellar career. Phil owned cars that had become my favorites and shaped my passions from age eight through twelve.

Phil Hill was a brilliant driver. But where did the money come from to buy those exotic cars he raced early on?

Phil was known as quiet and introspective, quite intelligent, with a ready smile, not favoring large crowds. Alma Hill, his wife, says he was a perfectionist when it came to his cars. His knowledge of them was encyclopedic and people would always ask Phil questions about them. Alma and he went through Lamaze classes and Phil assisted with the birth of two of their three kids, Vanessa and Derek, in the hospital. The pediatrician thought Phil was a doctor. Phil loved animals and the family raised dogs and cats, especially a Spaniel named Chumley, and a big white cat named Enzo. They seemed to favor Phil's lap. The Hills and Gurneys were close friends and travelled together. Alma remembers most the laughter from those trips.[60]

---

[60] John Lamm and Peter Egan, http://www.roadandtrack.com/car-culture/interviews/a17497/life-with-a-champion/

The Scream of an Engine

By 1952, Phil was racing for other owners, like Charles H. Hornburg, Jr., the Jaguar/MG importer in New York City. Driving Hornburg's Jaguar XK 120 C, Phil won the SCCA National at Elkhart Lake, WI in June 1952, and at Torrey Pines, CA in December 1952.

The early MGs, Alfas and Jaguars are my tie-in with Phil Hill, a man I never met but feel I know personally because of his connection with my favorite cars. Phil quickly migrated away from racing MGs, Alfas and Jaguars to racing Ferraris. His first Formula 1 race came at the German Grand Prix in 1958, the very race in which his close friend Peter Collins was killed. Phil was living on Collin's yacht in Monaco at the time.

You can imagine how that felt. But Collins' death opened a door for Hill to achieve a permanent position on the Ferrari racing team.

Phil raced to win and usually did. His first win in Formula 1 was in the 1960 Italian GP, the last win ever for a 2.5-liter Formula 1 car and for a front-engine Grand Prix car in a championship race. In addition to winning the Formula 1 World Championship for Ferrari in 1961, with the new Ferrari 156 V-6 car built to the 1.5-liter formula, he also won two of my favorite races, the Le Mans 24-Hour Race and the Sebring 12-Hour Race, both three times. His first Le Mans win was in the Ferrari 250 Testa Rossa sports car in 1958 with co-driver Oliver Gendebien.

As *Road & Track* put it: '*One thing most automotive enthusiasts didn't realize about Phil when he was racing was that long before competing and long after he was fascinated with things mechanical. Big things, like Packards and Pierce Arrows, but even their smallest component parts. Large clutch plates, but also tiny springs. Heavy engine blocks and light carburetor floats. One of the books on the main table in his living room was the bible of mechanical devices,* "The Way

The Scream of an Engine

Things Work." *It wasn't just a matter of aptitude, but also a big dose of simpatico with mechanical devices. If you had met Phil Hill and looked at his fingers you'd have likely found a little grease ground into the creases and swirls.*[61]

Phil Hill at Elkhart Lake, WI in 1952, winning in Charles Hornburg's Jaguar XK 120 C, the story featured in Burt Levy's fictional book, The Last Open Road. *This was the first win for the XK 120 C in the U.S.* Google

Phil Hill has the distinction of winning his first race in an MG TC in 1949 and his last race driving a Chaparral in the BOAC 500 at Brands Hatch, England in 1967.

Following his retirement from racing, Hill built up an award winning classic car restoration business in the 1970s called Hill & Vaughn with business partner Ken Vaughn, until they sold the partnership in 1984. Phil remained with the buyer until the sale of the

---

[61]http://www.roadandtrack.com/car-culture/interviews/a17651/phil-hill-50-years-later/

business again in 1995. Meanwhile, Hill also worked as a television commentator for ABC's Wide World of Sports.

So, Phil Hill was a classic gearhead under my definition, just like Dan Gurney. And completely unlike his close friend, Peter Collins, who could care less about technical issues in cars and just liked to win races.

Phil Hill passed away peacefully in Salinas, CA in 2008, victim of an Alzheimer's-like disease, at age 81, a confirmed and serious gearhead.

John Cooper Fitch

John Fitch served our country as a WWII fighter pilot in the U.S. Army Air Corps based in England. He made the rank of Captain, flew the P51 Mustang as bomber escort and shot down one of the new Messerschmitt 262 jet fighters. Then he in turn was shot down and ended the war in a POW camp.[62]

After the war, Fitch owned an MG car dealership in White Plains, New York, and raced an MG TC. But he also loved Jaguars, raced an XK-120 in 1950 and later a Jaguar Special of his own design before becoming a protégé of Briggs Cunningham's. He and Briggs became best of friends.

The Jaguar 'Le Mans' Special, as Fitch called it, never raced outside the U.S. The design featured a lightweight aluminum cycle-fendered body based on the XK 120 chassis, huge Alfin drums replacing the original Jaguar brakes, wire wheels for cooling. The car was the concept of the two enthusiasts and friends, John Fitch for engineering and Coby Whitmore, a magazine illustrator, for design.

---

[62] Wikipedia, May 2017

The Scream of an Engine

In 1951, Fitch was asked to participate in the Gran Premio de Argentina by Briggs Cunningham in an Allard J2 X. He won the race and the award of a kiss by Eva Peron – *Don't Cry for Me, Argentina*.

Also in 1951, John raced SCCA and won at Elkhart Lake in the Jag Special and at tracks in the northeast. Fitch won the first ever SCCA National Championship that year.

Then Fitch joined the Cunningham team and continued while racing the Jaguar special into 1952 in New York and Connecticut events.[63]

Fitch was a prolific racer in 1952, and found himself in German cars, a Porsche 356 at Nürburgring and a Mercedes 300SL prototype in the Carrera Panamericana road race in México. This was seven years after being rescued from a German POW camp. He dismissed this conundrum by saying, 'During the war we were soldiers. By the early fifties, we were drivers. No problem.'[64]

At the peak of the Cunningham team racing experience, Le Mans 1952-1954, Fitch placed third in the C5-R in 1953 with Phil Walters. Cunningham himself finished seventh that year in the older C4-R with Bill Spear. The Moran/Bennett C4 RK finished tenth in the same race.

At Le Mans in 1955, Fitch was paired with Pierre Levegh in the Mercedes 300 SLR. Fitch's first turn behind the wheel was close at hand. He was finishing a cup of coffee in the pits when Levegh's accident occurred.

---

[63] Jaguar Club of North America, http://www.jcna.com/library/news/2001/jcna0033.html
[64] http://autoweek.com/article/alms/racing-legend-john-fitch-dies-95

The Scream of an Engine

After Le Mans 1955, which claimed so many lives, Fitch started a company that focused on safety innovations for racing. His engineering solutions were cost effective and popular, especially the plastic sand-filled drums used to prevent vehicles from hitting sharp objects on public freeways, like the ends of steel guard rails. This is called the Fitch Barrier. It's seen everywhere on U.S. highways and is produced and sold by Impact Attenuation, Inc.

Returning to the Cunningham team in 1956, John drove their new D-types. Fitch racked up four second places and one first place trophy on U.S. race tracks, such as Thompson, CT and Elkhart Lake, WI. Most of those second places were one-two Cunningham team victories for Jaguar, with ace Walt Hansgen taking first.

The Fitch Driver's Capsule is a special seat which causes the seat back to rotate with the seat belt, reducing inertial forces on the driver. A further development attaches the helmet to the seat back to prevent driver whiplash and basilar skull fracture. Fitch obtained

John Fitch at Sebring 1957 in Zora Arkus-Duntov's Corvette SS Number 1, Piero Taruffi co-driving

patents for other designs, like the Fitch Fuel Catalyst which reduces short chain molecules in gasoline and inhibits oxidation in both gasoline and diesel fuels.

Fitch raced in many SCCA events and briefly in Formula 1, his best finish in Formula 1 ninth in the 1955 Italian Grand Prix in a Maserati 250 F. In sports cars, Fitch also won the 1953 Sebring 12-Hours in the Cunningham C4-R, a lap ahead of the Reg Parnell/George Abecassis Aston Martin DB3.

John joined the Mercedes Benz factory team in 1955. At the Mille Miglia that year, Fitch was assigned to the production class in a 300 SL road car. With his navigator Kurt Gesell, he finished fifth overall, the first across the line in the production class. Fitch was first of three 300 SLs to finish.

This is the race won by the Stirling Moss/Denis Jenkinson 300 SLR – that fabulous driver/navigator combination still a high-water mark in motor racing history.

Not so well known is that Fitch invented the famous scrolling map box that Denis Jenkinson used so successfully during the 1955 Mille Miglia.

In 1960, John co-drove the Corvette C1 at Le Mans with Bob Grossman, winning the over 5-liter class.

Fitch retired from racing in 1964 after nearly twenty years at it. He became the manager of the Lime Rock Park race track. Fitch lived nearby the track for the next forty plus years.

That's when he formed John Fitch and Co. to design and build custom cars. The company engineered a lightweight Chevy Corvair called the Fitch Sprint. John Fitch and Co. went on to develop a two-seat sports car based on the Corvair called the Fitch Phoenix, which resembled the Corvette Mako Shark concept car of 1963. His buddy Coby Whitmore helped with the design. Only one was built before GM pulled the plug on the Corvair.

After a rich life in airplanes and automobiles, John Fitch passed away at the age of 95 in Lime Rock, CT in October 2012. Into his '90s, John consulted on safety issues. It's amazing to me that he and his wife Elizabeth raised three sons, John, Christopher and Steven, while accomplishing so much in the automotive world. He also found time for sailing.

Fitch: another ultimate gearhead.

Masten Gregory

I was crazy about this character from an early age.

Masten Gregory, known as the Kansas City Flash, influenced me because of his success racing Jaguars, but he was so much more than that. Gregory is in a distinct club of motorsport being only one of seventeen drivers to compete in all three legs of the Triple Crown of Motorsport: Indianapolis 500, 24-Hours of Le Mans and the Monaco Grand Prix, and to have won at least one of those events.[65]

Gregory dropped out of school and married his sweetheart when he was nineteen. Then he used his inheritance to buy a Mercury-powered Allard, which he drove in his first race, the fifty-mile SCCA race in Caddo Mills, Texas, November 1952. He retired from that race due to head gasket failure so then installed a new Chrysler hemi-powered engine in his car to race at Sebring in 1953, where he again

---

[65] Wikipedia, April 2017

retired, this time due to a rear suspension failure. Gregory's first win came in just his third SCCA race, in Stillwater, Oklahoma. Switching to a C-Type Jaguar, Gregory won several races in America, including the Guardsman's Trophy in Golden Gate Park, San Francisco and a race at Offutt Air Force Base in Omaha, Nebraska.

In 1954, he won the inaugural Bahama Speed Week main event in a Ferrari.

Gregory moved to Europe to race Ferraris in 1954 and 1955, and returned to the U.S. in 1956, winning several SCCA races. During this time, he developed his unique way of escaping impending racing crashes: he'd stand up on the seat and jump out before wrecking. This led to serious injuries, anyway, so he missed many races recovering. Gregory performed this maneuver on many occasions, two that I remember: Silverstone, England, and Sebring, FL.

He crashed a lot of cars in the early years through about 1960, like a Lister Jaguar in 1958 and a Tojeiro Jaguar in 1959. His style matured. Crashes almost disappeared.

After winning his second attempt at the 1000 KM of Buenos Aires, he was offered a ride in a 250 F Maserati at Monaco in 1957. He placed third becoming the first American to make a podium finish in a Formula 1 race. His next podiums were racing for the factory Cooper-Climax team in 1959 with Jack Brabham and Bruce McLaren, heady company: Masten was third in the Dutch Grand Prix, and second in the Portuguese Grand Prix. Brabham went on to win the World Championship for Cooper that year. Gregory might have had a shot – good car, good driver – but he wrecked and missed the last four Grands Prix due to injuries. His Cooper contract wasn't renewed for 1960, possibly for that reason.

The Scream of an Engine

After the 1964 and 1965 seasons with Centro Sud, resulting only in one sixth place finish with uncompetitive cars, Gregory retired from Formula 1 racing for seven more years. After his close friend, Jo Bonnier, was killed at Le Mans in a 1972 accident, he fully retired from racing and moved to Amsterdam to become a diamond merchant. Later, he opened a glass blowing business there.

Masten passed away at the age of fifty-three from a heart attack during sleep. He was at his winter home in Porto Ercole, Italy, on the Tyrrhenian Sea north of Rome. He left his wife and four kids, Masten Jr., Debbie, Scott and Michael.

Gregory was a personality. I loved his glasses and quiet demeanor and the way he'd step out of a car about to crash. Like Peter Collins, Gregory liked to race, not build cars. An extreme fan.

Chapter Eleven: Characters

There are literally thousands of men and women who've made monstrous contributions to one hundred and fifty years of automotive history. This chapter is about the ones who most influenced my early years, in the Fifties, when cars were raced on street tires, men were men and women knew what to do about it.

Sir William Lyons

Starting with owning a motorcycle in 1919, as noted above, Lyons built an automotive legend capped with five Jaguar wins in the Fifties at Le Mans. And many first-place finishes in Fifties decade races around the world. While Malcolm Sayer gets design credit for the 1950s Jaguars that set the future of the company and so inspired me, Lyons had his hand in on the clay mockups.

Bill – as he was known to everyone in the early years - also had an uncanny sense for competitive pricing and promotional activities, like delivering the first production XK 120 to Clark Gable, the American actor, in 1949. Or speeding a prototype XK 120 on May 30, 1949 down the empty Ostend-Jabbeke motorway in Belgium to a two-way record of 132.6 MPH, timed by officials of the Royal Automobile Club of Belgium. And promoting the new XK 120 in 1950 with a photo shoot of Tazio Nuvolari, then 58, sitting behind the wheel in his classic yellow and blue racing suit.

That promotion was followed up just over a year later in October 1950, when Leslie Johnson took a Jaguar XK 120 to Montlhéry, a banked oval built in 1924 a few miles outside Paris, France. He and Stirling Moss drove the car for twenty-four hours at an average speed of 107.46 miles per hour.

In 1952, Lyons sent a Jaguar back to Montlhéry. Leslie Johnson returned along with co-drivers Stirling Moss, Jack Fairman, and Bert Hadley to drive an XK 120 fixed-head coupé LWK 707 for seven days at an average speed of just over one hundred miles per hour. Near the end, the car was running on a broken spring from rough spots on the concrete track surface.

Finally, the XK 120 returned to Jabbeke on October 23, 1953, tuned for speed with a full tonneau cover, side exhaust and plexiglass bubble over the driver. Norman Dewis, Jaguar's test driver for many years, drove the car to a two-way average flying mile of 172.416 MPH.

That's the promotional landscape Lyons produced. How's a ten-year old kid going to resist?

The Scream of an Engine

William Lyons married Greta Brown in 1924. Together, they raised three children: Patricia, the oldest, John Michael and Mary. Patricia married Leeds Jaguar-distributor and rally driver Ian Appleyard, and was his co-driver in many international rallies from 1949 to 1953, mostly in XK120 NUB 120.

The XK 120 in final Jabbeke record configuration, October 1953. The XK 120 sports cars were produced from 1948 through 1954, following the last SS 100 sports car made in 1940, and preceding the XK 140 which arrived in 1955. LA Times Photo

Lyons' management style was autocratic. Some reports say there were rarely Board of Directors meetings for Jaguar Cars, Ltd. until the 1960s when globalization pressures started to force consolidation of the car industry in England. In 1966, faced with challenges from more competitive markets and the need to invest larger sums of money in the business to survive, Lyons merged Jaguar with the British Motor Corporation – BMC - to form British Motor Holdings, which was later absorbed into British Leyland Motor Corporation.

The final years of Lyons' tenure were a struggle before he retired as managing director near the end of 1967. Lyons remained Chairman, trying to retain the identity and independence of Jaguar Cars, Ltd. and its engineering department within the larger company.

Chapter Eleven: Characters

The Scream of an Engine

Lyons retired completely to Wappenbury Hall in 1972, his three hundred twenty-nine-acre estate about half an hour drive from the Jaguar factory. The estate features a swimming pool, two tennis courts, formal gardens and greenhouses and was on the market in 2016 for $9.8 million. Lyons refocused his energies on golf, travel, gardening and raising prize-winning Suffolk sheep and Jersey cattle. His health declined in retirement a bit, but he enjoyed another thirteen years until he passed away in 1985 at home. His wife Greta followed him a year later.[66]

Frank Raymond Wilton 'Lofty' England

Less well known than Lyons, but extremely important to the Jaguar success story, is 'Lofty' England. The nickname Lofty comes about because he was 6'4" tall. But what better last name can you imagine to be involved with and succeed with English car manufacturers?

Lofty came up through the ranks of the racing sector of the English car industry with the well-known Sir Henry Birkin and Whitney Straight.

After leaving a five-year apprenticeship at Daimler in 1932, England became racing mechanic for some of the best-known names in motor sport. Lofty managed a stint at the Brooklands track where his first employer, Sir Henry 'Tim' Birkin, campaigned his Bentley, Maserati and Alfa Romeo race cars. When this connection ended, England joined the American Whitney Straight's team in 1934.

Later Lofty worked for ERA - English Racing Automobiles - which qualified him to maintain Richard Seaman's vehicles and eventually, the Siamese Prince Chula's White House Stable, which

---

[66] Wikipedia, April 2017, Business Insider, April 2016

prepared cars for Chula's cousin 'B. Bira' to drive. B. Bira, a nom de guerre, became an accomplished Grand Prix driver.

Lofty was determined to see active service so joined the Royal Air Force 1941. After qualifying as a pilot in the United States in 1943, he returned to Britain and flew Lancasters on hazardous daytime bombing missions.

England arrived at Jaguar in September 1946 and became manager of the Service Department. The job came about through a long-standing friendship, cemented during his Brooklands days, with the Jaguar development engineer Walter Hassan who let England know about the opportunity.

Lofty worked a second job while Service Manager: Jaguar racing team manager from 1951 to 1956. Lofty oversaw four of Jaguar's five Le Mans victories in the Fifties. He earned the reputation of being first at work and last to leave after every detail was attended to and done.

Joe Sutton, a factory mechanic for the racing team, observed, 'Lofty England was a one-off. You'll never find a bloke anything like him, anywhere in the world.....But one of the things that really endeared him to me was his pit counter manner – there were cars bashing by at 150 MPH, but Lofty didn't have a loud hailer like some of 'em. He used to lean over and say, Joe have you checked so and so.' [67]

Others felt England emulated Alfred Neubauer, racing team manager at Mercedes, who ruled his team with an iron hand. Lofty demanded allegiance from pit crew and drivers alike. At Reims, France in early 1956, Le Mans hero Duncan Hamilton ignored England's pit

---

[67] Jaguar, the Sporting Heritage, Paul Skilleter, Virgin Publishing, 2000, page 8

signals and passed another teammate to win the race. England fired him on the spot.

A successful competition debut by the new XK 120 model in the 1949 production sports car race at Silverstone encouraged William Lyons to support a team of cars at Le Mans in 1950. That result was sufficiently encouraging for him to make a bid to win the event in 1951. And who better to run the team than the lanky Lofty England with his commanding presence and wealth of racing knowledge and experience?[68]

Norman Dewis, Jaguar's Chief Tester from 1952, was another more of less behind the scenes personality that lead to Jaguar's Fifties success, along with Bill Heynes, Engineering Chief, Harry Weslake, Walter Hassan and Claude Baily who worked for Heynes.

But Lofty fired my imagination the most of this group. When Lyons retired in 1972, Lofty became Jaguar's Chairman and Chief Executive. This assignment lasted only two years as Lofty railed under the restrictions imposed by British Leyland, Jaguar's new owner.

Lofty was twice married, had one daughter and passed away in 1995 at age 83.

Henry Ford

A more politically controversial character than William Lyons, Ford started his long adventure in automotive history by building his first car in 1896, the second one in 1898 and developing and racing his number 999 Ford car in 1901. Then he was seriously ready to build cars

---

[68] Portions of the above taken from: http://www.independent.co.uk/news/people/obituaries-lofty-england-1585535.html

The Scream of an Engine

that would appeal to the market for lower cost transportation. He succeeded.

I wrote my Business History term paper on Henry Ford while pursuing an MBA degree. I was marked down on the paper for focusing too much on his achievements and not enough on his faults. Some of his achievements:

- Gained a reputation as a watch repair expert at an early age
- Apprenticed as a machinist for James F. Flowers Co. in Detroit at age sixteen
- Joined Edison Electric Company in 1891 and rose to Chief Engineer by 1896
- Started work on building an automobile while at Edison, met Thomas Edison who approved of his work to develop his first self-propelled vehicle: with four bicycle wheels, a tiller for steering and a two-speed transmission, no reverse. He finished a second car in 1898
- Started his own company, Detroit Automobile Company, in 1899. Ford vehicles failed to gain market traction. Ford was forced to close. He then continued car development and convinced the Detroit Automobile Company shareholders to form the Henry Ford Company in 1901
- Issues with the shareholders forced Ford's departure and that company was renamed Cadillac Automobile Company after he left, which, of course, succeeded in its own right
- Henry continued undaunted with pursuing his goal of building cars. He developed a race car, the famous '999', which he drove himself. In 1903, Henry formed the Ford Motor Company, turning racing over to Barney Oldfield
- The original investors in Ford Motor Company included Henry Ford, Alexander Y. Malcomson, the Dodge brothers, and John S. Gray

The Scream of an Engine

- The Model T was launched in 1908 and the moving assembly line in 1913. By 1918, half the cars on American roads were Model T's which took about two hours and thirty minutes to assemble from parts and drive out the door. Model T's were offered in the marketplace at lower prices each passing year due to Ford's steady improvements with innovative production methods. Fifteen million were sold
- From number one, Ford fell to number three in the U.S. by the mid-1930s at the bottom of the Depression, after General Motors and Chrysler

The knockoffs on Ford: he was autocratic – see Lyons above – didn't delegate, didn't change his models fast enough to keep up, was anti-Semitic, embraced nepotism by employing his family in the business including making his son President, was against war and had an isolationist outlook.

There. I've done it again.

Ford also outlasted over 1,800[69] other companies that tried to build cars from 1886 through his death in 1947 at age 83. His wife Clara died the same year.

Terrence Steven McQueen

Why is a movie star in a car book?

Think about it: Steve McQueen owned over two hundred-ten restored and unrestored motorcycles and fifty-five antique cars and trucks at the time of his death in 1980; he won his first sports car, an MG, in a high stakes poker game; Stirling Moss gave Steve racing lessons at Brands Hatch; Steve drove his new brown 1961 Austin

---

[69] Wikipedia, July 2017

Chapter Eleven: Characters

The Scream of an Engine

Cooper S, after coaching by Moss at Brands Hatch, to lapping within a second or two of Moss' time.

Steve's constant push into motor sports caught my attention. He raced a Sprite at Sebring in 1962 when my Dad was winning every race he entered in his Sprites. Steve owned and raced a 1961 Austin Cooper S; I later owned a 1963 Morris Cooper S, the only differences being the grille, the color and that I never raced my Mini.

Steve raced so well that BMC offered him a full-time position on their race team at Sebring, FL in 1962. The choice was between acting and racing. Steve chose acting.

The rest is history. Steve's movies included *The Magnificent Seven, The Great Escape, The Sand Pebbles, The Thomas Crown Affair, Bullitt, The Getaway, Papillon, The Towering Inferno, The Cincinnati Kid,* and of course, *Le Mans*.

Steve acquired and raced his own Porsche 908 successfully at the Sebring 12-Hour in March 1970. He did this 'to prepare himself' for making the movie, *Le Mans*. With Peter Revson, Steve almost won overall in the 3-liter Porsche until the end when nipped by Mario Andretti in a 5-liter V-12 Ferrari by less than twenty-four seconds. McQueen and Revson did win their class.

When McQueen made the movie *Le Mans* in 1970-1971, he refused to let stunt drivers do his part in the racing. Steve is quoted as saying about the movie, 'I enjoy the fact that we're playing for big marbles.'[70]

The period around the movie *Le Mans* became Steve's undoing. He'd wanted to make the movie for a decade. And he wanted to do it

---

[70] Ibid., page 298

his way, closer to being a documentary than a story. With his consummate star power at this point, he got his way.

Le Mans was not received well in the U.S., the primary target. *Le Mans* grossed $22M while *Bullitt* grossed $50 M two years earlier. The critics said there was no plot in *Le Mans* and didn't like the ending in which McQueen didn't win the race or get the girl. The movie did well in Europe and Japan where *Le Mans* means something. The absence of dialog and plot was especially well received in Japan, where understatement is valued by the movie public.

Steve lost money on his investment in *Le Mans*, and was forced to close three companies he'd founded, including Solar Productions which provided part of the funding for the movie, had purchased the Porsche 908 and was insolvent. At the time, he also received a $2M 'tax due' notice from the IRS.

And Steve lost his wife Neile of fifteen years to divorce.[71]

But Steve wasn't just a star. He was a friend to many. His friendship with Stirling Moss led to them exchanging letters after Moss' career-ending accident in 1962. Steve was friends with Graham Hill and stayed in John Cooper's home.

At the bottom of it all, Steve McQueen was a lifetime gearhead, motivated in that direction by his mechanical skills, his ego needs to beat competitors in races, his romance with danger and his love of fine machinery, like his XKSS and numerous Porsches and other cars and motorcycles.

---

[71] Ibid., page 310

The Scream of an Engine

Henry N. Manney III

    Now for a journalist who was also a character and race driver.

    But it was Henry Manney that I remember most from the day, probably more appropriate to be placed in the Character chapter. But he did race.

    Bearded Manney shaped a generation of car enthusiasts. My generation. But I didn't catch up with him until 1961 when he joined the 'faculty' at *Road & Track*, succeeding the colorful Bernard Cahier as the magazine's European Editor and race reporter. Previously, he'd worked for motoring magazines, based mostly in England from 1954, where he met the beloved 250 GTO Ferrari owned by race driver Jean Guichet. Henry bought the car from Guichet and drove it on the street until 1970.

    Henry was born in America and majored in English at Duke University. Afterward, he did a three-year stint in the U.S. Army as a radar mechanic.

    Then Manney used the G.I. Bill to fund ballet lessons. Annie Statz, the ballerina he met as a result, became his wife and gave Henry deep enthusiasm for dance. Henry's father-in-law was Arnold 'Jigger' Statz, a Major League Baseball outfielder. Jigger was one of only a few to amass four thousand hits in his baseball career. Henry's love for and knowledge of baseball came from that connection.

But Manney was so much more. His passion for the automotive field was his own doing, starting with a Crosley Hot Shot he raced at places like Pebble Beach, CA against MG TCs in the early 1950s. He later added a supercharger to the car to make the Crosley go faster.

Between 1961 and his debilitating illness by stroke in 1980, Henry wrote race reports, auto show reports and travel stories for *Road & Track's* 'good grey pages.'[72] These were thoughtful pieces but always with a sense of mischief and humor which bordered ending on the cutting room floor.

Manney's byline was Henry N. Manney III. Never a contraction, although he ended his own column at *Road & Track*, called *Henry Manney at Large*, with '*Yr. Faithful Svnt.*' He earned the respect of the racing community, whose stories he covered accurately and completely. Manney painted local color into his pieces, especially idiosyncrasies about the French, their food and their wine.

Manney's photographic masterpieces are still available almost thirty years after his death, like the shot of Graham Hill in the 1961 BRM with upright headers which sells for $50 a copy on the Internet.

A news report on the rumored $52 million sale of Ferrari GTO No. 5111GT brought back good memories about Henry for me. Manney drove this GTO on the street for years, selling it in 1970 for a lot less than $52 million.[73]

His most famous line: the then new Jaguar E-Type was '*the greatest crumpet-catcher known to man.*' In Manney's report on the 1961 Monaco Grand Prix, Dan Gurney's silver Porsche 718 eventually finished fifth. But for much of the race, Dan ran third between the red

---

[72]Dennis Simanaitis, SimanaitisSays.com, 2016

[73] http://www.velocetoday.com/henry-manney-and-the-52-million-dollar-gto/, November 7, 2013 by 'Pete'

The Scream of an Engine

Ferraris of Phil Hill and Wolfgang von Trips. Manney described Gurney as being *'Like an anchovy embedded in a pizza.'* [74]

Road & Track has attracted many talented writers like John Lamm, Dennis Simanaitis and Sam Smith. Henry Manney III was one of their best and a part of my car culture.

---

[74] http://pilotesanciens.blogspot.com/2013/08/henry-n-manney-iii.html

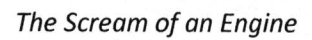

Chapter Twelve: Race Courses

The race courses that inspired me the most are in Europe but there is a good balance with several in the U.S. The European tracks had the most influence when I was between the ages of eight and ten. Then U.S. tracks took over the heavy hitting. Marlboro was an early high point as explained in Chapter Seven, *The MG A*.

Le Mans

For me, this historic race is the most influential and shaped my cultural introduction to cars. Mind you I was just eight when I picked up the vibes on the 1951 running of the race. Le Mans is where my passion started. Yet I've never been on-site for a race.

I've walked sections of the track and driven the portions of the course open to the public in a rental car. I've experienced every

Le Mans race vicariously since age eight. The recent races have been less interesting for me, those dominated by Porsche and Audi with Toyota threatening. These races seem too much like corporations pulling out all the stops: the personal emotion is missing.

The old spirit of motorsport was about individual fans or team owners buying a car and going racing. It was as much about the drivers and owners as the cars. With intense factory participation today, the drivers seem more like cogs in the wheel than memorable heroes. But maybe that's just me.

Once hooked on Le Mans, I continually updated my databases through the Fifties and into the Sixties. What stokes my passion for Le Mans, France happened more than sixty years ago. But the early passion is still there. It's still a big deal for me that the XK 120 C averaged 105 MPH in the 1953 race – over the full twenty-four hours – so long ago.

My favorite historical races at Le Mans are the Alfa Romeo wins of 1931-1934, the Jaguar triumphs of 1951, 1953, 1955, 1956 and 1957, and the Ford checkered flags of 1966-1969. I call that cultural bias. After all, Porsche has won more Le Mans races than any of my favorites.

For me, Ferrari The Car was the enemy in the Jaguar-Ferrari battles of the 1950s. We all choose sides, and at the age of eight, I chose Jaguar. Mercedes became the enemy in the 1950s as well. They threatened Jaguar by winning Le Mans in 1952.

By 1988, when Jaguar won again, the cars and the people who built them were all new. It was difficult to identify with machines which didn't look like Jaguars and drivers who came on the scene after my allegiances were established.

The Scream of an Engine

Long-time racer, Francophile and science teacher friend Chuck Engberg offered me a $100 gift certificate to a French restaurant in San Diego. The catch? I had to fly to Le Mans, France and find a mark he'd left for me somewhere out on the course. I had to photograph the mark and present it to him to receive my reward.

Of course, I met the challenge. The French restaurant in San Diego was outstanding, following equally special meals throughout France during the reconnaissance.

One of the meals in France was at the Hotel de France near the race course. My wife Brooke and I sat at the table that Stirling Moss, Carroll Shelby and Maurice Trintignant did for breakfast before driving their Aston Martin to the course and winning the 24-hour race in 1959. Race cars were driven to the Le Mans track in those days before the idea of transporters came into vogue.

Watkins Glen

I saw my first road race at Watkins Glen, NY in 1953 at age ten. My passion for motor racing was sealed then and there.

In the fall, the Finger Lakes Region where the town of Watkins Glen is nestled, is a bouquet of colorful sights. The leaves are turning red and gold, the sky is a crisp, dark contrasting blue light. The five Finger Lakes, including Lake Seneca spreading to the north of Watkins Glen, are a deep blue with sunlight glistening off wind driven waves.

The Finger Lakes are relicts from the last Ice Age which ended about 25,000 years ago and took another 10,000 years to melt all the ice. The ice gouged out deep, long basins between rock ledges too hard to carve. Today, the rock ledges are famous for providing waterfalls, like Taughannock Falls on Cayuga Lake, that displays a spectacular two hundred fifteen-foot water drop off four hundred-foot high ledges. The rivers must go somewhere; why not over the edge?

Cameron Argetsinger, a lawyer by trade, was one of the forces behind bringing racing to the Finger Lakes Region of upstate New York, at the foot of Seneca Lake, in the late Forties. Dad visited the original track in 1951 and recorded the races on 16mm film. I still retain these films and watch them from time to time. In 1951, the race was conducted on city streets and public roads – the original 6.6-mile course.

I was ecstatic to be able to see my first ever racing event there in 1953. My recollection is that the 4.6-mile course was new, the first time the races didn't go through the city streets of Watkins Glen. Since then the course has been changed several times but the location, the jet-black asphalt of the newer tracks and the sheer history of the place are part and parcel of my memories.

I was fortunate in returning to the same 4.6-mile road course in 1955. Both these introductions to The Glen resulted in Jaguar-powered cars winning races: Walt Hansgen - Jaguar Special in 1953, Dick Thompson – XK 140 MC and Sherwood Johnson D-Type Jaguar in 1955.

For the September 1953 races, our family drove up from Maryland to participate in the spectacle. Walt Hansgen won the feature event, instantly becoming one of my heroes.

We returned to the same spot on the track in 1955. This time we brought a raised platform which put us about six feet off the ground behind the retaining fence. And the fence was thirty yards from the track, a big step forward in safety from oil company banners on the edge of the street course in 1951. The views of the track, at our location on

The Scream of an Engine

the high speed back straight ending in a sharp hairpin turn, were the best. The loud speakers nearby permitted us to hear the start of the race, the announcer describing the positions of the leaders as they went out of his sight, and what happened as the cars returned from each lap's foray.

Briggs Cunningham's racing team brought a new D-Type Jaguar up from headquarters in Florida, white with blue stripe, the American racing colors. Sherwood Johnston was driving in this 1955 event. His nearest competition was Bill Spear in a bright red Maserati 300S which sounded so Italian, revving considerably higher than the Jaguars. On the first lap, Johnston led over the crest of the hill in front of us by six car lengths.

The rest of the race I had my fingers crossed that the Jag would run away with this one. It did. I was two for two with Jaguar wins at successive Watkins Glen race weekends.

Dad and I returned to Watkins Glen in 1961. I was a freshman at Cornell on Lake Cayuga, one lake over from Lake Seneca. We drove over from Ithaca to watch the Formula 1 race that September.

By 1961, there was yet another new course, shorter at 2.35 miles. The excitement of seeing these Formula 1 stars in person is still a vivid memory from the mind of this eighteen-year old.

Watkins Glen drew 100,000 spectators for the first U.S. Formula 1 race, long before Long Beach, CA or Austin, TX snagged calendar events.

One sage observer and newspaper columnist at the time wrote about the new Watkins Glen course as 'A biscuit reincarnated as a brioche.'

The Scream of an Engine

For the race, we bought pit passes and, as we walked in, discovered ourselves standing near Graham Hill. We inspected his V-8 1.5-liter BRM-Climax with headers that exhausted straight up into the atmosphere. What a sound that combination produced. We also got close to Jimmy Clark and his green and yellow Lotus, Jack Brabham and Stirling Moss. Innes Ireland won the race in his Lotus, Ireland's first Formula 1 win, also Lotus' first Formula 1 win.

I felt connected to the vehicles these men drove and especially the drivers.

The outcome of a race becomes more meaningful with these prior connections. Mostly these bonds came through reading *Road & Track* which has always covered some of the races.

Sebring

Many epic Sebring, FL races fired my imagination before my first visit to this fabled venue in 1966. My graduate school roommate, Dan Krez, and I drove from Ithaca, NY, to Sebring for Spring Break 1966 with a stopover in North Carolina, in about twenty-six hours. He owned a reasonably new, red Volkswagen Karmann Ghia coupé and drove. Fast. Usually with his throttle foot to the metal. Our ultimate destination was Ft. Lauderdale, FL.

I twisted his arm to stop over for the race. We knew we'd be late, held up for exams in Ithaca, and trying to make up time on the roads of the day. We arrived with about eight hours left in the twelve-hour race at 2 PM. We found a spot on the straight just after the pits on the inside of the course.

Then Bob McLean pulled out of the pits in his 289 Ford GT 40. When he braked for the turn, it appeared to us his right front wheel broke or came off the studs. His car flipped onto the roof, hit a telephone pole and caught fire. This was before the era of fuel cells which would prevent this kind of fire. We stood literally one hundred yards from the accident, protected by an American wire fence with red metal posts.

Within a minute or so, two corner workers with hand held fire extinguishers were discharging the white vapor, trying to put the fire out. We could see McLean was trapped inside. Flames were shooting fifty feet into the air suggesting McLean had just completed a refueling stop as well as a tire change.

Many more minutes passed before a fire truck with heavy duty extinguishers arrived. But Bob McLean perished. With this as an introduction to Sebring, Danny and I decided to leave a few hours later, well before the 10:30 PM end of the race, and complete the trip to Ft. Lauderdale. This experience was a real downer.

Lest it appear that I'm an ambulance chaser reporting these terrible incidents, Sebring is much more than accidents over the years. As a 12-hour precursor to Le Mans, it had no equal in the Fifties. Then Daytona, FL upstaged Sebring by holding a 24-hour endurance race for sports cars in February 1962, one month ahead of Sebring. This Daytona race continues today and is a definite competitor with Sebring for top endurance race in the U.S.

Before we left that day in March 1966, just after nightfall, we noticed the faster cars' disk brakes glowing orange as they slowed for the hairpin turn after the pit straight. Seeing this for the first time, the immense energy transfer this represented impressed Danny and me, both engineers.

Andrews Air Force Base

Andrews represents my second race experience, the first being Watkins Glen the prior September 1953.

The Scream of an Engine

On May 2, 1954, one hundred sixty-five cars showed up for this SCCA National Race. This was a warm spring day with sunny blue skies. The Andrews AFB course was 4.3-miles on airport runways, the course within sight of the Capital Building in Washington, DC, but located in Maryland. SCCA had never achieved this many entries for a race, an indication of how popular U.S. sports car racing had become in just a few short years.

An estimated sixty thousand fans showed up to watch.

Dad and I drove just over an hour to get there from our farm in Maryland. We stood at the end of the back straight, watching the races and the cars braking for the ninety-degree left.

The first ten lap race was between Porsches, Triumphs and Austin Healeys, billed as production cars under 3000cc. W.P. Kincheloe eked out the win in his Healey over Dr. Dick Thompson, the flying dentist from Washington, DC., in his Porsche 356. A Triumph was third followed by four Healeys, so the next Porsche to finish was eighth. Thompson was good.

I was just amazed at the sounds of racing and the colors of the cars, but with my English cultural bias, rooted for Healeys. There were plenty of them racing.

But the real reasons I was excited at Andrews were the two C-Type Jags entered. I didn't know Ernie Erickson in the C-Type from Chicago, but had seen 'Doc' M.R. J. Wylie race an XK 120 at Watkins Glen in 1953. I couldn't wait to see what they could do. In their C Modified class, though, were two V-12 4.5-liter Ferraris driven by Bill Spear and Jim Kimberly. Kimberly was well-known from the Chicago Kimberly family which made a fortune developing and selling Kleenex. Kimberly won almost everything in sight in 1954 and won the SCCA Class C Modified Championship at the end of the year.

Chapter Twelve: Race Courses

The Scream of an Engine

After the ten-lap second race for Modified and Production cars under 1500cc, won by Rees Makins in an OSCA and followed by – you guessed – Doc Thompson in his Porsche, the stage was set for me having a heart attack.[75]

The seventeen-lap third race, a 'Preliminary' for the main event, placed Modified and Production Cars over 1100cc on the grid. This race would mix up the very fastest C Modified cars – which were faster than the larger engined B Modified Allards and Kurtis racers - with the slowest D Production Healeys. Who knows why? I figure it was to give more cars more track time.

Jim Kimberly's 4.5-liter Ferrari was clearly faster than Ernie Erickson's green 3.4-liter C-Jag. Ernie did finish second and beat two other Ferraris, a pair of Maseratis an Allard, a Kurtis, and Doc Wylie in the other C-Jag. Bill Spear didn't race his 4.5-liter Ferrari.

Second place. I couldn't bear this outcome and wondered if the new D-Type Jag would have fared better. But they weren't racing in America yet. I'd soon see the D-Type win the following year – 1955 - at Cumberland, MD and Watkins Glen; NY.

In the fourth race, CP and FP, ten laps and forty-three miles, was a feast for this eleven- year-old Jag fan. There were so many Jaguar XK 120s – thirty-eight - and Porsche 356s – twelve - entered that a separate production car race was held for just these two makes. This was early days for Porsches, so Jaguars took the first eleven positions before Doc Thompson showed up again in his Porsche, winning the FP segment of the race. Charlie Wallace took CP honors in his Jag.

---

[75] http://www.ferrariexperts.com/SCCA%20results%201954.htm#AND. The finishing order in the races, for cross checking purposes, and a photo of the race program for the day is shown

Chapter Twelve: Race Courses

The Scream of an Engine

Following the hotly contested MG race, the main event commenced. This was the race for the President's Cup, a long two hundred-mile chase. Bill Spear, a huge man, was last into the first turn after stalling his 4.5-liter Ferrari 375 MM on the starting line. But Spear was already thirteenth after the first lap and a distant second by the second lap. Kimberly held a huge lead in the early going. By the end of the race, though, Spear had caught him, passed him twice and been repassed twice. This was a real motor race. But on the last lap, Kimberly's motor expired. Spear won.

President Dwight D. Eisenhower presented the huge President's Cup to Spear. In the photo, Al Momo, Spear's Ferrari mechanic, appears 70% the size of Eisenhower, who was considerably shorter than the towering Spear.[76]

I wonder how SCCA pulled that off? Must have been General Curtis Lemay, who started Strategic Air Command racing on Air Force bases to entertain the troops, working on Ike behind the scenes. Ike held Lemay in high regard for his contributions to Allied World War II bombing in Germany and Japan.

To finish me off for the day, Bill Lloyd came second to Spear in another Ferrari, Briggs Cunningham had an amazing drive in the small OSCA that had won Sebring in March to place third, and Doc Wylie brought his XK 120 C home fourth. Wylie had done much better than his ninth place in the third race. Wylie also beat another 2.9-liter Ferrari, Sherwood Johnston in an OSCA, the two Maseratis, Walt Hansgen in a

---

[76] http://www.cliffreuter.com/etceteriniSCCAresults1954.htm#AND The race report is also available here, so this section of the book is not just from my memory which is left with red Ferraris and green Jaguars whizzing around the track

Chapter Twelve: Race Courses

modified Aston Martin, and several other fast cars powered by big V-8 engines.

Two weeks later, Doc Wylie would win first place at the Cumberland, MD national main event, and his wife would win the Ladies Race, both in their C-Jag.

But I wanted more at Andrews. I was an ungrateful wretch that day, a sore loser, even if the racing was sure exciting. Congress got involved asking why Lemay was using government facilities for sports car racing, and that wonderful three-year era of racing on Air Force bases soon came to an end.

Lemay probably saved the SCCA. Street racing in the States was ending due to devastating accidents like the one at Watkins Glen in 1952. The SAC races filled the gap between the street venues and the purpose-built race tracks that started to fall into place later.

Mid America Raceway

This idyllic race track just forty miles west of St. Louis holds many memories. The six-inch drop off at the edge of portions of the race course macadam, for instance. If a driver made a mistake and went wide, those drop offs had to be taken head on or risk ending upside down. Another memory is the rough surface on turn four – the only rough surface on the entire track - as the course headed back toward the pits, then veered off left again into the country side.

This was my home race course from 1972 to 1975.

Then there was the back axle on the Alfa, plastic shims replaced by metal on the triangular locating rod fixing the axle in place. This modification by the previous owner was to reduce compliance. As a result, the axle clattered like mad under heavy braking on the rough turn

The Scream of an Engine

four paving. The clattering stayed loud until the rear suspension loaded up again once into the hard-left hander. More memories: the sound of the Alfa engine accelerating between 4000 and 8000 RPM continually, the butter smooth transmission, using second through fifth gears every lap, the ability to keep the loud pedal down longer going into the turns and out-braking the competition. With the notable exception of a 2-liter Formula B car I tried to out-brake on turn eight one memorable occasion. I ended up looping off the course backward.

Regional races could have big speed differentials between Production classes and the faster Formula cars. That wouldn't stop me from trying to avoid being lapped.

The deep mud in the pits on rainy days. A Triumph TR 2 engine blowing as the driver just ahead of me downshifted for the turn before the main straight, engine bolts and pistons flying into the air, the loud sound as one of the pieces hit my racing helmet. Remembering to take care when lapping a car, for many reasons, like this one.

The satisfaction of earning an SCCA Regional Driver's license here, and later achieving enough points here to earn the SCCA National License.

Watching lap times drop every time racing here.

See more about this course in Chapter Fifteen, *My Turn*.

Elkhart Lake

My favorite track to race is found in the beautiful rolling hills of southern Wisconsin. The 14-turn course is smooth as a baby's skin. The main straight long and fast, but providing time to catch the breath before starting again. The color of the trees turning brilliant reds and yellows in the fall. Meeting drivers again you've met at Mid America

The Scream of an Engine

or Blackhawk Farms. Finding drivers who are real gentlemen, here to win races but unwilling to compromise their fenders to do it.

Racing a venue where your early heroes fought their epic battles.

See my personal racing story at Elkhart Lake in Chapter Fifteen, *My Turn*. It was at Elkhart Lake that I began to appreciate fully the dedication, time and cash required to turn this passion of part time racing into a full time racing national championship. Namely, a lot.

Brands Hatch

On a vacation in England in 1972, I arranged to watch a local club race at Brands Hatch, England. From photographs I took there that weekend, I realized that MG, Lotus and Mazda racer Chuck Engberg had taken photos at the same corner on the same weekend that I was there. Of course, I didn't meet Chuck until 1995, twenty-three years later. Chuck was living in San Diego in 1972 and I in St. Louis. When he shared his photos with me in San Diego in 1996, I almost fell over. This was no coincidence: we were meant to meet.

Club racing at Brands Hatch is typical of racing on English tracks: well laid out and paved, and chockablock – a word first used in 1799 according to Miriam Webster - full of closely matched cars, especially the Minis racing on this day in June 1972. In the summer, these tracks seem overgrown with green things. But that's racing in England.

For me, Brands Hatch is like many of the other English tracks, as in Snetterton and Mallory Park. They provide excellent club racing on a low budget. Silverstone, on the other hand, is where the Formula 1 cars and other top European series race. It's a different story. The

The Scream of an Engine

support buildings, spectator stands, and pits are all much more impressive. Read expensive.

On one stop at Silverstone on a 1994 trip to England, half a dozen cars were testing. The sounds were magnificent. But the stands were empty. There was nothing to absorb the screams of these engines but your ears.

Long Beach

When I moved to California from St. Louis in 1976, a whole new vista of race tracks presented itself: Long Beach, Holtville, Riverside, Buttonwillow….and Laguna Seca. I was aware that many other famous California tracks no longer operated, like Edwards Air Force Base that got its start with the Strategic Air Command in the early 1950s, or the Lakeside oval track that held the first California race in 1907. I concentrated on the living tracks.

The Long Beach Formula 1 Race in March 27, 1976 was the first, watching Ferrari cars numbered 1 and 2 finishing 2nd and 1st respectively. Mercedes brought the 1955 W196 Formula 1 car, driven by Fangio in an exhibition with other 1955 Formula 1 cars, a spectacular return to those exciting days of racing.

The Long Beach race course turns were tight and lined with concrete barriers. Driver helmets were often visible, but often not the cars themselves. This wasn't a spectator course. My home movies of the event reveal the beautiful concrete barriers and not much else.

But it was a Formula 1 race on U.S. soil.

The Scream of an Engine

Laguna Seca

My favorite California course is Laguna Seca on the Monterrey Peninsula south of San Francisco. The ups and downs, the short straights and sweeping turns, the 'corkscrew' turn, and fabulous spectator visibility. I've been there many times, not to race, but to see spectacular racing. The most famous turn on this course is the 'corkscrew.' Located at the end of the back straight, and after heavy braking, cars literally drop off the hill and through an esses, accelerate through a short straight, then take a 90^0 left onto the main straight. Spectators can see all of this, plus an overview of the entire pit area, from a hillside on the outside of the main straight. Pulse quickening.

The most exciting driver to watch I've seen here is Marnix Dillenius, hands down. He drove an Alfa Romeo TZ, the coupé model that won the European Touring Car championship in 1964. He attacked the corkscrew without hesitation. In fact, he hesitated nowhere. The result? Win after win with Marnix passing cars that should have beaten him handily. I vividly remember watching him thread through several much larger engined Ferrari GTOs, whose drivers were apparently unsure what racing vintage cars was all about. Dillenius showed them.

In 1978, Mercedes brought the factory W-196 300 SLR sports racer to Laguna. This was Mercedes weekend. Juan Manuel Fangio drove the car. Stirling Moss drove a D-Type Jaguar. The two provided an exhibition run, passing and re-passing each other every lap. They re-created the exciting racing in Europe of 1955, twenty-three years earlier, when these two cars battled for supremacy in road racing. I found this hugely entertaining since I cut my teeth on the race reports of the mid-Fifties. I'd never seen these two cars race together in the flesh until this moment.

I attended the 1985 Laguna Historics, too, with the following outcomes: Race 1, Pre-1926 Sports Cars, 1st 1924 Alfa Romeo; Race 2,

The Scream of an Engine

1926-1939 Sports Cars, 1ˢᵗ 1932 Alfa Romeo 8C 2600 Monza; Race 3, 1947-1955 GT Cars, 1ˢᵗ 1954 Jaguar XK 120; Race 4, 1956-1962 GT cars under 2-liters, 1ˢᵗ 1957 Alfa Romeo Giulietta. This was the famous Al Leake, Jr. Alfa that won 262 races and 26 national championships, a 750 F, like my Dad's Alfa described above – beating a passel of fast Porsche 356 cars in the process; Race Five, 1959-1965 GT cars under 2-liters, 1ˢᵗ 1964 Alfa Romeo TZ. The wild Marnix Dillenius drove this Alfa.

It wasn't until Race 6 that something other than an Alfa or a Jag won, and in Race 6 a D-Type Jaguar was a close third after a Scarab and a Lister Corvette but ahead of two beautiful Ferrari 250 Testa Rossas. These weren't small fields either: often twenty or more cars were on the grids. What a thrill for a kid, now grown up, whose favorite cars in the mid-Fifties were Alfas and Jags. A 1932 Alfa Romeo Tipo B P3 then won the seventh race and a Jaguar Special the tenth race. No Alfas and Jags were entered in the races they didn't win, except the last one, the fourteenth race, in which Jags finished out of the money.

Lime Rock Park

Since I lived in Connecticut for nearly five years in the late Sixties, Lime Rock Park was a natural destination. As noted, Lime Rock Park was being managed by retired race car driver John Fitch, who was attracting top competitors and upgrading the track safety features at the same time. This was a much better spectator course for me than Thompson, the other active Connecticut race track at the time. And Lime Rock continues to provide outstanding racing today. The green rolling hills around Lime Rock are beautifully decked out with trees in summer, providing a gorgeous back drop for red, yellow, green, white or blue cars streaming around the race track.

I especially enjoyed the Trans Am Sedan Championship racing: Mustangs, Camaros, Cougars and AMC cars roaring and thrashing

The Scream of an Engine

about in the over 2-liter sedan category. Alfas and Porsches – again – battled it out for under 2-liter sedan honors in 1967. Porsche had successfully petitioned the SCCA to let the 911 join the fray for 1967. But then, none of these cars were really sedans with four doors.

In the inaugural 1966 U.S. Trans Am series, Ford Mustangs won the over 2-liter class. Alfa won the under 2-liter class, Horst Kwech and Gaston Andrey scoring 39 of 57 possible points for the Manufacturer's title for Alfa. Jochen Rindt drove an Alfa GTA to first overall at the Sebring Trans Am race, beating all the over 2-liter Trans Am cars.

With friends Bob and Salle Evelyn from Noank, CT, we sat on the hill for one Trans Am race overlooking the end of the Lime Rock main straight. Bob successfully raced a lightweight Morgan, purchased at the Morgan factory in England, and a British Daimler SP 250. He maintained a running commentary on how these drivers and cars stacked up, many of whom he raced against in other series.

From our perch, we could see the sweeper turn at the end of the straight before the cars head back up the hill and disappear again. The braking prowess that let under 2-liter cars pass the larger-engined beasts at the end of the straight was obvious from where we sat. The smaller-engined cars pulled through the sweeper faster than the big boys could. Of course, after the sweeper, the big V-8s took over again up the hill, through more turns and back to the main straight. V-8s are hard to beat on main straights.

On this day in 1967, the Austrian-born Australian transplant Horst Kwech led the 1570 cc Alfa GTAs, the factory Ford Lotus Cortinas and soon all the larger 1991 cc Porsches. Then amazingly, Kwech started passing the big boys to finish fourth overall – including passing Ed Leslie's well-prepared Bud Moore Mercury Cougar which ended fifth. This I found immensely satisfying. Little cars passing bigger ones. Where does that come from? David and Goliath? And by the way, Alfas do beat Porsches.

Jerry Titus finished third overall in a beautifully prepared 4727 cc Mustang; second overall was Roger Penske's 4956 cc Camaro driven by Mark Donahue; and the runaway winner by two laps was Peter Revson in a Bud Moore prepared 4737cc Mercury Cougar. Since the Mercury used a Ford engine, I suspected the 10 cc larger Mercury-identified engines were for marketing purposes.

I was soon to meet Charlie Rainville and ask his racing shop to re-build the engine in my Alfa Giulia street sedan. He did a terrific job on my car. Charlie drove a Plymouth Barracuda this day at Lime Rock with Tony Adamowicz to finish thirteenth overall.

As it turns out, I employed experienced race drivers who also built Alfa Romeo engines to care for the engines in my street Alfas and in my race Alfa.

For the year 1967, Ford went on to win the over 2-liter Trans Am championship and Porsche the under 2-liter championship. The power advantage of Porsche 911s couldn't be overcome by the nimble Alfas, especially on the longer courses. Lime Rock was a short course anomaly.

Silverstone

This track captures the imagination of car enthusiasts around the world. English race courses like Aintree, Brands Hatch, Castle Comb, Cheshire, Goodwood, Oulton Park, or Snetterton are exciting. But Silverstone, the modern home to the British Grand Prix every year since 1987, stands head and shoulders above the rest for prestige.

The Scream of an Engine

This is a fast course. Like elsewhere, speeds have risen. The first post war British 'Grand Prix' at Silverstone on October 2, 1948 was won by Luigi Villoresi in a Maserati 4CLT/48 – Maserati was still using the build year to identify its race cars - at an average speed of 72 MPH, followed by Alberto Ascari in another Maserati. In 2017, Lewis Hamilton averaged 145 MPH in winning the British Grand Prix at Silverstone in his Mercedes.

Silverstone isn't just about Formula 1. Superbikes race here as well as older cars in the Historic Sports Car Club Championship, the latest sedans in the British Touring Car Championship and marque club racing as in Ferrari Racing Days and the Aston Martin Owners Club Racing. There are more.

Silverstone first opened in 1948 just after the war when the Royal Automobile Club was casting about for a place to stage races. The Air Ministry which owned the airport near the town of Silverstone agreed to let the RAC stage races. The course was laid out using oil drums, ropes to keep the spectators back and tents for the race organizers.

Epic races abound in the history of Silverstone. During my culturally formative years, the Fifties, I was aware of the English Vanwall and Connaught attempts at victories and the use of exotic names to identify corners like Woodcote, Copse, Maggots, Becketts, and the high-speed Abbey and Stowe. Race reports in the day referred to these names when describing passing maneuvers.

Amazingly, Juan Fangio won only once in the British Grand Prix. The year was 1956 and Fangio was driving the Lancia-Ferrari 'D50' with side gas tanks between the front and rear wheels.

Vanwall – a contraction of founder and race driver Tony Vandervell's name and the main product, Thinwall bearings –

constructed their first cars to race in the 1954 Formula 1 season. Vandervell had notable help from staff members Colin Chapman and Frank Costin. The chassis was designed by Owen Maddock and built by the Cooper Car Company. The 2-liter engine was designed by Norton engineer Leo Kuzmicki, essentially four Manx single-cylinder 498cc engines with a common water jacket, the cylinder head a copy of the Norton's with induction by four AMAL motorcycle carburetors.

The team achieved their first race win in the 1957 British Grand Prix at Silverstone, with Stirling Moss and Tony Brooks sharing a VW 5 model, earning the team the distinction of constructing the first British-built car to win a World Championship race. Vanwall won the inaugural Constructors' Championship in Formula One in 1958, before the parent company Vandervell Products – famous for the Thinwall bearings brand for automotive engines - collapsed financially, ending the effort.

But a major part of the charm of Silverstone for me was the British saloon car Championship dominated by Jaguars in the Fifties and early Sixties. This included the Jaguar 3.4 Mark 1 and 3.8 Mark II sedans, as well as the huge Mark VIIs.

Between the privateer teams like John Coombs Racing, Peter Barry Racing and Equipe Endeavor, Jaguar saloons were victorious in a majority of British Saloon Car Championship – BSCC – races from 1958 through 1963. Not only did a Jaguar sedan take first in most races, they also consistently took second and third place. Meanwhile, in France, the Jaguar saloons were incredibly successful at the Tour de France Automobile road race, winning the Touring Car class from 1959 through 1963.

The Scream of an Engine

I'm still in love with the Jaguar 3.8 Mark II. At the Mark II introduction in 1960 at the New York Auto Show, all the bright work on the show car was gold plated. Barrett-Jackson Auction, Scottsdale, AZ, January 2017

Jaguar saloon cars won every International Tourist Trophy Race at Silverstone from 1952 through 1962. The first five years were with the then-newer Mark VII, followed by the smaller 3.4 and 3.8 sedans starting in 1957. Winning drivers included Stirling Moss, Mike Hawthorn, Ian Appleyard of Jaguar rally fame, Walt Hansgen, Ivor Bueb, Colin Chapman, Mike Parkes and Graham Hill.[77]

Phew. I love Silverstone.

---

[77] Wikipedia July 2017 supplies the statistics and color and for much of the Silverstone story

The Scream of an Engine

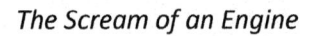

The Scream of an Engine

Chapter Thirteen: Kit Cars

For my money, kit cars held great fascination when I was in high school in the Fifties. Kit cars had the least impact on my car culture. But I still found them hugely interesting and a few inspired my passion.

The most popular in my book was the Devin kit car. These bodies looked great to a high school kid trying to figure out how to find a vehicle to both impress girls and drive to school.

This thinking and discovery effort was part of my high school culture.

That car problem was solved for me when Dad bought our second Austin Healey Sprite named Nellybelle, or Nelly, for short. She required body work. Then we selected the Ferrari blood red paint color – the reddest red we could find – for her. She looked sexy and Italian in that vivid red. But I must admit the stock red seats clashed with the body color.

Bummer.

Nonetheless, Devin got my mind going and the passion boiling.

Devin Enterprises is a good gearhead story, begun by a passionate man named Bill Devin in California. Devin Enterprises made kit car bodies for nine years from 1955 to 1964. In other words, Devin covered my high school years and a little more.

The company produced high quality fiberglass car bodies sold as kits. They also produced automotive accessories and complete automobiles. The business commenced in Fontana, CA and ended up in El Monte, CA, another indication that California has always been car country.

When Bill Devin sold his Ferrari 250 MM coupé to a buyer in Michigan in 1954, he took a 1953 Deutsch-Bonnet Le Mans barchetta in trade as partial payment. Devin also bought out the stock of a Panhard dealer in California, acquiring ten chassis with engines but no bodies.

Devin designed his own ladder frame for a custom race car that would use the engine and front-wheel drive transaxle from the Panhards. The wheelbase of this chassis was eighty-four inches. Devin also took a mold of the body of the DB Le Mans, made some changes, and began to produce custom bodies for his new car.

With help from Norton motorcycle racer Don Evans, Devin adapted the cylinder barrels, cylinder heads and pistons from the Norton Manx motorcycle to the two-cylinder boxer Panhard crankcase, roller-bearing crankshaft assembly and piston rods. He then fabricated a

The Scream of an Engine

custom manifold that would accept two-barrel side-draft Weber carburetors. These alterations didn't affect the displacement of the engine, leaving the 79.5mm bore and 75mm stroke unchanged: total displacement 745cc.

By comparison, the engines in the first Austin Healey Sprites were an immense 950cc.

The Devin-Panhards went into production in 1955 with engine options that included OHV, SOHC and DOHC variations of 745cc and later 850cc displacement engines. Another version of the engine came with a MAG supercharger, which bumped the car up into the 1100cc class.

After gaining experience making complete fiberglass bodies with the Devin-Panhards, Devin Enterprises expanded in 1956 into production of fiberglass bodies to be sold to builders of custom and one-off specialty cars.

Devin produced distinctive and attractive roadster-style bodies that high school kids loved.

1957 Devin with a Chevrolet V8 engine – who wouldn't want to drive this? Devin phot

The Scream of an Engine

Chapter Thirteen: Kit Cars

Chapter Fourteen: The Sprite

Family culture evolves. In my late high school days, Sprites arrived as noted.

Dad met an English car mechanic in 1960, Charlie Parsons, who talked him into the new passion: Austin Healey Sprites. Charlie was friends with a University of Puerto Rico professor who owned a gray 1960 Sprite. The professor asked Dad to drive it at the new Autopista de Caguas track in the mountains forty minutes south of San Juan. Without checking anything on the car, Dad jumped in and won his first SCCA HP Class race going away.

The stock Dunlop bias ply street tires were down to the cords by the end of the race.

The Scream of an Engine

Sprites were first delivered in 1958, so this was still at the front end of the Sprite craze. Sprite popularity continues to this day nearly sixty years later in the form of vintage cars on the street and Sprites in the winners' circle at the SCCA National Championships. In the early Sixties, when Dad raced Matilda, factory Sebring Sprites - from British Motors Corporation or BMC – were winning races around the world including the Sebring 12-Hour. In class of course. Steve McQueen drove a Sprite for BMC at Sebring 1962 and earlier in another BMC car, the Mini, at Brands Hatch in 1961.

Dad bought the car, now named Matilda, from the professor. And Charlie kept suggesting ways to make Matilda go faster. Soon Matilda was re-classified to GP. Later, Matilda was converted to Sebring Sprite specs with wire wheels and an Alexander cross flow head. That last feature forced Charlie to cut holes in Matilda's hood to accommodate the twin SU carburetors. As a result, the SU dashpots stood up out of the hood.

By now, with Dunlop R 5 Racing tires and many laps under his belt, Dad was moved up in class several times to ultimately run in Class C, way above Matilda's original pay grade, Class H. He set the lap record on the beautiful Autopista de Caguas in C Production that lasted for eight years.

The only faster cars on the track were a 327 Corvette coupé and a Mustang 350 GT which ran in BP class; and a Ferrari 250 California, an Aston Martin DB4 GT and a bigger 427 Corvette which ran in AP. The Ferrari often won the AP race because Rafi Rosales was a good chauffeur. And he played games. Like the brake light switch he rigged so he could flash the brake lights from the dashboard: anyone following him would see the brakes flash on way early and start to back off the throttle. Rafi was still pedal to the metal.

The Scream of an Engine

But these AP and BP cars weren't much faster than Dad's Sprite. And Dad talked about installing one of the new all-aluminum Buick V-8 motors into Matilda and going after the AP cars. Installing V-8s in small cars was in the air, recognized by Fred Puhn in his Santee Cars, Carroll Shelby in the AC Ace 'Bristol'/Cobra cars, and Bill Devin with his kit cars.

Bud Suiter, Sr. with Matilda in SCCA H Production form before the 'Sebring Sprite' conversion. These are just a few of Matilda's many trophies. 1961

The fallout for my brother Ron and I is that we got to drive Sprites to high school. Mine was just senior year, but Ron lucked out and had one to drive sophomore through senior years. How did that happen? We owned five Sprites at one point. But three were for parts. The remaining red Sprite, now named Nellybelle, and gray Matilda complemented the family yellow Volvo 122S four door sedan.

I met a Puerto Rican lass at the dance after one of our high school basketball games. Milca Marietti had just won runner up in the Miss Puerto Rico contest and showed me the photos from the big event.

I asked her out for an afternoon movie as a first date. Matilda and I pulled up to Milca's home and I bounced up the steps to knock on the door.

When Milca opened the door, she said, 'I'd like you to meet my sister. She'll be going with us.' The chaperone requirements in Puerto Rico are very real. No way out. I'd forgotten to ask. Milca's sister sat on Matilda's metal hump between the seats while I tried to shift gears around her left leg, an unenviable task at best for the unfortunate sister. Milca and I had a fun but unromantic first date.

Later, I drove red Nellybelle home from school one afternoon into a traffic jam in Santurce. I'd left the top in the garage. At a red light, a Puerto Rican 'agua cero' – literally 'downpour' so intense you can't see through it - struck and dumped huge quantities of water on the stopped cars. Fellow travelers in other cars around me rolled up their windows and pointed and laughed at my dilemma. The agua cero was short, probably less than ten minutes. But three inches of water accumulated in Nellybelle's foot wells. And of course, I was no longer dry, either. Even if I'd had the top, the storm was over before the top could've been erected. Risks of driving a sports car in Puerto Rico.

Then there were rallies and other car games in high school. Dear friend Gilberto Vals owned a Renault Gordini, a hopped-up Renault sedan. We talked and decided to form a racing team, Equipo Ass Verde, for Green Ass Racing Team. We'd enter rallies.

Our first rally was in the mountains of central Puerto Rico, the Cordillera Central. We both placed diagonal white sticky tape stripes on our front doors, signifying our race team colors. Both cars – the Gordini and Matilda - were the same shade of grey.

At one point during the rally, co-driver Ibsen Morales and I were stopped at the top of a mountain decoding the rally instructions.

We were lost. A straight road stretched before us down our mountain headed to the top of the next mountain: a gray car on the top of the next mountain was hurtling toward us. We raced down our mountain hoping to regain the course somewhere ahead. At the bottom, the other car passed us going at least as fast in the opposite direction – I figured a relative speed of at least 120 MPH.

It was our teammate. As we passed each other, Gilberto and I both shrugged shoulders to indicate neither of us had a clue. Within minutes the road became so rough that Matilda bounced violently and stopped running.

I pulled to the side of the road, jumped out and raised the hood. A crowd of onlookers drifted out of the jungle surrounding both sides of the road to watch. I quickly diagnosed our problem: the high-tension ignition wire had fallen out of the coil. I asked my co-pilot Ibsen, little brother of one of my best friends, to see if the bystanders could come up with pliers and a screw driver. Race team preparation is notably weak if these items aren't aboard.

Within seconds, the tools appeared. The ignition wire clamp was re-tightened to the frame and the wire re-inserted into the coil. We returned the tools, closed the hood, fired up Matilda and accelerated down the road. To cheers and clapping from our new-found fans along this previously 'deserted' jungle road.

We then took a short cut to the finish line, missing out on qualifying for trophies. However, we felt like we'd just finished the Mille Miglia in Italy. Great fun and excitement that I remember fondly fifty-seven years later.

After my brother and I were off to college in the States, Nellybelle was breathed-on by Charlie Parsons and Dad raced her in

The Scream of an Engine

class G Production. So, Dad always raced twice on Caguas Raceway weekends, G Production and C Production.

Chapter Fifteen: My Turn

Now culturally attuned in my own unique way, I've grown up. It's my turn to buy cars.

My first ever car purchase was an Austin 850. Why not a Jaguar, an MG or an Alfa which as described, I'm already hooked on?

At the time, I was still in the Cornell Graduate School of Business in Ithaca, NY. Cash was hard to come by. Needed wheels. Paddy Hopkirk had just won the 1964 Monte Carlo Rally in a Mini Cooper. The press was full of good stories about Minis impressing permanent grins on drivers' faces.

Friends in New England owned Minis. We all had the same English car bias.

The Scream of an Engine

A 2017 poll by British motoring magazine *Auto Express* to determine the fifty best British cars of all time has put the classic 1959-2000 Mini in the number one spot, edging out the Jaguar E-type and the Land Rover Series. Those polled included unidentified members of the magazine's staff, as well as ten 'expert' judges from the car manufacturing industry.[78]

Auto Express said about the Mini, 'The car became an icon of British innovation, a fashion accessory and a motorsport hero that also brought affordable motoring to the masses.'

First Mini, an Austin 850. Ran like a top but not quickly. I later painted the wheels yellows to emphasize their 10" size. At Connecticut College, New London, CT.

There were a lot of well-used Minis, like Austin 850s, running around eastern Connecticut then. So, I found one and bought it. My bird's egg blue Austin cost $175 running. Except for seats, the interior

---

[78] Hemmings Motor News, April 24, 2017

The Scream of an Engine

had been gutted. Sears blue/green, indoor/outdoor carpeting made fine floor mats and door lining. I was in business with a four-passenger car powered by an 848cc engine, weighing 1411 pounds.

So, fall of 1965 and spring of 1966, I owned a Mini to drive on campus and take many trips, one to New London, CT to visit my future wife at Connecticut College.

The way home to Ithaca, NY from Connecticut College required a trip through the mountains on Route 79 in Upstate New York. On one such trip, the ice and snow were thick on the freeway. The heater had never worked. It was cold in the car. By the time I came through late Sunday night, the ruts cut by cars and trucks on the freeway had frozen solid. I bounced around like a cork floating on stormy seas.

Then the ice on the edge of one of the ruts ripped the muffler off. The car now roared like a large commercial airliner on takeoff. Finally, the engine began to lose power. The roar diminished. The car made only 34 BHP to start with; I reckoned I was down to seventeen. Pulling over to the side of the road, covered in snow and ice, I stopped and popped the hood to see what the matter might be.

I found ice buildup around the air intake for the single SU carburetor. No air! I grabbed a screwdriver and chipped the ice off, jumped back in and was pleased to find the engine would start and run. The ice quickly returned. I stopped again.

When I finally arrived in Ithaca at my apartment on 125 Heights Court, the trip had taken ten hours, twice the normal five. My ears were ringing from the immense noise the car made. I climbed the steps to the second floor and collapsed on the landing. My roommate Danny Krez heard the racket and helped haul me to bed.

The Scream of an Engine

At one point, my Phi Kappa Sigma fraternity brothers lifted the Mini onto the front porch of the fraternity house; the doors close against stone pillars couldn't be opened.

The following summer of 1966, between years in the business school, I landed a sales job with IBM in Groton, CT. Our three-week IBM System/360 training class was held in Poughkeepsie, NY. My classmates were entertained by seeing this little blue car with yellow ten-inch wheels in the parking lot.

One IBM classmate and friend later drove up to Groton to visit. I took him for a ride in the Austin 850.

He was impressed with how fast we could go, like 60 MPH zipping along the back roads of Eastern Connecticut, but laughed about how long it took to get to sixty, like twenty-four seconds. He drove a new Volvo sedan. Even that was fast by comparison.

I asked him if he'd like to meet the lady in the apartment next to mine. This lady had made it clear to me that she'd like my company one night soon, as her husband was at sea on a submarine and would shortly return. She'd made several passes. But I had a girlfriend. My IBM classmate, on the other hand, had no such restrictions. Or scruples. So, I introduced them. Next morning, my buddy allowed that she was better than she looked. I told him I'd hoped so. We laughed a lot.

By the end of the summer, I'd accumulated cash, enough to upgrade to another Mini, a Morris Cooper 1071 S. Old English White with a black top. Plenty of torque, a heater and classy grey/red upholstery. It was a rocket ship compared with my old Austin 850 and set me back only $750. I sold the 850 for $175, exactly what I'd paid for it the year before. This Mini offered 70 BHP, twice my first one.

The Scream of an Engine

Back on campus in the fall for my last semester in Business School, I took classmate and friend Scott Ledbetter for a test run, out the Phi Kappa Sigma fraternity driveway and right onto Ridgewood Road. Scott was a sharp dresser and for this event was wearing a full-length camel hair coat, white dress shirt, red tie and tortoise shell framed glasses.

He looked properly English.

To impress him, I nailed the throttle. I'd never done this on Ridgewood Road. The dog leg came up faster than I remembered. I used the whole road instead of staying in my lane and remember now the sound of the ivy on the telephone pole slapping the driver's side door. I slowed down. But as I let Scott out later, I think I noticed a brown stain on the back of his camel hair coat that I'd not seen before.

We often do silly things we later regret. Like the time my roommate Dave mooned a car full of young ladies out the back window of our other roommate's Plymouth Fury sedan. The three of us were headed for New York City and Thanksgiving our sophomore year. I'm sure Dave would like to take that one back, too.

As a side bar, Mike McCarthy was my classmate in the Business School. To make ends meet, I taught Hotel Engineering- mostly heating, ventilation and air conditioning - to undergrads in the Hotel School. Mike ran a slot car track just north of campus. I had a collection of slot cars including a blue Ford GT 40. I added a Mini to the collection, which I painted with black top and English white body to match the 1071 S Morris Cooper I was driving on the street by then. I built the chassis up from scratch using bronze tubes. I wanted a realistic front wheel drive slot car.

At the time, front wheel drive slot car kits weren't available.

Chapter Fifteen: My Turn

The Scream of an Engine

    Mike and I raced. He was quicker but always spun off and let me through for the win in the GT 40. I suspected he had more hours on the track than I did, too.

1965 Ford GT 40 slot car with magnesium frame and magnesium wheels. The large gum rubber rear tires were my only modification. Fast and quick enough to win many slot car races in Ithaca, NY.

Slot car model of my 1963 Morris Cooper 1071 S. Tubular hand-made frame, large gum rubber front tires to gain traction with front wheel drive. Authentic but no wins

Chapter Fifteen: My Turn

The Scream of an Engine

No one can study all the time. The Ford was fast but my Mini suffered acute wheel spin coming off the turns. My version of front wheel drive needed further development.

Still driving my 1071 S Mini Cooper and after commencing my first full time job at General Dynamics Electric Boat Division, I started my own car 'business.' I bought three more Minis to fix up and sell. One Austin 850 set me back only $20, a stripped body I bought for the windshield. A second Mini I found was in roadworthy shape, but lacked an engine and a windshield. This was the one to be completed and made into a fully working Mini.

I bought a re-built short block from Bob Evelyn in Noank, CT for $50. Then I transferred the head and transmission and other bits and pieces from the engine/transmission on the third Mini to the short block. The third Mini was a real beater and would never see road time again. I installed the now completed engine/transmission into the second Mini.

The heart transplant was conducted in a driving rainstorm on the outside driveway of the Mystic, CT carriage house we rented. Lots of barked knuckles and unrepeatable words accompanied this gearhead trick. I was soaked to the skin.

After I dried out and completed the second Mini, I sold it for $350. The transplanted transmission, I later heard, lasted only a year. I hadn't overhauled the transmission and the young fellow who bought that car had a very heavy right foot.

One cold February weekend in 1967, four of us drove our Minis from Connecticut up to Maine to watch an ice race. It was cold the morning of the race, twenty below before wind chill. We extracted jumper cables from one Mini and connected two Minis together to start one, then continued until they were all four fired up. British

Lucas electrics were famous for these idiosyncrasies. As Maine is famous for cold.

Ice racing is different. At the start of the race, a huge roar erupted from the twenty-three cars on the grid. But none of them moved. Slowly, as if tied together, they all moved off, snow stud tires biting on the ice. Once underway, the spectacle was even better: the cars tried to stop for the turns, often failing. An ice bank marked the outside of the turn at the end of the first straight. This ice bank arrested several competitors on the first lap at the cost of a bent fender or bumper.

We cheered for the Minis, but the three-cylinder Saabs had their measure. Undoubtedly Saabs were winter trained in Sweden before they left for the Americas. They also had bigger wheels and larger tire contact patches on the ice.

Driving my Minis on the streets and roads of eastern Connecticut was exhilarating. Friend Salle Evelyn, editor of the *Sports Car Penny Pincher*, named one of the hills on Route 1 between Groton and Mystic 'Third Gear Hill.' This was because none of the four speed English and Italian sports cars of the day, including Minis, could make it up without shifting down to third.

These Minis left me with aching face muscles after drives, from the continual grins. I was hooked on Minis.

Then two years later, a friend pointed out a black 1965 Alfa Romeo Giulia TI sedan sitting on a Chrysler dealer lot in Mystic, CT. The price was $500 for an immaculate three-year old car with 30,000 miles on the clock, but with a catch: this Alfa needed pistons, liners and rings. So, for $500 I drove that Alfa home, smoking like a chimney. The pistons, liners and rings later set me back another $250 installed by Charlie Rainville, an Alfa and Trans Am Plymouth racer and mechanic in Rhode Island.

The Scream of an Engine

My new Alfa drove like a dream, growling like 1600cc Alfa Normales do on takeoff, with four-wheel disc brakes that meant business and me wading through the five-speed gearbox like a hot knife through butter. The Minis were all four speeds. Everything on the Alfa worked.

I was hooked on my first Alfa.

Two years later, in July 1970, I drove the black Giulia an hour down Interstate 95 from Mystic to the Performance Auto dealer in New Haven, CT. The Giulia needed a brake job and Performance Auto was the nearest Alfa dealer. The rear pucks on the Dunlop disc brakes were frozen.

I walked through the show room. The salesman threw me the keys for a brand new 1969 white boattail 1750 Spider which was just sitting there beckoning to me. And shouted, take her for a spin. I obliged. And bought the car on the spot. I still loved this Alfa forty-two years of ownership later.

Second Alfa, the 1750 Spider sporting the original Connecticut license plates. June 1971

The Scream of an Engine

I was now hooked on 1750 Spiders. It was only a matter of time before I'd go racing.

I'd been thinking about racing and the tradeoffs between that and owning more exotics to drive on the street.

We moved from New York City to St. Louis with the General Dynamics Corporate Office relocation in June 1971.

A Cornell friend and fellow volleyball player, Al Kohn, and I tested a new 1972 De Tomaso Pantera Ford V-8 off the showroom floor in St. Louis. When I hit 6,000 RPM, the redline, all the instruments crumped out. I figured that was a signal to pass on this one.

Then I visited the Alfa dealer in St. Louis to see if I could work a deal to service and build my imagined new Alfa race car. This was before I found my own garage. A gleaming black 1964 289 Cobra sat in the showroom: for sale for $12,000. This was before black was popular. I never worked the deal to house a race car at the dealership and I decided to hold off on buying the Cobra until after the race car.

Which also turned out to be black.

Now I had to go racing. By mid-1972, I'd admired a black 1750 Spider race car – like my white street Alfa, also a 1969 model - at a Mid America Raceway race weekend. The track was just forty miles west of St. Louis.

Prerequisites for racing are figuring out what it's all about. Watching races – I'd been to dozens by now – isn't enough. So, I bought and read Alan Johnson's *Driving in Competition* and Piero Taruffi's *The Technique of Motor Racing*, with foreword by Juan Manuel Fangio. Alan Johnson had creds: he'd been four-time SCCA National Champion and his advice is awesome and still available on

Amazon forty-five years later. Taruffi was one of the greats of Grand Prix racing in the Thirties, Forties and Fifties. The foreword in Taruffi's well written book is so good I figured someone ghost wrote it for Fangio. On the other hand, maybe not, and Fangio's no longer here to defend himself.

Everyone said buy a race car already built. Don't try to convert a street car into a racer.

I called Dave Coman the owner/driver of the black Alfa race car at his home in Tulsa, OK, and the deal was struck. I bought a new 245 Volvo station wagon for a tow car - fearing the inadequacy of my wife's then new lightweight Datsun 510. Then I drove to Tulsa and picked up Number 99 – an abbreviated version of Henry Ford's 1901 racing number, 999, which Barney Oldfield was later to use while racing and winning for Henry Ford.

We search for these little clues that we're on the right path. I liked the car number.

The black trailer was so big and heavy the Volvo would barely maintain highway speeds. So, when I arrived back in St. Louis, I immediately bought a new Clark lightweight trailer from the manufacturer in Perkasie, PA and had it delivered.

When it arrived, the new white trailer turned out to be a gem and a dream to tow. We could now handily exceed the national speed limit of 55 MPH imposed after the petroleum shortages of the early 1970s.

The new brick apartment building my wife and I lived in had two closed-garage parking spaces underneath – one for my tow car and one for my street Alfa, I imagined. But I knew I needed more space for the race car.

I found a private, unused, standalone two-car garage in Clayton, MO, a few minutes' walk from our apartment. The garage was covered in age-blackened wood shingles. A knock on the door of the owner's home led to a very accommodating relationship for the next three years. Mrs. Kreutz, the garage owner, a silver haired, slender, elderly lady who lived alone, insisted only that I keep the noise to a minimum. She rented me the garage for $20/month. I used one bay for the new trailer and one for the race car.

For a race car, the Alfa was surprisingly quiet, so that part was easy. I kept the doors shut when the engine was being 'tested' and minimized engine-on time while loading the car on the trailer outside her garage.

Dave Coman's mechanic told me they'd just finished the Brainerd, MN five- hundred-mile race, but the car had been checked out and was ready to go. With short notice, I took his word for it and signed up for the driver's schools that October 1972 at Blackhawk Farms and at Mid America Raceway.

I was immediately in trouble. The front end was so loose at Blackhawk that I had to steer constantly just to keep the Dunlop R5's pointed in the right direction. Then I blew the head gasket at Mid America a week later.

That winter, I shipped the engine to Ward and Deane Racing in Los Angeles, CA. Alfa racer Alan Ward was the hot Alfa shoe on the west coast at the time and did all his own engine work with partner Don Deane. I told Alan I wanted a strong motor. He tried to talk me into a two-liter upgrade, but I insisted on the original size and matching serial numbers. The finished product produced 156 BHP on the dynamometer, tested as part of our contract. This was a good step up from the stock 129 BHP. I was pleased.

The Scream of an Engine

Ward and Deane added an incredible combination of cams, pistons, racing main and rod bearings, new head – the old one had been shaved once too often - and new Weber carburetors. My advisors at the time said that the Webers were peakier but stronger in the power band than the original Alfa-Spica fuel injection that Coman had used. So, I switched.

The clutch plate and flywheel were replaced with lightweight aluminum racing versions. Just in time: I noticed at my last driver's school before this overhaul that most of the pressure plate springs were broken on the old clutch. That's why I limited the RPMs to 6500 before the overhaul. I suspected I was hanging on by a thread. Alan confirmed I was.

I also rebuilt the front suspension with Ward and Deane parts, Koni shocks, and lots of new bolts, including the longer Alfa 2000 Spider lug bolts and nuts so the wheels could be moved further out from the center of the car. I replaced the 'drill rod' – heaven forbid - Coman used to hold the lower front A-arms to the chassis at proper camber. One mechanic rolled his eyes when he saw the drill rod: implying I was lucky to be alive after my driver's schools.

I bought two new Alfa Autodelta Quadrifoglio green four-leaf-clover-on-white stickers for the front fenders. This historical touch reproduces the first Quadrifoglio painted on the Alfa that won the Targa Florio road race in Italy in 1923 by owner/driver Ugo Sivocci. Autodelta, the Alfa factory racing arm, adopted the Quadrifoglio as the official symbol for Alfa Romeo racing. Autodelta produced complete factory race cars and a whole catalog of speed parts for us gearheads to drool over and buy for our cars.

My pit crew at this point consisted of Gary Barfield who liked cars and Coors. He'd drive clear across Missouri to Kansas in his Camaro to buy Coors beer before it was available in St. Louis. And Gary's buddy, the strong silent type who took his instructions from

The Scream of an Engine

Gary. Gary was employed as a General Dynamics accountant where I worked as a financial analyst. Gary found out through the grapevine I was racing. He hustled in the pits. I don't remember his buddy's occupation, but he followed Gary's orders quick-step.

The third driver's school on March 23, 1973 was a cold forty-five degrees but a different story: the Alfa was strong and tight. I could spin wheels in third gear with new Dunlop R5 CR82 compound tires on the car. Amazing throttle response combined with a clean, new inspirational engine bark. My contemporary notes show tire pressures of 34 PSI front and 31 PSI rear, 1 ½ degrees camber, 1 ½ degrees castor, 20-minutes toe in, 4.78 rear end, NGK 9E cold sparkplugs.

NGK was my only sponsor: they donated spark plugs, both several sets of race plugs and a set of street plugs. I always warmed the race engine with warmer NGK 7Es and switched to 9Es for the race. In turn, I put their sticker on the front fenders, just behind the front wheels.

And I was awarded my SCCA Regional driver's license that day.

My first race was a seven lapper as part of the driver's school on Saturday. As you can see from the photo of the start, the Alfa was at the front of the grid based on qualifying times. The photo below appeared on the front page of the *St. Louis Globe Democrat* Sunday sports section the following day. On the second lap, I spun on turn eight, recovered and finished eighth out of forty-nine cars on the grid, second in class to a Datsun 2000. I fought heated battles with the Datsun 2000s, especially later at Road America, overcoming their larger engine sizes – 2-liters vs 1.8 - with better brakes. When I could.

Sunday dawned bright and sunny for my first official Regional race. The only part I didn't overhaul on that race car over

The Scream of an Engine

the previous winter was the lightweight motorcycle battery. When I started the Alfa Sunday morning for the Regional race practice, that battery exploded in smoke and sparks.

Start of first Driver's School Race, on a cold Saturday in March 1973. Alfa center front. Photo: St. Louis Globe Democrat

    I sped down the road into the nearest town, Wentzville. A Western Auto store was open Sunday morning. They stocked an uncharged garden tractor battery, the only size that would fit without modifications. I bought it and chewed nails while it was charged.

    Back at the track, the new battery went in quickly, in time to make the grid for my first real race, even if at the back of the pack. The track was wet from rain. I had no rain tires. But the R5s were intermediates, so it wasn't as bad as it sounds. The car was a lot quicker than I was at this stage. We threaded through traffic and managed a fourth place in DP in the wet the first time out.

The next race was the Regional at Blackhawk Farms, west of Chicago on May 5-6, 1973, on a 1.8-mile course that required my 5.12 rear end which was home in the garage. It's necessary to run a track once or twice to get the setups right. I could hit fifth gear using the 4.78 rear end for no more than one second on the main straight. My pit crew this weekend was a couple who stayed in their tent all weekend - their first date. They sure were happy the one time they came out of the tent to eat.

I qualified the Alfa ninth out of thirty-one cars on the D, E, F, G Production, D Sports Racing grid and finished second overall and second in class, this time behind John Schmidt's cherry 3-liter Yenko Stinger. This was Schmidt's home track. I beat him later at Mid America, my home track. We enjoyed an intense but friendly rivalry.

The Alfa was now fast and I was learning the limits. Practice helped this second time out on the track, but I mastered Blackhawk Farms during the race.

The following weekend we were back at Mid America Raceway for my first National race. I qualified for earning the National license based on completing two Regional races.

The Group 44 racing team, previous year National Champs in my class and in several other classes, brought all their hot shoe drivers and cars for C, D, E, F and G production: five cars. Their cars are immaculately prepared and painted in their white with green accent livery that intimidates the competition.

Bob Tullius, principal of Group 44, is an American success story. When Tullius' boss at Kodak forced him to decide between his day job and his racing hobby, Tullius chose racing. He talked Triumph into giving him one of Kas Kastner's Sebring Triumph TR4s. But in that era, racing was a rich man's hobby if you wanted to be on top of the pile. It still is. Bob had a family to support. To continue racing

The Scream of an Engine

full-time, he knew he had to find a way to make racing into a profitable business. That's when Group 44, Inc. was born.

The road racing team, named for Tullius' racing number, combined Tullius' race and sponsorship savvy, Brian Fuerstenau's mechanical ability and Dick Gilmartin's Madison Avenue advertising expertise. They produced professionally prepared race cars, racing results and major publicity for sponsors which included Triumph and Quaker State.

Their team look was featured on the race cars, team uniforms and one of the first-ever team transporters in the motorsports world. Group 44 made quite a statement when they arrived at the track.[79]

I was very nervous before this first national race. I'd be meeting the best cars and drivers in the country.

Our race was DP, EP, FP, B Sedan and C Sports Racing. Group 44's Brian Furstenau qualified first in his MG-B and Group 44's John McComb won in a Triumph GT-6. Their motors sounded like they turned 9000 RPM. Factory money! I qualified 21st out of 52 cars on the grid and finished 25th after a pit stop to check out the cause of a banshee scream coming out of the engine compartment. Seems a bolt holding the alternator body together had backed out into the alternator cooling fan. What a noise that made.

Don Stewart and I couldn't figure it out in the pits, so I went back out at reduced speed to protect the engine, if that turned out to be the problem. Stewart was an Alfa owner, did his own engine work, and was the best – especially technically - of my many crew members over the three years I raced.

---

[79] From Moss Motoring writeup at http://www.mossmotoring.com/bob-tullius-group-44-inc/

Chapter Fifteen: My Turn

That's the thing about racing: if it can happen, it does. Parts that are fine for two hundred thousand miles on the highway break in a season of racing. Every part must be checked and re-checked between races. For example, I retorqued the original 1750-wheel lugs before going out on the track for a practice or a race. The original lug nuts always backed off while running on the track. Scary, but that's the way it was. I figured the bolt and nut threads had worn out over so many removals and would no longer hold a given torque. Over the winter of 1972, I installed new, longer lug bolts and nuts from the 2-liter Alfa catalog. They never backed off. I checked them every time anyway.

I have a regret from my first National race. Fifty-two cars on the grid, I'm in the middle. After the start and between the second and third turns of the first lap, the cars ahead of me are in a line to the left of the road, the proper line at speed. However, we weren't at speed. The cars were all nose to tail at perhaps three quarters speed. Knowing the course, I almost whipped the wheel over, pulled out of line and passed ten cars before turn three. And I'd have been on the inside of turn three. I could've done it.

I didn't. Why not? It's a race, for heaven's sake! That's what you're supposed to do. But I was intimidated. My only consolation is that no one else did it either. We were all intimidated.

But the best race of all, and the best race course for me, was Road America, Elkhart Lake, WI on September 23, 1973. Lots of great memories: a sleek, orange 'A' Sports Racing Lola with a big Chevy V-8, lapping me on the carousel with me pointing for him to pass inside as we exited the turn. That momentary concentration lapse – keep two hands on the wheel, brother - on my part caused the left rear wheel of the Alfa to drop off the pavement. We twitched a bit. After that race, the driver of the ASR car dropped by in the pits and apologized. What a gentleman. Especially considering the bobble

The Scream of an Engine

was my fault. Those are the kinds of drivers who make you glad you were part of SCCA in the 1970s.

First National SCCA race at Mid America, May 1973. Turn 1, inside right rear wheel lifting

In my class race, I had a nose to tail race with a 2-liter Datsun 2000 roadster. One lap I'd be in front, next he'd be in front. Late in the race, the Alfa was ahead coming down the main straight, where the Datsun had the power/speed advantage. So, I went to my strength at the end of the straight, brakes, and held the throttle down in fifth gear twenty yards further than normal. I really had to mash the brakes to slow down for the right hander.

The Datsun didn't have a chance: he banged right into the back end of the Alfa and spun off into the weeds. Finished that sucker right off.

But getting second in class behind that 3-liter Yenko Stinger – yes, again - wasn't the real story. That course is fun to drive: a smooth, wide macadam surface, elevation changes, fourteen turns, challenging for drivers, high speed straight, carousel turn, and history of epic motor races. Like the 1955 main event: held on the then brand new 4.0-mile track. That year the course was down from the six miles it used to be on the original public roads. Phil Hill in a Ferrari Monza nipped Sherwood Johnston in a Cunningham D-Type Jaguar by inches for the win. These memories I'd cherished as a twelve-year old kid reading about it in *Road & Track* came right back. I relished driving the same course my heroes eighteen years earlier raced.

The scenery in the Kettle Moraine region of Wisconsin is gorgeous. I'd go back in a heartbeat. The rolling farmland is dotted with colorful flowers and hard-working bees. Snowshoe hares are now brown by summer's end, river otters have raised their spring young, grouse are drumming and the wild turkeys strutting. Red-winged blackbirds, grackles, and robins are abundant in late summer, with lesser numbers of killdeer, song sparrows, bluebirds, and eastern meadowlarks.

For geology buffs, the continental glaciers during the last Ice Age dropped huge quantities of rocks and earth here, scraped from parts north. The Great Lakes were scooped out by the moving ice. The Wisconsin moraine was created when the Green Bay Lobe of the Laurentide Ice Sheet, on the west, collided with the Lake Michigan Lobe of that glacier, on the east, depositing sediment. The western lobe formed Green Bay and Lake Winnebago.

The moraine is dotted with kettles caused by buried glacial ice that calved off the terminus of a receding glacier and got entirely or partly buried in glacial sediment and subsequently melted. This process left depressions ranging from small ponds to large lakes and enclosed valleys. Water-filled kettles range in depth from three to two hundred feet deep. Elkhart Lake and Geneva Lake are the larger kettles now filled by lakes. The topography of this area is widely varied between the lakes and kettles. The hills of glacial deposits are up to three hundred feet above the level of the lakes which is reflected in the race course.

Road America's six hundred and forty acres are southeast of Elkhart Lake and about an hour north of Milwaukee along Route 57 and Lake Michigan. But this trip was a big one from St. Louis where I lived at the time, taking over seven hours even with the new trailer.

The race committee in the early to mid-seventies was superb. Wisconsin food, especially sausage and cheese, just can't be beat. The local beer is good, too.

There were other races and other stories to tell at Mid America and Stuttgart, AK. For example, I showed up for a practice-only weekend at Stuttgart with the race car still in red primer paint. But I was headed for the finish line.

The Scream of an Engine

Chapter Sixteen: The Finish Line

Sooner or later, we assess whether racing is the right thing to be doing. In my case, racing an Alfa could not have been a better choice. The sound of that Ward and Deane Alfa engine still screams in my ears. My heart rate never slowed completely until Wednesday following a race weekend.

For brief moments on the track I was Tazio Nuvolari in an Alfa P3 beating Mercedes and Auto Union at Nürburgring, Juan Fangio in an Alfa 158/159 winning the 1951 World Championship, or the Australian Horst Kwech in an Alfa GTA at Lime Rock passing 2-liter Porsches to win the under 2-liter Trans Am race.

I especially relished out-braking the competition into the corners: Alfa had the best production sports car brakes going in those days. Street stock, the 1750 Spider would stop from sixty MPH in one hundred and nine feet per *Road & Track*. With at least two hundred-fifty pounds off my race Alfa compared with street stock, plus the addition of huge Dunlop R5s, I'm certain my stopping distance was even shorter. Sure felt like it. Today, only the Porsche Turbo level-car stops that quickly. Go ahead, check it out. Well, almost only the Porsche.

Never mind that I used the street stock pads which worked so well on the track – and wore out completely in one weekend. Brake dust turning silver wheels black. I installed a new set of pads for every race weekend.

But in 1974, my wife and I were expecting a first baby. I was now as fast a driver as the car was fast, so I was taking too many chances. Another rebuild would be required over the winter. I also figured that at 31 years young I was not headed for a World Championship; should've started sooner with a bigger budget. The 1.8-liter Alfa had been dropped from DP to EP which made me more competitive in the lower class, but how do you compete with the Group 44s?

Even the guys at the top echelons of racing get bonked on the head. Or worse.

So, I crossed the finish line. Dave Coman saw how much I'd improved the car. In 1975, he bought the Alfa back, new trailer and all.

The Alfa GTAs walloped the Porsche 911s back in the mid-sixties before I got started. Alfas do beat Porsches every now and again. My Dad made the right move with the Alfa 'Super Spyder.' Too bad Dad never got a shot at Bob Holbert's 1300cc Porsche coupé.

Chapter Seventeen: Time for a Maserati

By 1984, my street Alfa was fifteen, my daily driver all those years. With crowded commuter traffic on freeways increasingly ill-adapted to the strengths of a small, nimble, back road-mastering Alfa Spider, I decided to buy a coupé. Quieter, safer, I reasoned. On Interstate 8 West one morning nearing Interstate 5, at 75 MPH, the Alfa in the fast lane, a rear-ender accident in the far-right lane bounced car parts in front of and behind me. Risky out there in a soft top.

I could take my three kids with me since two door coupés also offer a back seat.

The Alfa would get a mid-life overhaul at Ward and Deane in Los Angeles, with a racing clutch, aluminum flywheel and higher compression pistons, and new paint in the engine bay. And become the first 'collectible' car in our garage. As it turned out, the Alfa was also the only car ever in my collection. I owned the car for forty-two years, beating Dave Garroway with his SS 100 Jaguar by twelve years.

We gearheads sure are competitive.

The Scream of an Engine

For my first fifteen years with the car, my street Alfa was driven every day; the last twenty-seven only on weekends, in car shows or car parades. Except when my second daughter Elizabeth drove the Alfa one mile each way to school her senior year – the only one of my three who did stick.

I especially liked cramming my wife and three kids in Sophia – so named after a certain Italian actress I admired - for Fourth of July parades in the neighborhood. Complete with flags, bunting and costumes. I was Lee Iacocca in one parade, Tom a race car driver.

I sold Sophia in 2012 when we moved to Spain for two years. Who would charge the battery while we're gone? She sold for six times the new car purchase price. Beats a savings account.

But back to the time line. After consideration, a dark blue new Maserati Bi-Turbo showed up in my home garage in 1984. How could that be?

Everything about that car made sense from the specifications: 2491cc 90⁰ V-6 with twin Japanese IHI turbos. Turbos were new on production cars but the Japanese in 1984 made the best. The Italian engine produced 185 BHP at 5500 RPM, 208 ft. lbs. torque at 3000 RPM; ATE four-wheel disc brakes, just like the Alfa, the best; five speed ZF gearbox with fifth an overdrive ratio of .87, again like my Alfa five speed; aluminum alloy wheels; limited slip differential; full sized spare, Pirelli P6s; dry weight 2560 lbs.;[80] sumptuous, comfortable all leather interior, wool carpets, great smells; rare, not one on every street corner.

I talked to my boss, Edward T. Keating - President of the company I worked for, DatagraphiX, Inc., to discuss the dilemma of

---

[80] Maserati Bi-Turbo Specification Sheet

The Scream of an Engine

buying the right new car. He knew I was an Italian car fan having seen me drive my Alfa to work for nine years at that point - during his watch. I mentioned the turbo Thunderbird that had caught my attention. He said, 'You don't need a Thunderbird. You need a Maserati.' He knew that a Bi-Turbo was on my final list. His comment pushed me toward a decision.

But the real reason for buying a Maserati was that I loved the 250 F Maserati Formula 1 race car. After all, Juan Manuel Fangio won the 1957 World Championship, the fifth and last of his world championships, in a 250 F. I admired the Formula 1 Maser – a shorthand term of endearment - so much that my Bi-Turbo's CA license plate read, '250 F.' Twenty-nine 250 F Formula 1 cars were built by Maserati from 1954 through 1960.

Who says racing on Sunday doesn't sell cars on Monday?

Maserati has a rich history. In 1903, future founder Alfieri Maserati worked for high end Italian car builder Isotta Fraschini as a technician and driver, following in older brother Carlo's footsteps there. Alfieri was just sixteen and soon made a name for himself as a technician and driver.

Later, the Maserati brothers Alfieri and Ernesto, two of seven Maserati brothers, started their own company in Bologna, Italy on December 1, 1914. The war interrupted the automobile work of the new company. After the war, Maserati business resumed in the Ponte Vecchio section of Bologna, modifying 6.3-liter Isotta Fraschini engines and racing Diatto vehicles with these engines. In the early 1920's, Alfieri won many races, such as the Susa-Moncenisio, the Mugello and the Aosta-Gran San Bernardo.[81]

---

[81] Maserati, Volume One, Automobilia, 1984, Italy, page 9

The Scream of an Engine

By 1925-1926, the Maserati brothers started building their own race cars. Both Alfieri and Ernesto drove. They won the Italian Championship in 1926 and 1929. Their cars were model-numbered in the year they were completed: their first car became known as the '26'.

This start paralleled Enzo Ferrari's later path. Ferrari raced Alfa Romeos first, then managed the Alfa Romeo racing team before starting to build his own cars.

Maserati had developed a Grand Prix V-16 engine of nearly 4 liters by 1929 known as the V4; won twice with a twin supercharged V-8 powered 8CTF race car at the 1939 and 1940 Indianapolis 500, made beautiful, successful sports racing cars, like the 4.5-liter 450S in 1957, and delicate, lightweight designs like the very fast Tipo 60 through 65 Birdcage Maseratis. These were serious car people.

And they now offered me a chance to be part of this history at a reasonable price. The Bi-Turbo series of Maseratis were produced from 1981 through 1993. By 1984, I wasn't buying the first one off the assembly line.

If Italians know how to build any part of a car, it's the engine. I was confident in the new V-6 Bi-Turbo engine. Italian designers like Scaglietti, Zagato and Pinin Farina were the best in the world at making cars look fast standing still. The in-house body design of the Bi-Turbo notch-back coupé was crisp and effective with a fabulous, purposeful grille emphasizing the Maserati classic Trident symbol. Mario Maserati, the artist of the original Maserati brothers, first penned the Trident that is still in use today. The coachwork was excellent, no wrinkles, no 'orange peel' in the paint or unsightly door gaps. The doors slammed with a satisfying, solid 'thunk.'

Go for it.

The Scream of an Engine

Maserati was owned by De Tomaso Industries from 1976 through 1993 when Fiat S.p. A. acquired ownership. Under De Tomaso, Maserati headquarters were in Modena. The new Bi-Turbo announced in 1981 required volume production techniques which were soon implemented in the factory. Production increased from hand-building a few cars a month to hundreds to thousands. In May 1984, about the time I bought one, three thousand Maseratis were sold, mostly Bi-Turbos using the 2.0-liter version for the Italian market – taxes on cars were lower under two liters - and the 2.5-liter motor for export. By 2014, annual Maserati production had grown to 36,445 cars.[82]

The Bi-Turbo turned out not to be the best car I've owned, by a fair margin. But I still enjoyed driving it.

Three guys at work wanted a test ride, so I drove them to lunch one day. On the half-mile-drive back to the office after lunch, the temperature gauge pegged. Never happened before that, never since. But everyone aboard commented on this unusual event for a new car. Was this an electrical gremlin or a sticking mechanical thermostat? I never found out.

I had a go with a BMW E30 inline six 325i on Route 52, a freeway, from 60 to 100 MPH. Yes, San Diego freeways were virtually empty then by comparison with today. My advertised horsepower was higher than his 168 BHP so I was sure I had his measure.

But we were even. At the end, I smiled first to let him know I'd won. I hadn't. Afterward, I concluded he'd tweaked his E30. Only way I can explain the outcome. Certainly, wasn't the driver of the Maserati.

---

[82] Wikipedia, 1-17

The Scream of an Engine

The Maserati Bi-Turbo in June 1984. The license plate was the best feature

From notes and letters to Maserati's U.S. headquarters in San Francisco, including one dated August 19, 1986, several nuisance items cropped up that weren't being fixed during visits to the local dealer. Surprising to me, most centered on the engine. I'd figured this would be the car's strength. The worst was an oil leak on the right cam bank, resulting in puffs of white smoke out of the engine compartment at stoplights, or out the back at speed, with puddles of oil under the car and friends saying, what's that oil smell?

This required three trips to the dealer to fix.

In the meantime, Maserati was going great guns, having introduced two more models to the marketplace, the four-door 425 and the Spyder convertible. The ads in *The Wall Street Journal* dated February 26, 1986, noted the tie in to Formula 1 – see my history and love of Formula 1 – the $27K-32K price range, and more technical

The Scream of an Engine

details than you ever see in car ads. The technical details and the tie-in to Formula 1 had brought me into the fold two years earlier. They were appealing to my kind of buyer. Oh, and they mentioned that 6,000 Masers would be shipped to the U.S. in 1986, the exclusivity hook, noting no one else offered twin turbos in the U.S. market.

But the biggie came later at the 33,000-mile point, October 19, 1987, driving north in front of a police car on Interstate 5. The engine lunched. Quietly. It just died. I put in the clutch, drifted off the road at the exit, parked and had the car towed into the dealer. The price? $3,500 for new valves, pistons and associated work. The dealer said I'd over-revved the engine. When the engine let go, I'd been in heavy traffic at about 60 MPH limit in fifth gear, probably turning 1,800 RPM.

After discussion, Maserati fixed the engine for free. Seems the rubber cam belts – Alfa used steel chains – hadn't yet been perfected. These belts were required to be changed every 30,000 miles and had just been changed by the dealer at the 30,000-mile service. Funny things valves do to pistons when the timing belt breaks and the pistons hit the valves.

I heard rumors that the IHI turbos were lasting 40,000 miles. I put the car up for sale at 35,000 miles, just in case. I'd owned the car for five years: the turbos were no longer warranted. The first respondent to my ad test drove very carefully, then said, 'I hear noise from the turbos.' I honestly didn't and said so.

The second respondent made several visits to see the car, then brought cash and smiled as he drove the car away. He paid my asking price.

Next day, the IRS rang our doorbell. The agent showed me a photo of the buyer and asked, 'Is this the man who bought your car?'

I said, 'Yes,' and relayed to them the sale price of the car. No sense in messing around with the IRS. They left and said they'd be in touch if they had more questions. They sent a letter with questions which I responded to as accurately as possible.

Apparently, my buyer was being watched closely on his cash purchases. Money laundering? The IRS never contacted me again after the letter.

I can hear the comments: what did you expect? The Maserati is Italian. But my forty + year experience with the Alfa Romeo was just the opposite: almost never a problem, ran like a top. Everything but the heater worked, which I never needed because I lived in Southern California.

Chapter Eighteen: First Ford

In keeping with the family tradition of owning Ford cars, a Thunderbird Super Coupé (SC) arrived in my garage just after the Maserati departed. My first Ford. This SC was a new model in 1989 and came with the Light Titanium Clearcoat Metallic paint and optional Special Value Package

Opposite experience from the Maserati. I kept this one for eleven years and 145,000 miles. That's an indication this was a good one.

Gearhead features abounded, such as independent rear suspension, like the Maserati; a Roots supercharged 3.8-liter V-6 meant instant throttle response, unlike the delayed response from the Maserati IHI turbochargers; 210 BHP; electronically adjustable nitrogen-over-hydraulic fluid shocks; four-wheel disc brakes, five speed manual transmission; limited slip differential and sticky Goodyear Eagle tires. This combination made for compelling performance over the road.

The Scream of an Engine

A switch on the console permitted selecting a firm ride for high speed work. I used the FIRM mode for the occasional stoplight grand prix or in minimizing travel time up twisty Route 79 in the mountains to Julian, CA, from San Diego. Otherwise, the normal setting was far and away satisfactory for non-Grand Prix conditions.

Maroon bucket seats with adjustable side bolsters to hold the front seat passengers in place made a nice contrast with the exterior color. The black on white instruments included a tachometer.

I was happier than the proverbial clam.

A friend owned an M30 BMW 635 five speed CSi coupé and a Thunderbird SC. His BMW was for weekends only. He said he preferred to drive the Ford. I can't verify that comparison since I've never driven that model BMW.

Make no mistake: this was a driver's car.

Ford raced this body silhouette in NASCAR with success. Mark Martin, racing for Roush Racing from 1988-1991 won at Rockingham in October 1989 and took six pole positions that year. Martin, who was voted into the NASCAR Hall of Fame class of 2017, ran the Folgers coffee colors on his Jack Roush-owned T-bird for just two seasons, 1990 and '91.

In 1990, Martin lead the NASCAR Championship until two races from the end of the twenty-nine-race season, aced out by Dale Earnhardt when Martin received a forty-six-point penalty over the thickness of a carburetor spacer.

During the time he carried the Folgers sponsorship, Martin won four races and posted thirty top-five and forty top-10 starts in just fifty-eight races.

The Scream of an Engine

Lyn St. James, one of many talented female drivers who broke the male-dominated sport of motor racing, owned a Thunderbird SC, specially built by Bill Elliott for the sole purpose of breaking closed-course speed records. Lyn proved to be a quick study. She set the record of 212.577 MPH at Alabama's Talladega Superspeedway in October of 1988 with this car. These are the stories circulating when I bought my SC. Lyn is selling the car in early 2017 at an Amelia Island, GA sale.[83]

My eldest daughter, Katherine, was ready for her learner's permit at 15 1/2. I figured if she could drive stick, she could handle anything. After practice with our automatic shifting 740 Volvo wagon, including a trip into the bushes at the church parking lot, I took her out in the SC to learn stick shifting.

After several stalls and restarts figuring how to coordinate the clutch, brake and gas, she calmed down. Once up to speed, she was fine. However, on the way back to the house, we stopped at an unsigned intersection before turning onto our street, allowing another car to pass. When she started out, the car stalled. She stalled twice more. In frustration, she flung the driver's door open, shouting she'd prefer to walk back. She did.

Katherine never drove stick again until living in England years later. She mastered the technique there. The English are fond of manual transmissions.

Daughter No. 2, Elizabeth, saw quickly that two out of our three cars were stick, so she'd play the percentages and learn manual shifting. Due to her planning, she drove the Alfa Spider to school her senior year in high school.

---

[83] Kurt Ernst, Hemmings Daily, February 3, 2017

The Scream of an Engine

Son No.1, Tom, was next up for training. Same SC, same intersection as Katherine, and the car stalls. After two more attempts at getting underway again, Tom flung the driver's door open, shouting he'd walk back home from there. He did. Tom never drove a stick again until the next Ford chapter.

1989 Thunderbird Super Coupé. Automobile-Catalog.com

I still prefer stick. Paddle shifters are gaining.

Chapter Nineteen: The Jaguar

At last, a Jaguar. It'd been years since I'd raced my hand carved wooden C-Type Jaguar on the garage floor in Maryland. But Jaguars were still a passionate favorite.

About the time the SC had reached trade-in time, an important event occurred. My oldest daughter was getting married in San Diego in August 1999. I quickly noticed that I'd been excluded from preparations and discussions about critical issues like which church, which minister, which guests, which menu items and which venues for the reception afterwards and the late-night party. Both my wife and oldest daughter are very strong minded: they duked out the details.

I was consulted about the budget. The budget was agreed upon.

So, I again requested clarification of my duties. OK, I'd walk the bride down the aisle. Good. Was there anything else I could do?

The Scream of an Engine

No. Wait. You're in charge of transportation. You'll make sure everyone gets to where they need to be. On time.

Suddenly, I could see daylight: I'd interpret my duties as broadly as possible. So, I sold the Thunderbird, and drove over to the local San Diego Performance Jaguar dealer in Kearny Mesa. I knew that the S-Type, just available for the first time as a 2000 model year car, had an advantage over coupés: it had four doors, like any good sedan. Perfect for driving the bride and groom around town.

To be honest, I even thought about renting an old Rolls Royce to squire them. But that was such a temporary solution.

My son Tom would be the chauffeur. Leaving me free to pursue my other responsibilities like greeting out of town guests.

Wedding chariot. S-Type Jaguar 4.0-liter V-8 with J-Gate automatic transmission, December 2000

The Scream of an Engine

Performance Jaguar Sales Manager Vernon Honore and I hit it off right away. His smile was as big as all outdoors. Of course, I was buying one of his cars. But it went further than that: he liked Jaguars and knew something about them. He told many stories, like the one about Tony Gwinn, the San Diego Padres Hall of Fame right fielder, buying two S-Types, one for himself and one for his wife, Alicia. I always admired Tony Gwinn.

There was a British Racing Green DOHC 4.0-liter V8 model available on site. I signed the three-year lease, remembering that it was a Jaguar, that this was a new model and drove it home. If it worked out, I'd buy it at the end of the lease.

As it turned out, it did work out, but I didn't buy it. My 2000 S-Type was as trouble free as a car can ever be. But Vernon pointed out at end-of-lease that certain features of the new model available in December 2002 were huge improvements over mine. Wait, he cautioned, for the new S-Type and buy that. I accepted his advice and turned our 2000 S-Type back to the dealer in July 2002 with exactly 35,985 miles on the odometer. The lease included 36,000 miles.

And never got the new one. But that's the subject of the next chapter.

As a *Road & Track* subscriber, I'd known about the S-Type much earlier. In the December 1998 issue, the full-on treatment that *Road & Track* delivers is laid out in savory detail.

Ford had purchased Jaguar in 1989 – or Jaguar wouldn't be here anymore.

The S-Type was to be a joint development using the new Lincoln LS platform. But *R &T* was quick to point out that even the platform had different metal stampings and welds and was stiffer than

The Scream of an Engine

the Lincoln version. While the 3.0-liter V-6 engine was a Jaguar-modified Ford Duratec engine producing considerably more power, the V-8 was an all-new Jaguar engine. It has all the latest tricks, including overhead camshafts and four valves per cylinder – beating the Maserati and the SC by one valve per cylinder. And with 281/290 BHP – DIN vs SAE rating - the power was significantly up from my previous Ford SC V-6.

I love the looks of this new Jaguar. Geoff Lawson, the Jaguar designer of the model, got it right. He claims never to have looked at the original 1963-1968 S-Type Jaguar sedan which was the inspiration, in name at least, for this new model. Right, Geoff.

I preferred the Mark II Jag sedans built from 1959 through 1967 – yes, there was overlap with the newer S-Type which arrived in 1963. The original S-Type introduced independent rear suspension and more luggage space, but for me the profile, especially the rear deck, didn't look as crisp and fast as the earlier Mark II model. I bet Geoff Lawson looked at those Mark II Jags, too, before penning the new design.

Later, I obtained autographs for son Tom Suiter from Hurley Haywood and Bob Tullius – Group 44 highly skilled Jaguar race car drivers who were hired for a promotional event at Performance Jaguar in San Diego. Hurley also had a fabulous Porsche racing career as well. I've saved the Jaguar brochure they both signed. Tom may still get the autographs.

At the Performance Jaguar event, I asked Bob Tullius which of his many race cars he preferred driving the most. He paused, gave it some thought, pointed to the XJR5 race car on display, and said, 'The XJR5. I had to reach down further inside to get the most out of that car.'

I'm still a big fan of the 3.8 Mark II sedans, almost as much as the Jaguar sports cars. *Road & Track* tested this car in the August 1960 issue – I keep all the *R & T* Jaguar road tests – and noted that for under $5K, Jaguar delivered a compact, high-performance, high quality sedan. Performance? The 220 BHP 3781 cc six-cylinder DOHC XK engine propelled the car to 125 MPH. 0 to 60 took just 9.2 seconds. OK folks, we've come some way since 1960.

However, *Road & Track* points out this is a nice step up from the 2.4 and 3.4 Mark 1 sedans of 1957-1960. The 3.4s won many British saloon car races during this period. The performance step-up to the 3.8 Mark II, now with overdrive, is noted:

Acceleration	3.4-L	3.8-L
0-30 MPH	3.4 sec	3.0 sec
0-60	10.5	9.2
0-100	27.5	25.1

By comparison, the new S-Type V-8 would do 0-60 in 5.8 seconds, 0-100 in 15.9 seconds and peak out at 156 MPH if I could figure out how to take the governor off, which limited the speed to 155 MPH. In theory. My new car was a bit faster than the 3.8 Mark II sedans I'd so craved.

The knockoffs on the 1990 S-Type? It was available only with automatic transmission, the Jaguar J-gate five speed with lockup torque converter, allowing manual shifting and the ability to hold a gear.

Also, the car must be described as 'smooth.' Everything about this car was smooth. The upshifts were smooth, the leather seats were smooth, the wood trim was smooth, the takeoff from parade rest was

The Scream of an Engine

smooth, and cornering and stopping were smooth. That's how Jaguar perceived we U.S.A. fans would prefer it. Maybe their market research was done in England where this was the correct response.

For me, sportier is preferred. The December 2002 S-Type was sportier and had many other improvements that were to my liking, including bucket seats with bolsters.

Here's an example of what happens in a 290 BHP car that's too smooth. I'm driving on surface streets in San Diego when I become aware that three gardeners in a Ford F-250 dually truck are on my bumper. Then I notice they're laughing and pointing at the funny little 'furrin' car.

I decide to get away from them, so I negotiate the on-ramp to 805 South slowly so they're still on my bumper, then halfway through the on-ramp, I nail it. When I hit 80 MPH, I glance in the rearview mirror. THEY'RE STILL ON MY BUMPER, STILL GRINNING FROM EAR-TO- EAR. That's what smooth means.

Later, I'm at Holtville Raceway east of San Diego with friends. It's open track. You pay a few dollars and run a few laps. No inspections, no corner workers. This ex-airport race course has a lot of weeds in the infield in 2001 and large gaps between cement slabs which cause tires to thump when running over them. The turns are blackened with rubber marks from forty years of racing, but the straights are pure white concrete. A trip around is 1.6 miles.

My friends, brothers Bob and Chuck Engberg, have raced cars since the Fifties. Chuck as noted raced a Lotus 11, broke a wheel hub at Phoenix International Raceway and flipped.

But this day at Holtville, Chuck was teaching his early-twenties daughter Anna how to drive his Mazda RX 7 race car at speed. Bob

The Scream of an Engine

Engberg was a spectator. Bob and Chuck and Chuck's wife Janet, were trying to entice me to drive the race course in the Jag. I hadn't done anything like that for thirty years.

But I borrowed a helmet and out I went. I passed Chuck and Anna at one point. Chuck recalls today that I was then showing Anna the 'correct line through the corners.' Later, Chuck said I looked exceptionally smooth. I didn't tell him it was the car, not me. Afterward, Bob said my times would be competitive with BMW 3 series times on the track. After twelve laps. I had trouble getting braking points consistently right. Once at the wide right hander before the main straight, I'd braked so early that I had to accelerate long before the apex to get back up to cornering speed.

But I wasn't driving an S-Type out there: it was a C-Type or D-Type.

I was so crazy about these Fifties Jags that one time I stopped into Symbolic Motors in La Jolla. Sitting on the floor was Steve McQueen's D-Type Jag – not his XKSS which was one of the originals - in British Racing Green. This one was a replicar, but a good replica, down to the exposed aircraft rivets on the beautiful, flowing lines of the D-Type body.

The salesman opened the car door for me and in I went. Almost. Couldn't get my left knee around the fixed-place wood-rimmed steering wheel at first. Then my size thirteen shoes wouldn't fit into the pedal box. My mind was racing: I need to buy a pair of racing driver shoes which are more like gloves, then come back and try it again. I never did. Bummer. It just didn't fit.

So, I figured that a C-Type replicar would be just the thing: this would complement my wooden racer in my model car collection, but I could drive it on the street. And surely the earlier C-Type would have

The Scream of an Engine

more room for the large driver. The Proteus Company in England makes beautiful examples of the C-Type, very true to the original, over two hundred at this point.

British Racing Green is the color of McQueen's replica D-Type as is this 1955 D-Type Jaguar sporting Stirling Moss' favorite racing number. What Fifties kid could resist this? North Island Naval Air Station, October 2000

I saw a newspaper ad when in England visiting family. A Proteus C-Type was offered for sale in East Anglia. Fortunately, we'd planned a sailing trip on the Broads that day. On the return trip to Herne Hill, a suburb of London, we stopped by the East Anglia farmhouse where the C-Type was garaged. It was nearing 10 PM, quite dark. My contact met us on the paved road with a lantern in his hand, marking where we turned into the farm lane.

The owner, secretary of the Lotus Club, leads the four of us into his barn. Twenty-four cars under individual car covers appear. He makes a show of guessing where the C-Type is, then walks over to one car and whisks the cover off. It's the Jag.

The owner then asked me to step into the car and see what I thought. I must say it was immaculate, the British Racing Green paint perfect, reflecting the overhead lights. This next bit was déjà vu once more: I couldn't get my knee past the steering wheel.

He said, here, let me show you how to get in. He then stood on the driver's seat – I'd never do that - grabbed the wheel with both hands and slid into the seat. I used a modified version of his method, but realized that his 5'9" frame worked much better than my 6'2".

My feet didn't fit into the footwell. Same as the D-Type earlier in San Diego.

So, I said, thanks, I'd think about it. Should've said, no way José. He invited us into his 14th century farmhouse for a cup of coffee. This immaculately restored home featured stained wood ceiling beams on eighteen-inch centers, doors and ceilings so low I had to duck my head and keep my knees bent, and an open-hearth fireplace about fourteen feet wide. A large fire was burning. This was summertime. On the other hand, this was England which almost never gets completely warm.

As we left, the owner ran along-side our car, rapped on the window and lowered the price twice. I just couldn't buy a car that didn't fit.

The Scream of an Engine

The Scream of an Engine

Chapter Twenty: Second Ford

Instead of showing up for work in a Jaguar – work now being teaching high school physics after a twenty-eight-year business career - I imagined a simpler vehicle would be appropriate this time around. Besides, the new S-Type wouldn't be available for another three months.

I've always liked small cars best. After looking at Toyota and Volkswagen offerings, I preferred the VW GTI Turbo with 180 BHP and told the VW salesman that.

But as an afterthought, I dropped into the Ford dealer for the fun of it. In advance, I knew that the Focus wasn't sporty enough for what I had in mind. My salesman friend Steve Etheridge was on duty. I'd previously bought a Windstar from Steve for family transportation that worked out well. I used it to transport the members of the budding Francis Parker Sailing Team to practice. My oldest daughter was crazy about buying a purple van: this met her needs. My second daughter

The Scream of an Engine

then drove the Windstar back East to college her sophomore year and Steve sold us a Taurus for family transportation at home to replace it.

This is Steve's third time around. I told him what I wanted. Salesmen prefer selling larger cars for bigger commissions. But Steve went along with me and suggested we go for a ride in one car he thought I'd like.

The car was a gray Ford Focus. But it was a model I'd never heard of: SVT. What does that mean, I asked? Special Vehicle Team, he said. Wrong: the correct answer is FUN. The first thing I noticed was the white gauges with a tachometer bandwidth redlined at 6750-7300. When I grabbed the gearshift, I could see the six-speed pattern on the insert. Then I let the clutch out. I was hooked.

2002 Ford Focus SVT – a driver's car

This Ford handled better than anything I'd driven recently – including the GTI – and maybe the Alfa. But that's an unfair comparison. Thirty-three years of automotive development had improved the driving experience on all cars, especially this SVT. The Continental ContiSport Contact tires on this car were by far wider,

The Scream of an Engine

stickier and more predictable than the Pirelli P6 tires on the Alfa at that time. The Alfa had been upgraded to 15" Panasonics – Minilite look-alikes. The SVT had 16" wheels. The Alfa pulled strongly at 7,000 RPM. The Ford did, too, but with considerably more power. The brakes were fabulous on both cars. But with thirty-years development, the Ford brakes had better feel even if it took them nine feet longer to stop from 60 MPH. The difference in weight shows up here.

The 170 BHP double overhead cam four, normally aspirated, was sheer joy to hear and feel pulling the car through the gears.

I signed the papers when we returned to the dealership. I'd take the Alfa home and come in later to pick up the SVT. As I left, I told Steve that I'd stop by the VW dealer and tell him I'd changed my mind and wouldn't be buying his car. Steve almost had a heart attack. 'No need to do that' he said. 'That's part of the car business. He'll understand.'

Of course, I knew that the VW salesman would try to unhook the Ford order. And that wasn't going to happen. I followed Steve's advice.

How could I tell a $16,000 car is better for me than the $50,000 car I'd just turned in? Pulse. My pulse rate in the SVT soared every time I drove it - like never in the Jag. I'd absolutely lucked into another driver's car.

Mind you that this Focus offered 170 BHP compared with 132 BHP on a stock Focus. No big deal in absolute terms. But the way this extra 40 BHP left you feeling with the exhaust sound, the buttery smooth six-speed with perfect shifts every time and the heart pumping need to find a twisty road somewhere, told the story. And this was a very happy story.

Chapter Twenty: Second Ford

The Scream of an Engine

The purple cloth inserts on the otherwise leather seats distinguished this model from the others. I'd never experienced purple seat inserts. They feel quicker. Fast forward to the 2017 Focus RS and you can see where the design team was headed, even in 2002.

The 2017 Focus RS is the culmination of Ford's efforts to stay competitive with the GTIs of the world. They succeeded. The all-wheel drive, 350 BHP-version of what I owned for seven years is just an extension of the 2002 SVT. Albeit a big extension.

Then I joined the SVTOA – SVT Owners Association – Ford's attempt to build esprit d' corps in the performance oriented ranks of Ford owners. Get togethers of the SVTOA included race weekends at various circuits across America.

Buttonwillow, owned by the California Sports Car Club of the Sports Car Club of America, is one of those tracks. I just had to try it.

The Focus SVT at Buttonwillow, CA on the front of the grid in 2004. I knew I'd end up here the moment I first drove the car in San Diego in 2002

Chapter Twenty: Second Ford

The Scream of an Engine

Over one hundred cars were entered for the weekend on the 2.9-mile Buttonwillow race course. The grids were set up in groups of twenty-five cars, roughly. My group consisted of twenty-two Mustangs, two Focus SVTs and one Raptor pickup truck.

I was amazed at how fast that Raptor flew around the race track.

The course marshal came over to my car on the practice grid to check that I was wearing the mandatory safety equipment. When he saw the Alfa Romeo logo on my old driver's suit, he called out, 'Who let this guy in here?' There was a big grin on his face.

First time on this track for me, first time racing the SVT. Liked both immediately. With 17,000 street miles on the SVT, I was familiar with how the car worked. I'd asked everyone in the pits who would listen what I should do with tire pressure. Street pressures were 32 lbs. front, 32 lbs. rear. I boosted them to 35/33. That sure didn't work. The car felt slippery. Came back in dropped the pressure to 32/32. Cold. Worked.

I was second fastest in practice in our group behind a Stage 3 Roush Mustang, 390 BHP. His car was brand new, brought in on a trailer – we drove our car up from San Diego - and he'd never raced before. He drove hard so had to change brake pads Saturday for the Sunday races.

We both had great fun chasing around out there. He'd disappear down the main straight, but on the wiggles, I came right up behind him. Every lap. On the main straight, he'd nail it and get away again. Several times I'd enter the straight faster and get by him for a few feet before he lit off the big V-8 and was gone again.

The Scream of an Engine

We did this all weekend. I could never pressure him into spinning out. I told him afterward that he had a good future in racing if he wanted to pursue it.

Several memorable moments: in the first practice session, the other SVT Focus in my group spun right in front of me in turn 3, the uphill esses known as the Phil Hill turn. In avoiding him, my borrowed – from Chuck Engberg - driving gloves, oversized for some reason, bumped the windshield wiper stalk. Turned on the wipers and scared myself silly what with the spinning car and others all around me.

Later, I was lapping an older red Mustang. The Focus was right behind him coming onto turn 12 before the start-finish straight. I could see his huge eyes in his left outside mirror, watching me. He missed his braking point and went straight off into a gigantic puddle from rain earlier in the week. His rooster tail was at least twenty-five feet high. I almost lost it watching him muff it.

Then I tried to go faster on the right-hand sweeper at turn 11 before the left turn onto the start/finish straight. I got out on the 'marbles' – bits of rubber and pebbles pushed out of the correct racing line through the corner. I cranked on more lock, then felt the four-wheel drift come on, the G-forces diminish, not sure what would happen. Made it through without spinning.

Wonderful memories.

Chapter Twenty-One: Hail Storm at a Classic Car Show

The Julian Classic Motoring Car Show, May 22-23, 2010

My Alfa Spider was a nice car. Reliable. Clean. Fast. I'd never have kept it forty-two years otherwise. Lots of shows, parades and Sunday drives. The enthusiast does them all. I cleaned the car myself for the shows. This is the story of one of the shows entered with this car, written at the time and first published in *Romeo and Giulietta*.[84]

Gearhead stuff.

Bob Engberg, one of the Julian Classic Motoring Car Show organizers, sent the email asking if I'd enter Sophia, my 1969 Alfa Romeo 1750 Spider Veloce. The answer was easy. Yes! Little did I

---

[84] The publication of the Alfa Romeo Owners Club of San Diego

suspect that this simple 'yes' would lead me and my car enthusiast friends to fall victim to the Fastnet 79/Sydney-Hobart 98 Syndrome.

These were both sailboat races that didn't end well.

Anticipating a three-hour round trip into the mountains east of San Diego and back, I took Sophia in for a tune up, the first in well over a year. A trip to Midnight Oil Motors, LLC and my favorite Alfa mechanic, Dan Pluth, provided the mechanical security I need in a three- decade old + car before setting off on such an adventure. Oil change and filter, lube all points, check for a persistent oil leak, and check and adjust valves as necessary were on the list. Everything was done to my complete satisfaction, including replacing the front crank shaft seal, which was the leaking oil culprit.

The seal had been new in 1987 when Alan Ward overhauled and upgraded the engine. I'm thankful for the happy motoring that last seal provided over the past twenty-three years, before starting to squirt oil around. And the exhaust valves were a little tight, so it's a good thing we checked.

Perhaps more important to car show judges are cosmetic issues. So, I then embarked on two days of intensive care with Brite Boy metal polish, Turtle Wax paint polish, and Armor All cleaner/polisher for the vinyl and rubber surfaces to bring Sophia's cosmetic appearance somewhere near new. I cleaned the trunk, the engine compartment and the door jambs so they gleamed, too. A little polish on the engine, especially the cam covers on an Alfa, never hurts.

The two beneficiaries of the profits from this show were the Julian Medical Association and the Julian CERT (Community Emergency Response Team) Organization. Little did these two organizations know what the weather would do to those profits.

The Scream of an Engine

Julian is the town made famous by the gold rush started in 1869 when A. E. Coleman found placer gold on nearby Coleman Creek. By 1872 there were already fifty homes in Julian. Today there are five hundred residents focused on the local tourist industry. Over four thousand more live in the area surrounding Julian.

My wife and I were staying with friends Dave and Olivia Bantz who lived nearby. So, we missed the popular Julian B & B's this time.

But back to the car show. On Saturday, May 22 at about 3 PM, we started lining our cars up, backing into curb on the north side of Main Street in Julian. This recreated the famed Le Mans start. First used in the Le Mans, France 24-hour sports car race on the streets and roads of France an hour's drive southwest of Paris, this uniquely exciting method to start a motor race must be seen to be believed. The wind was by now brisk, the air cold, the sun still shining. My wife Gaynor and I found the next to last available space in the lineup – farthest away from the starting line - for the Alfa, positioned between a Porsche Carrera and a Corvette Z06.

At 5 PM sharp, a cannon sounded. Forty drivers sprinted across Main Street, jumped into their waiting cars, started their motors, and peeled out. They all turned right toward the Menghini Winery for the reception. Police cars abounded. Cops stopped cross traffic while the assortment of roaring, wheel spinning Cobras, Porsches, and Ferraris took off. There were single examples each of Alfa Romeo, Jaguar, Morgan, Lamborghini, Lotus Ford Cortina and a Rambler custom race car. For the record, Bob Spriggs, a car and boat friend, was first to his Lotus Ford Cortina, and first to get his wheels turning. A boat friend said later that Bob lifts weights, which of course explains everything.

Engines hit red lines as spectators and cops grinned and drivers re-lived their youthful lust for speed and high RPMs. The Lamborghini ahead of Gaynor and I in the Alfa blasted past the Ferrari just ahead of

The Scream of an Engine

him, so we stuffed the Alfa up the Ferrari's exhaust pipe just to keep things moving and close. The twisties on this smoothly paved route are cambered, well-marked and taken in second and third gear in the Alfa, mostly well below our nominal 8000 RPM redline. I haven't had so much fun in years.

A few minutes later all the cars arrived at the winery off Wynola Road and parked in the grassy area reserved for the Sunday show.

Several race cars and transporters were already there, such as DiLoreto's. DiLoreto brought a blue 1964 Cobra coupé and several other cars. These cars were not drivable, or the owners didn't want to risk them in the Le Mans start melee. Fred Puhn's 1962 Santee roadster was without transaxle, but you couldn't tell it, as the blue Number 5 Olds-engined race car designed and built – guess where, in Santee - sat proudly in the grass among California oak trees and the stunning mountains that surround the vineyard. Similarly, Bob Engberg's 1956 Elva race car, finished in shiny polished aluminum, was race ready but already in place by the time the rest of us got there. The Elva had just finished a major winter overhaul in preparation for the vintage race in Sonoma, CA, in two weeks. No sense in taking chances.

The reception featured barbecued lamb chops, stuffed mushrooms, and bruschetta which were served by smiling ladies dressed in parkas. Yes, folks, by now it was 6 PM and COLD and WINDY. None of the rest of us could smile who were still dressed in short sleeve shirts or, at best, cotton sweaters. For $5 you could secure a plastic cup of wine. My choice was the Menghini cabernet sauvignon. The wine was good and offset the cold a bit.

Guest of honor Alan Girdler, past editor of *Road & Track* magazine, liked the lamb chops the best. That's what he said. However, he did drink more than his fair share of the red stuff, indicating that was his real preference.

The Scream of an Engine

Gaynor and I left because of the increasing cold. We made for Jeremy's Restaurant on the corner of Wynola Road and Route 79, about ten minutes driving time from the winery. Owner Teresa, whose son Jeremy is the chef at the tender age of twenty-three, also started the fire in the fireplace for us. Libby our waitress soon came over and provided Gladiator cabernet sauvignon, a Napa Valley product that improved our moods considerably.

Soon our friends Dave and Olivia Bantz arrived from Warner Springs and we ordered four of the salmon salad specials. But there were only three specials left, so I switched to the blue cheese iron steak, fries and spinach. All of them were quite good.

After dinner, Gaynor had a chill, so Olivia volunteered to take her to the Bantz home in their new Lexus SUV with giant heater. This is about a thirty-minute drive if you follow the speed limits. Dave volunteered to freeze with me. The Alfa heater has not worked for the last twenty years or so. But you never need a heater in San Diego, so until this Saturday night it hardly seemed worth the effort to fix it.

At Casa Bantz, we exchanged stories with the Bantz' and retired early under heavy quilts, an electric blanket, with the furnace turned up to 70.

Now the tale turns to the comparison of a car show with yacht races of yesteryear.

Dave loaned me a chamois which I wet. I then removed the dust from Sophia in a driving wind at thirty-eight degrees Fahrenheit. The wind was mixed with the occasional drop of rain. At this point, we should have packed it in and headed for San Diego. Dark clouds were swirling in from the west, promising more havoc.

More havoc it was: we encountered TWO hail storms and intermittent showers all the way back to Julian and the winery Sunday morning. The hailstones were about 1/8" in diameter and they collected along the Wynola Road before melting. They bounced on the roads, too. They made noise.

Who in his right mind would continue? Almost all the car owners as it turned out. In the Fastnet 1979 and Sydney-Hobart 1998 yacht races, the weather forecasts were terrible, but the sailors went to battle anyway. The storms in those two sailing races were so horrific that many boats sank, many men died. I was now experiencing the Syndrome: so much invested in time and money at this point with a commitment to friends and organizers to be there. We continued despite the warnings. At least no one died at the car show. That I know of.

Unfortunately, the weather was so foul that spectators didn't bother to show up. The profits to the Julian Medical Society and the Julian CERT could not have amounted to more than a handful of change.

Bob Engberg emailed Sunday night that they had fired the Weather Committee of the Julian Classic Motoring Auto Show. Glimpses from this milestone event follow.

The Scream of an Engine

This 4.4-liter V-12 Ferrari didn't compete in the Le Mans start Saturday: something about protecting the fenders.

Friend Bob Spriggs parks his Lotus Ford Cortina at the Menghini Winery. This level of intensity – and fast feet - won him the Le Mans start

Chapter Twenty-Two: Automotive Design

I grew up at an almost ideal time, becoming a gear head during the Fifties, a time of unbridled excitement and optimism in the automotive field. Sports cars were taking firm hold in America as they had earlier in post-War Europe.

In design, stunning, innovative ideas emerged from specialist groups like Creative Industries in Detroit, Scaglietti, Pinin Farina and Touring in Italy, and Figoni et Falaschi in France. These businesses supplemented the in-house design departments of car manufacturers.

Design and the excitement it engendered was a big part of my expanding Fifties car culture.

Italian Giuseppe Figoni of Figoni et Falaschi, the artistic partner in the successful and well-known partnership, drew the exterior design for the more conventional Alfa Romeo 8C 2300 that won Le Mans from

The Scream of an Engine

1932 through 1934. I would argue that the later stunning automotive designs by Figoni for Talbot Lago, Delahaye, Bugatti, and Delage contributed to other designs with long hood and sweeping fender lines, like the 1948 Jaguar XK 120.

Ovidio Falaschi, a skilled Italian businessman and financier, joined Figoni in the business in 1935 and his skill in establishing strong financial relationships with car builders assured the success of the partnership.

Malcolm Sayer penned his epic designs in Coventry, England for Jaguar's XK 120, C-Type, D-Type and later, E-Type sports and racing cars. The designs, with the E-Type winning the Architectural Digest Award in 1961 – the first such award going to a car - took place under the watchful eyes of Sir William Lyons. Sayer manually employed mathematical formulas for ellipses and parabolas to describe the shapes of these cars, later emulated by computer in most all automotive design shops.

Harley Earl, the famous GM designer, pushed the envelope as he was wont to do. He's remembered as the first styling chief in the United States automobile industry, the originator of clay modeling of automotive designs, the wraparound windshield, the hardtop sedan, factory two-tone paint, and tailfins. Sir William Lyons beat him with two tone paint on his early Austin Swallow cars in the mid-1920s. But that was in Europe.

Earl said in 1954, 'My primary purpose for twenty-eight years has been to lengthen and lower the American automobile, at times in reality and always at least in appearance.' The extremely low and long

The Scream of an Engine

American cars of the 1960s and 1970s show the extent to which Earl influenced an entire industry and culture.[85]

Just a few of Earl's designs include the Corvette, new in 1953. Although Zora Arkus-Duntov is credited today as father of the Corvette, Zora's immense effect came after Earl's design was introduced. Even Arkus-Duntov needed a design component on his later Corvette team.

Corvettes starting with the first one in 1953 featured Earl's wraparound windshield. Google Images

---

[85] Wikipedia, April 2017

The Scream of an Engine

Harley Earl's 1938 Buick 'Y-Job.' Route 66 Pub Co

Three of hundreds of Earl's designs: GM's Turbine Powered Firebird I, II and III, 1954-1958, https://silodrome.com

Lesser known Creative Industries in Detroit, designer of many products but especially cars, produced inspiring project cars like the Ford Mystere, a one off that never made it into production. Some of the design concepts shown here did.

The Scream of an Engine

Ford Mystere developed as a rolling chassis capable of being powered by a gas turbine. This advanced-looking car was later scrapped. Google Images

Why was the 1955 Ford Mystere interesting to me? We owned Fords that included some of these design elements like similar tail fins and swooping side molding. But you can also see elements of Cadillac front ends of the Fifties in this design. Just some of the features: the car was a rear engine concept without an actual gas turbine installed; the entire glass dome roof lifted up, hinged at the rear which seemed to make this feature into a giant air brake – not too smart at speed; air flowed through the periscope-type scoop to cool passengers in the cockpit; and the steering was a control stick that could be swung from one side to the other for operation by either front seat passenger.

Many individual designers, like Virgil Exner and Gordon Buehrig, made immense contributions to creating the passion of enthusiasts. They were enthusiasts themselves.

All the car manufacturers built in-house design teams. The names of most of the individual designers in the Fifties are lost to history. Their contribution to creating the passion was inestimable.

The Scream of an Engine

The Scream of an Engine

Chapter Twenty-Three: Rally

The idea of a rally is a collegial drive through the countryside. Bunch of friends get together and go for a drive, two in a car, a driver and a navigator. Two or more cars, set some rules and you have a real rally.

The European Monte Carlo Rally stands as the event that most captured my rally imagination in the Fifties. By the mid-Sixties, English Mini Coopers were winning the Monte Carlo overall, beating the Ford Falcon Futura team cars in 1964 in the process. The Fords had 305 BHP, 289 cubic inch motors, front disk brakes and limited slip rear ends. I used this win as part of the justification to buy my first Mini in 1965. For me, it was about which cars won.

In the 1960s and 1970s, more than half of the competitive distance on the Monte was run at night, with long sections running through the Chartreuse mountains between Chambéry and Grenoble before crossing the Rhone valley and continuing in what was often the deeply snowbound and ice covered Ardeche, all in the same night.

In addition to the Monte Carlo Rally, there were other rallies everywhere: Peking to Paris; Dakar, Africa to Paris, France; the now defunct U.S. Cannonball; the Rallye Aicha des Gazelles in Morocco, North Africa;[86] the international FIA World Rally Championship since 1973,[87] and the Liège-Sofia-Liège Rally, a flat-out drive from Belgium to Bulgaria and back, through the roughest roads the length of Yugoslavia and over the difficult passes like the Gavia and the Vivione in Italy.

You get the picture.

But the Monte Carlo was the big cheese in rallying when I become interested in this form of entertainment. There were plenty of local rallies to sink your teeth into, like the one entered by my rally team, Team Ass Verde, in Puerto Rico.

My wife Brooke and I drove the eastern Connecticut Frozen Fanny IV rally in 1968 in our new British Racing Green MG 1100 sedan. Comfortable and smooth driving, this latest incarnation of the Alex Issigonis' original 1958 Mini in a larger form factor was a good rally car. The heater worked. Brooke was a good sport to go along with my car shenanigans.

Driving that seat-of-the-pants rally, meaning no rally calculators were allowed, we quickly learned that it was better for Brooke to drive and me to navigate. Sure didn't work the other way around. We finished third in our first ever rally. That was also our last

---

[86] Ladies only: three hundred competitors from eleven countries now duke it out

[87] The Series consists of thirteen three-day events held around the world on ice, snow, gravel and tarmac in one million-dollar, 1.6-liter turbo charged four-wheel drive rockets based on production-sedans

ever rally: too much tension, doubt, second guessing, interpretation of vague instructions. That quickly became my reality in rallying.

Rallying sounds easier to do than it is. 'Cast 30 MPH until you see a stone wall with a milk can on top' is an instruction fraught with peril. 1) Cars don't accelerate from 25 MPH to 30 MPH instantaneously, so the car must go faster than 30 MPH on this new leg for a time to make up for acceleration time – but how long? 2) What if you can't find the milk can? What do you do then? And then there are the other thirty-two instructions.

Some fans of rallies enjoy the confusion, missed milk cans and doubt created by instructions dreamed up by a bonkers Rally Master.

I'm not patient enough for that. What's needed is lots of patience and intense focus for extended periods of time. Not my cup of tea then, still not. But I did find outlets for my competitive juices in an event called an autocross, developed by the Sports Car Club of America.

Rally Cars

Can't hold a rally without cars. Big international rallies are very different affairs: virtually road races on narrow, twisty often unpaved roads, with gravel, ice and snow for traction.

Mini-Cooper

With John Cooper providing performance versions of Minis, it wasn't long after the Mini was first introduced in 1958 that they were out there racing and rallying. The epic Mini rally was the Monte Carlo Rally in 1964. As reported by *Sports Car Digest* on January 24, 2014:

The Scream of an Engine

'On 21 January 1964, the Mini Cooper S won the Monte Carlo Rally for the first time. The pairing of Northern Ireland's Patrick "Paddy" Hopkirk with co-driver Henry Liddon pulled off the big surprise. They defeated significantly more powerful rivals in their small British car. Hopkirk crossed the finish line just seventeen seconds off the pace set by his chief adversary Bo Ljungfeldt in the far more powerful V8-powered Ford Falcon. The Mini's faultless run over country roads and mountain passes, ice and snow, tight corners and steep gradients laid the foundations for the underdog-turned-giant-slayer to cement itself in both the hearts of the public and the annals of motor sport legend. Indeed, the Mini's dominance of the Monte Carlo Rally continued over the years that followed, Hopkirk's Finnish team-mates Timo Mäkinen and Rauno Aaltonen adding two further overall victories — in 1965 and 1967 — to the British manufacturer's collection.'

Paddy Hopkirk and his 1964 Monte Carlo Rally winning Mini Cooper S, 33 EJB. Photo taken much later. Courtesy Mini Turns 50 – see footnote

The Scream of an Engine

The success of the Mini Cooper S in the 1964 Monte Carlo Rallye was lauded as a sensation by motor sport fans around the world. But this wasn't a success that came entirely out of the blue: the small car developed by Alec Issigonis, then Deputy Technical Director at the British Motor Corporation, possessed an inherent sporting talent from birth. The first person to spot this potential was John Cooper. The sports car designer was the driving force behind construction of a more powerful version of the car. The Mini produced only 34 BHP at launch, but its front-wheel drive, low weight, wide track and comparatively long wheelbase made it an extremely agile four-seater and paved the way for its forays onto race circuits and rally courses.

As early as 1960, big-name racing drivers like Graham Hill, Jack Brabham and Jim Clark were spotted testing the cornering flair of the John Cooper-tuned small Mini on the Silverstone Formula One track.

However, the classic Mini was most at home in rally racing. Pat Moss, sister of Grand Prix driver Stirling Moss, piloted it to wins in the Tulip Rally and Baden-Baden Rally in 1962. And by the following year, the diminutive British car was ready to burst into the public consciousness at the Monte Carlo Rally. Preceding years had been a tough learning experience for the works team, but now they would make people sit up and take notice. Rauno Aaltonen and Paddy Hopkirk drove the Mini Cooper to a 1-2 finish in their class in 1963, which was good enough for third and sixth places overall.

Identifiable from a distance with their tartan red bodywork and white roofs, the six small racers dispatched by the BMC works team for the Monte Carlo Rally in 1964 were — at least on paper — fighting against the tide once more. The Mini Cooper S lined up at the start for the first time. Its new four-cylinder engine now had an increased

The Scream of an Engine

1071cc capacity and output had also been boosted to around 90 BHP – other sources say 70 BHP. This was a lot more than in previous years but still modest in the face of competition from the likes of the Mercedes-Benz 300 SE and Ford Falcon, whose six-cylinder and V8 units had three or four times more power at their disposal.[88]

The 1966 award winning French movie with Anouk Aimée, *A Man and a Woman*, captured the essence of the Monte Carlo rally with a bit of Le Mans thrown in for good measure.

Rallies are now dominated by factory teams from Peugeot, Lancia, VW, Ford and so on. Their performance in the worst possible road conditions is staggering to watch, depicted on YouTubes of the World Rally Championship.

But in 1964, a diminutive giant killer struck at the Monte Carlo Rally and won. And I remembered this when I bought my first car, a Mini, a year later.

---

[88]Photos and Mini Cooper stories from Mini Turns 50 - Racing History and Photo Gallery, Car Profiles, August 26, 2009, and Monte Carlo Historic Rally 2011 Information, Vintage Car Racing, December 21, 2010

Chapter Twenty-Four: Autocross

With rallying behind me, in November 1970 I switched to Sports Car Club of America Autocross. A group of like-minded friends from eastern Connecticut joined me for the competition. All three of us worked at General Dynamics Electric Boat Division. We built nuclear submarines for a living.

We three were new to the idea of autocross and remember calling this event a gymkhana. But technically, a gymkhana – from a Hindu and Persian word combination that described a ball game on a court in the mid-1800s – is more than an autocross. In addition to a one to three minute 'race' around orange cones, a gymkhana may add a 180 and 360 degree turns or parking in a box then reversing out, or both. Reversing out, you can imagine, might involve grinding the gears when trying to do the maneuver quickly. Gymkhanas are popular in England, Ireland and Japan.

Automobile slaloms, another way of describing what we were up to, are now called autocrosses. And since I first tried that cold, gray November day, autocrosses have become more competitive and more organized. The Sports Car Club of America publishes rules about what you can and cannot do to your car or to the tires. The idea is to allow friendly competition yet make it easy for first timers.

Tom O'Donnell drove a new grey Porsche 914, Tom Wadlow a well-prepared and maintained red Triumph TR-4A, and I drove my just purchased white Alfa 1750 Spider, now four months old. We hadn't done this before, but it sounded like fun. To make it more interesting, we had an informal bet going, combined with chest thumping. We each thought we owned the best car for the job.

This first competition for us is near New Haven, CT and the venue is a parking lot. A large one. We take the spare tires out of our trunks, as well as the jacks and tool kits. That's how you can tell we're serious. I then remove the hubcaps on the Alfa and of course tightened the lug nuts on each wheel just to be sure. I'd pumped the stock Pirelli Cinturato tires up at a gas station on the way in, from street pressure of 32 PSI/front, 30 PSI/rear to 40 PSI, front, and 37 PSI, rear. In retrospect, I think that was way too high. But this was the first try.

There are cars of every description at the meet, but I check out the Porsche 911s. With considerably more power, they get going fast on the one long straight section. But their drivers have their hands full on the turns. One green 911, with screaming engine and tires and lots of oversteer, scares everyone watching on each run.

Each driver gets three runs. Times are posted. The competitive juices in each of us were running hot. We agree we three are our own class. Don't have to worry about the 911s.

At the end of my third run, I have O'Donnell's 914 by half a second and Wadlow's TR 4A by six tenths of a second. The grey Porsche 914 is where the Porsche should be, behind the Alfa.

But when Tom O'Donnell goes out the last of us on his third run, he charges out of the gate like a mad man. Clearly, he would set his fastest time. When it was over, he'd won by half a second. But we noticed that when he left the gate, he bumped the first orange pylon on his right, which teeter-tottered several times, and finally fell over.

We didn't know it until times were finalized. But that pylon cost O'Donnell a one second penalty. The Alfa won!

On the way home, Wadlow and I raced up Interstate 95 – there was absolutely no traffic in those days – until I showed 115 MPH on the clock and backed off. Credit to Wadlow who might have hit 116.

With this auspicious start, you'd expect I'd be doing this every weekend.

No. I soon received a promotion from Electric Boat in Groton, CT to the General Dynamics corporate headquarters in New York City. With all that change and excitement, I never ran another autocross.

Retired undefeated.

The Scream of an Engine

The Scream of an Engine

Chapter Twenty-Five: The Heart of the Matter

In addition to my own experience, I've interviewed enthusiasts like Roy E. Disney and Lynn Hitson, and asked three of them, Fred Puhn, Chuck Engberg and Ken Braun, to write their own stories which are included here.

The result of these field interviews is a clear understanding of the motivations of those who hold passion for their cars. Every story is unique, yet many of the principles are the same.

Enthusiasts are fans or gearheads. You'll notice the line between them can blur from the stories that follow. I start with the story of a fan and then move to two gearheads, followed by another group of stories from a range of enthusiasts.

But the common threads of passion, loyalty, mobility, nostalgia, competitiveness, ego, need to express mechanical or engineering talent, peer interest, youthful memories, family involvement and the search for adventure are compelling and provide a profile to answer the question: what are the keys to a car enthusiast becoming hooked?

Roy Edward Disney

This story illustrates what one fan is like. Of course, not all fans are like the late Roy Disney.

I met Roy, Walt Disney's nephew, at the Anteater Regatta in Newport Beach, CA in 2004 through a Francis Parker School parent who knew Roy well. I was managing the Parker Sailing Team which I started in 1998. By now we'd hired a delightful, competent lady coach named Kate Sheahan, so I'd passed the coaching responsibilities to her. Managing the team was enough challenge for me now.

Roy was an active Board Member and at one point Vice Chairman at The Walt Disney Company, then Chairman of Walt Disney Animation. In that creative role, he's credited with *The Lion King* which opened in 1994 and many other animated features. With his second wife, Leslie, he later created the sailing documentary *Transpac—A Century Across the Pacific* in 2000. Roy and Leslie were also executive producers of the sailing documentary *Morning Light*, which follows the selection and training of eighteen to twenty-three-year-old sailors on a boat for the 2007 Transpacific Yacht Race.

Roy was a big advocate of high school sailing. At the time, eighty schools competed in California alone in what's known as the Pacific Coast International Sailing Association, or PCISA. Roy contributed $500,000 for brand new sails to the PCISA. The sails were to be used only on the fourteen-foot long Collegiate Flying Junior sailboats raced in the championship series. The sails leveled the playing field: sails were a variable now held constant. Everyone had new sails in the races.

Roy successfully raced his own eighty-six-foot sailboat *Pyewacket* for many years which he donated to Orange Coast College's School of Sailing and Seamanship on his 75th birthday.

I told Roy that day I first met him that I admired his new V-12 Ferrari Maranello. He immediately lit up. I'd seen the car in the parking lot at Newport Harbor Yacht Club, the host club for the PCISA Anteater Regatta.

Roy responded, *'Let me tell you a story about that car. I was coming up Route 73 in the Ferrari when I glanced down and realized I was doing 120 MPH. I thought I'd better slow down cresting the next hill because it would be a perfect spot for a radar trap. So, I slowed to 90 MPH as I crested the hill. Sure enough there was a speed trap.*

'The arresting officer came up to the window and said, "You were going too fast. Driver's license and registration, please." I passed them out to the officer. He glanced at them and then said, "You're not Roy Disney".

'I responded, "Yes, I am."

'The officer then passed the driver's license and registration back, saying, "I can't give Roy Disney a ticket." Then he leaned into the car and said, shaking his finger in my face, "Don't you EVER do this again." And left.'

Roy Disney was a fan of Ferraris. He loved his car. Ferraris are pretty, expensive and fast. Available only to those like Roy at the top of the economic pyramid. But Roy didn't work on it or spout statistics about Ferraris he's known or owned in the past: Roy wasn't a gearhead.

The Scream of an Engine

And after this episode, I suspect Roy was also a fan of the California Highway Patrol. And probably never got another ticket, either.

Fred Puhn and Chuck Engberg

Now let's turn from fans to two examples of gearheads, friends of mine who represent an exciting part of the universe of gearheads.

These two guys had already built and raced gravity cars – like Soap Box Derby cars but without the rules – by the time they met in ninth grade at Grossmont High School, La Mesa, CA. They're still good friends all these years and adventures later.

On May 19, 2017, we three met for breakfast at the Jalisco Café in Bonita, CA, one of four favored San Diego-area Mexican restaurants we frequent to talk about cars. We do this at least every year.

At breakfast, we even order the same thing: chiliquiles and three eggs with beans. Except that Fred orders scrambled eggs, Chuck orders over hard, extra cheese, and I favored sunny-side up. We all ate extra salsa. Chuck's extra cheese never showed up.

We discussed what made Fred and Chuck into extreme gearheads. Fred said he was drawn in because cars in the Fifties were so unreliable: you had to be able to fix them, including flat tires. And why not change the oil?

'Service stations were invented for girls,' Fred says, describing the feeling about gas stations at that time.

There were two groups of kids at Grossmont High, Class of 1956: hot rodders and sports car nuts. A hot rod at Grossmont may have been a family sedan with a dual exhaust, or been lowered, or sometimes, sported dual radio antennas. Serious hot rods would emerge after high school for those inclined.

The two groups didn't mix.

Chuck said he was hooked on sports cars in 1953 when a friend, and later brother-in-law Dallas Dickson returned from U.S. Army duty in Germany. Dallas was accompanied by a 1938 white BMW 328. Chuck remembers the Michelin radial tires which didn't squeal on corners but gave little warning about incipient breakaway, the small size and the wind-in-the-hair speed of this exotic imported sports car.

Fred explained that he built his gravity racer when he was eight – Chuck was nine when he built his – and describes his motivation for building the car as 'looks, mobility and the urge to kill yourself.'

Fred was drawn in further when he was about fifteen and found two car books which he still owns, *World's Fastest Cars* and *All the World's Cars,* in 1955. He recalls today that the photo of the 1937 Mercedes W125 Grand Prix car at speed with all four wheels off the ground in *World's Fastest Cars* really stuck with him. That publication cost him $.50.

Fred owns hundreds of car books today. He's also written a few.

Chuck and Fred remember driving to Torrey Pines to see the races there in 1955 and to Pomona, CA and to Hourglass Field, Mira Mesa, CA, all in a Model A Ford. Canvas was missing on part of the Ford's top, so they could dangle their legs into the car while watching the races from high up on their rooftop perch.

Back at Fred's National City barn after breakfast, Fred describes details to Chuck and me on several of his project cars. He's

The Scream of an Engine

pleased to show off the 1934 Nash Big Six with overhead valves – progressive in the day – and two spark plugs per cylinder. He noted his 1935 Diamond T truck is now running.

Then he brought us up to date on the 1948 Alfa Romeo 6C 2500 SS Touring Coupé which is out at Alan Taylor Company, Inc. in Escondido, CA, for final restoration work. Fred bought this Alfa because of the nostalgia he felt over another 6C 2500 SS he owned in his younger years and sold. The proceeds from the original Alfa he'd invested in an MG TF to race, the opposite of my Dad's experience in going from an MG to an Alfa to beat Porsches.

Fred's original 6C 2500 SS was not a race car

This second Alfa restoration is costing a bunch today, with Fred telling us it was a bad idea financially. Fred points out the axiom of buying an already restored car in lieu of restoring one yourself. Bill Evans, a local hotelier and Cornell University Hotel School grad, just bought a newly restored 6C 2500 SS to add to his family's car collection. Fred thinks this would have been a better course of action he should've taken for himself.

Fred's 1935 Maserati Grand Prix race car isn't present this day and is stored off site. The story of this car is so compelling that its told separately by Fred below.

In addition to two Morris Minors, both restored and one of which is a woody, Fred owns and drives a nicely restored, street-driven 1950 Packard. He then shows us his Quasar, serial number one, built in 1970, stored up on the mezzanine in the barn. This is the car Fred designed from scratch, raced to first in the Southern Pacific Division of SCCA and was responsible for his being named Driver of the Year in 1970.

That's how Fred designs, collects and restores cars: all the information, all the details, no part of a restoration less than fully accurate, no matter the time or cost involved.

Frederick Arthur Puhn

Fred Puhn quickly became a good friend in 1997 when Chuck Engberg introduced us. I knew Fred's reputation by following car news for decades before this fortuitous meeting. I'd purchased a set of four 'monocoque' racing wheels with my Alfa race car in 1972, developed by Fred's company, Chassis Engineering, Inc.

This is Fred's story in his own words. His passion, like mine, comes from the Fifties. Fred helps answer the question of why some of us become gearheads.

'I was born in 1939 and was interested in cars since I was a young child. My childhood was spent in a country environment near Lakeside, California. We lived on a dirt road and played outdoors most of the year. A big activity was the design, construction, and driving of 'coasters', gravity powered race cars. We were poor so we scrounged materials such as old shopping cart or wagon wheels, scrap lumber, and old bolts and nails. Our coasters ranged from pretty to very crude and we spent many weekends and summers riding down hills, crashing, and rebuilding. I learned how to throw a coaster sideways in the dirt to stop it because they never had any brakes. During these early years, I learned to control a vehicle and to design and build one.

At age sixteen I got my driver's license, but I had money problems. I really wanted to buy a Cord roadster that was for sale for $1000, but could not float a loan from my parents. I finally had to settle on a 1948 Studebaker 4-door sedan because that was the only car my dad would loan money on. He was very much opposed to the sporty cars I had my eye on. He really got mad when I told him I could get a

The Scream of an Engine

Graham Hollywood with a supercharger for less than $500 on a used car lot. I didn't dare mention a Ferrari.

I learned to drive on the Studebaker, I customized it, and modified it slightly for better power. However, the car was slow, handled like a pig, and had bad brakes. I drove it on the door handles trying out sports car racing techniques, but all it did was scare my friends and break the front spring. I was really glad to get rid of it and buy a Morris Minor convertible. It was very slow, but it handled like a real car and had bucket seats and a 4-speed gearbox.

I discovered Road & Track *magazine in 1955 and went to my first race that year at Torrey Pines. The sound of a V-12 Ferrari was something from another world and I was in love. I watched the driving skill of Phil Hill, Carroll Shelby, Masten Gregory, and Ken Miles among many others. On weekends, my friends and I would sneak out to Torrey Pines and take a few corners at speed.*

In the late 1950s, I discovered a local enthusiast who was importing used Italian sports cars. His name was Bill Brehaut, and he was one of the two people who started Road & Track magazine! I visited Bill to look at his cars for sale and was instantly hooked on Italian sports cars. I rode in cars such as a Cisitalia, Ferrari, and Alfa Romeo. All these cars were on sale for about $2000, and that was well above my budget. I begged Bill to find me a car I could afford. He reluctantly helped me and found a 1949 Alfa Romeo 6C 2500 SS Farina cabriolet for $500. I worked all summer in a grocery store and saved up enough money to buy it. That Alfa was my daily transportation and I drove it to work and to school. My friend Gerry Sullivan bought his Fiat 8V from Bill at this time. I think he paid $1200. It was a pure race car formerly owned by Lorenzo Bandini. He also drove it to school.

'At that same time, I spent lots of time hanging around a foreign car sales and service shop called the La Mesa Pit Stop. George

The Scream of an Engine

Peterson was the owner, and his uncle was former racer Lou Fageol. When Lou bought a race car for George to drive I was happy to work my spare time on the pit crew. I was going to college at the time, studying to be a mechanical engineer. What I wanted to do was design high performance cars. At this time, I worked for free as a helper to a master mechanic Al Bond, and learned a lot about how to work on cars. I went to races with Al, George, and Lou and really enjoyed the experience. I got to drive the race car in a test session one day and now I really wanted a race car. I later bought the car from Lou after it was wrecked, but I never managed to finish it.

'At the same time, I had several friends with race cars. I helped Chuck Engberg with a racing MG TC, and his brother-in-law Dallas Dickson with his BMW 328. Then I spent some time helping Walter Roach put a Fiat 8V engine into his Veritas and race it. The engine and gearbox came out of a Siata 208S owned by Joe Flores. Another friend Alan Taylor (now a well-known car restorer) had a Siata 208S with a Chevy V8 in it. I'm not sure if it was the same car owned by Joe Flores.

'Upon graduation from college in 1961, I found my first engineering job at Gyrotor Inc., a small helicopter research and development company. The firm was looking for a product to build while they were waiting for litigation on their helicopters to be settled. I talked them into building a sports car. It helped that everyone at the company liked sports cars. That was the start of the Santee sports car project. Part way through the project the assets of the company were reorganized into a new company, Santee Automobiles, Inc. I was Chief Engineer. Now I was living my childhood dream. Some design features I liked in my friend's Fiat 8V were the aluminum V8 engine, the 4-wheel independent wishbone suspension, and the smooth sound of the 180-degree firing order. I liked the space frames and the rear mounted transmission of race cars of the day. I incorporated all these ideas into the Santee. The exhaust sound I captured in the Santee SS race car by inventing the 180-degree exhaust system, aka bundle of snakes.

The Scream of an Engine

This new exhaust system Fred designed soon appeared on many race cars.

'Soon after the recession of 1962, Santee Automobiles, Inc. folded. I found a job at General Dynamics developing the Centaur rocket. The Centaur launched the Surveyor, the first soft-lander on the moon. At this time, I was working on race cars and helping my friend Chuck McCarty with his Gemini formula car. Wide tires were first starting to be used so there was a need for wider racing wheels.

'The few manufacturers in this business could not keep up with demand, and Chuck could not get delivery on special magnesium wheels for his racer. As an engineer, I did the natural thing, I 'reinvented the wheel' and made a set for him. I called these new wheels 'monocoque' wheels. They were made of three parts, an inner half, an outer half, and a center spacer. The wheels were spun formed and heat-treated aluminum sheet rather than the magnesium castings being used in racing. The wheel halves were bolted together near the rim. This 'modular' wheel was copied by many people and is now quite common in racing, particularly drags, dirt track, and off-road racing. My wheels were lighter and much stronger than the cast magnesium wheels and I could make a custom set in two to four weeks. I started a business to manufacture the monocoque wheels and I called it Chassis Engineering, Inc. I built wheels for all the big names in racing including McLaren, Honda, Dan Gurney, Alfa Romeo, Nissan, and Cragar Industries.

'In 1963, I designed a dragster with some unusual specs. The car was so light – two hundred fifty pounds today - I was worried about the aerodynamics. A colleague in the aerospace industry analyzed the dragster and found it to have lift at high speed. As a fix for this I designed and built a wing to hold the car down. Later I tested the wing on Formula 3 car and it worked well. As a product for my company,

The Scream of an Engine

San Diego gearhead Fred Puhn sits in his Oldsmobile V-8 engined Santee Super Sports, July 4, 2012. Fred was Chief Engineer for Santee Automobiles, Inc. which produced three cars. Author photo

I decided to try to market the wing for use in road racing. My first ad for the wing appeared in Competition Press *classifieds*. In that issue, the front page announced that Jim Hall's new Chaparral racer had a wing on it! Nobody was using a wing on a race car at this time, so this was big news. I thought this coincidence would be a huge success for my new product. However, nobody even inquired about my ad for wings. Apparently, I was too far ahead of the state-of-the art in this area.

'In 1964, I started racing. I had previously traded my beloved Alfa 6C 2500 SS for an MG TF, so I could race. I modified the MG and had some moderate success. But what I really wanted was an all-out race car like the one Lou Fageol sold me. As part of Chassis Engineering, Inc. activities, I decided to design and build an all-out race car. I sold the MG and with the $1500 I got for it I purchased a new Alan Fraser Sunbeam Imp racing engine. Along with help from two

The Scream of an Engine

other friends who wanted similar cars, I designed the Quasar sports racing cars. We built three. Mine was equipped with the 850cc Imp engine and the other two with 1300cc Ford Escort engines. I marketed the car as complete, as a kit, or sold plans and parts. I raced SCCA National races in 1970 – Southern Pacific Division - and won all of them for a perfect point score. I was voted San Diego SCCA driver of the year. I set lap records for the class at Riverside and Ontario tracks. A highlight of the season was a road test of my Quasar in Road & Track *magazine. I raced in the first SCCA runoffs at Atlanta and finished 4th. In 1971, I raced the car twice and let Carter Penley, my Vice President, drive it also. We both qualified for the SCCA runoffs that year, but I let him drive. He was faster than I was, but he fell off the track often so he had a poorer record. Then I sold my Quasar to Bill Hobbs in Atlanta who successfully raced it.*

Fred Puhn's designed-from-scratch Class D Sports Racing Quasar. Fred Puhn 1971

'At Chassis Engineering, I continued to develop race cars and manufactured wheels. In 1970, I designed and built a Quasar Group 6 car for Chuck McCarty to compete in the European 2-liter sports car championship. It was powered with a Cosworth FVA Formula 2 engine. The car weighed only 1050 pounds and used Formula 1 tires. In testing

The Scream of an Engine

in England, it unofficially broke the track record for 2-liter cars, but crashed. The car never raced again, but it has now been brought back to the USA for vintage racing. In 1973, I designed a series of Super Vees. These were the ultimate embodiment of the old air-cooled formula because the car was designed around the VW air-cooled engine. Before the cars were completed we had the oil embargo. That ruined the racing business, so I sold the company and took up a serious engineering profession so I could support a family.

'After starting work at General Atomics in 1974, I received an offer to write an automotive book. I wrote How to Make Your Car Handle *in two years of spare time. It has been quite successful and after 200,000 plus copies it is still in print. Later I wrote another book,* The Brake Handbook, *but that one is now out of print. You can still find it on eBay.*

'As a hobby, I started vintage racing and car restoring in 1974. I bought a famous little race car built by Martin Tanner and raced it at the 2nd and 3rd Monterey Historics. Then I bought an Abarth 207A Boano Spyder, but it took so long to restore that its first race was the 22nd Monterey Historics. I also bought a 1935 Maserati V8-RI Grand Prix car, all three of the Santee cars, two Quasars - including my old car - an Alfa 6C 2500 SS Touring coupé, two Morris Minors, and a bunch of other cars and trucks. They're in my collection.

'After racing it a few times, I sold the Abarth 207A, and that helped speed up restoration of the other cars. I finished restoring the Santee SS and vintage raced it three times. My Santee Sports is now being totally restored. I've gotten my 1935 Diamond T truck running. Both my wife's Morris Minors, convertible and woody, are now restored and running fine. The Maserati and the Alfa will be next on this list to complete after both the Santees are done.

The Scream of an Engine

Fred's Fiat Abarth 207A Boano Spyder, a friend driving. Fred Puhn

'Automobile Quarterly published a story on Santee Automobiles, Inc., and that makes me really happy.

'As a mechanical engineer and manager at General Atomics for forty years I worked on some very interesting projects. After spending twenty-five years managing design of large magnetic confinement fusion experiments, I switched to more near-term projects. In the commercial field, I designed the drive train for the world's largest mining trucks and power supplies for the BART trains. For the military I designed radar sets, electrical power inverters for the electromagnetic aircraft catapults, large electric motors, and electric actuators for ships. My final project before retirement in 2014 was back in fusion research. I designed tooling for the manufacturing of the central solenoid for ITER, the world's first fusion reactor.

'I still love cars. I hope to spend my retirement years in my barn doing restorations and using the old cars in vintage races, tours, and shows. I recently bought a 1934 Nash and a 1950 Packard to cruise in. I plan to do a bit more writing, too. My dream of designing race cars is less attractive now because the cars are so specialized. We engineers ruined the sport and I have to admit I participated in the effort. My engineering career was a success however, because I

The Scream of an Engine

accomplished what every design engineer wants to do: I reinvented the wheel.'

Why do gearheads act as they do, so passionate about bucket of bolts cars from long ago? Fred Puhn, San Diegan and gearhead from the get-go, wrote this next thoughtful piece that brings nostalgia to the table as one of the answers to this question. He owned an Alfa Romeo 6C 2500 SS in college – think about that for a minute - which he later sold and used the proceeds to buy an MG TF to go racing.

This is Fred's story about nostalgia in his words written December 16, 1994.

'The search for an Alfa Romeo 6C 2500 SS is finally over. I now own the car that was permanently etched on my heart as a youth. The encouraging response to my want ads in the Alfa club newsletter kept my spirits up during the long and frustrating search for the right car. I thank everyone who helped with advice and leads, including many new-found friends.

'But why would anyone want to spend a decade of savings on an old corroded car with a power-to-weight-ratio only slightly higher than a VW beetle? The answer is in the word 'nostalgia.'

'It all goes back to my youth in the mid-1950's. Cars were the hot item of conversation in high school, every year offering new exciting models with wild power and style. My schoolmates had hot rods, but I had discovered the world of exotic sports cars. My small circle of sports-car enthusiast friends eagerly awaited each new issue of Road & Track, *and we discussed our dream Scuderia for hours. The pages of* Road & Track *were filled with the most exotic, curvaceous, and macho machines, the best of which came from the automotive artists of Italy. Fantasies of driving these sensuous beauties were discussed daily. We*

The Scream of an Engine

continued to drive our Model A Fords, MG TDs, and Morris Minors while we dreamed of Alfa Romeos, Maseratis, OSCAs and Ferraris.

'I worked part time in a grocery store and took home $13 a week. This paid for gas for my Morris Minor, but left little to save for a new Italian exotic. Thus, the only hope was a used car, but where to find one? I scoured the classifieds each week, looking and wishing.

'One day in the San Diego paper was a classified ad for several exotic Italian used cars. I called immediately and talked to Bill Brehaut. Bill was importing and selling used Italian sports cars from his home. It turned out that Bill was one of the two men who started Road & Track magazine! He talked about OSCA, Cisitalia, Alfa Romeo, Lancia, and all the other exotics we had been dreaming of. He was selling them at 'used car' prices. We had to meet this man!

'My friend Chuck and I went to Bill's home that night to see the cars he advertised. It was a night to remember for all time. Sitting in his driveway was a machine I had never seen before. It was low and compact, but large for a foreign sports car, with a smooth sculptured curvaceous body that flowed from its long tapering hood to its rounded tail. The steering wheel was on the right side like a racing sports car. What could be more exotic? The speedometer on the left read to 200 on the dial, a sure sign of raw speed. It had a giant tachometer in front of the driver (another sign of speed). The massive finned aluminum brake drums glimmered behind the huge wire wheels. This incredible car seemed to crouch in the driveway like a giant panther ready to leap onto the road. I walked around to the front and immediately recognized the heart-shaped grill of an Alfa Romeo. Bill identified it as a 6C 2500 SS, a luxury Gran Turismo sports car of the immediate post-war period. This car had a hand-made convertible body by Farina.

'We talked about the Alfa and how good a buy it was for a mere $2000. I could not ever imagine saving that much money, but I had to act interested if I wanted a test ride. Bill was more than willing to

The Scream of an Engine

oblige, since he obviously liked these cars as much as I did. He offered a ride!

'To open the door, I had to figure out how to make the flush-mounted handle pop out by pushing a button. Such a complex door handle was obviously necessary to cut air drag at high speeds. The huge heavy door shut with an oily click like a bank vault. I slid into the dark cozy interior and experienced the feel and smell of soft leather seats. It was the ultimate sensual experience. Bill got into the right-hand seat, extracted the wild looking round key, and pushed it into a hole to activate the ignition. The starter button lit up! A blip on the throttle primed the engine with its triple Weber carbs. It burst instantly to life at a tap on the button. The 6-cylinder engine warmed with a smooth purr as I marveled at the huge ornate tach and speedometer dials which lit up their faces in front of me. Time seemed to stand still as we sat in the dark warming the engine.

'Then we were off into the night. The big Alfa rode firmly but was not harsh. It felt solid as an ingot with none of the usual rattles and shakes of a convertible. The thick leather seats soaked up any bumps the suspension didn't. We dashed around the winding roads of the Point Loma, San Diego, neighborhood listening to the mellow baritone of the twin-cam six singing off the canyon walls. We roared up a hill and rounded a sweeping curve at full noise in 3rd gear with no lean or tire squeal. The huge Pirellis gripped the asphalt like glue. It seemed like the best handling car on earth. I had never felt such performance.

'The ride was over way too soon, but I knew right then and there that I had to have a car like this. I moaned, sniveled, and whined to Bill about my poverty-stricken state and asked him if there wasn't a way to find a lower price used Alfa. He said he only wanted to bring in nice cars, but he promised to look for one closer to my price range. I would save my money and wait for Bill's Italian partner to find the right car.

The Scream of an Engine

'There were a number of visits to Bill after that to look at photos of available cars. My friend Jerry went with me because he too had the urge. We looked at photos of 2-liter Maserati sports-racers, Lancia Aurelias, Zagato bodied Fiats, Cisitalias, and so forth, all in the $1000 to $2000 price range. We rode in some of these cars as they came in but nothing clicked. Then one day, Bill's partner Michele Vernola notified him of a car that was right for me. It was a 1949 6C 2500 SS Farina convertible just like the one I first rode in. The cost was only $500 in Italy because it had 100,000 kilometers on it and needed paint. It wasn't the quality they liked to bring in, but they would import it as a special favor to me.

'My finances had to be firmly established to buy the Alfa. I asked my mother to look at the car I was buying in case I had to ask her for a loan. Luckily there was one for sale nearby that Bill had recently imported. Mom and I went there and took a ride in it. This was a 6C 2500 SS with a coupé body by Touring in really nice condition. We rode out into the hills in this wonderful, wicked-looking coupé and I was totally committed. Mom said OK too because she knew her son was in love.

'All summer long I worked in the grocery store full time and saved every penny. I trapped gophers at ten cents each to supplement my earnings. Time dragged on. Finally, I got the word that my Alfa would soon be shipped. Would the ship sink in a storm? Would someone steal my car on the docks? Would they drop it during unloading? Would the paperwork get lost in the mail? All these horrible worries were in my head as I worked and waited.

'Then one day I got the shipping papers, and I knew which ship it was on. I found the unloading date and went to the port of Long Beach to see it for the first time. It was beautiful! Faded grey paint and threadbare top aside, it was the car of my youthful dreams. Of course, I had to come back on another day to get it through customs.

The Scream of an Engine

'We traveled again to Long Beach to get the car. We put a little gas in it and it fired right up. The exhaust was a little smoky but otherwise it ran well. I was on a cloud as we drove down Highway 101 back to San Diego. We stopped at San Juan Capistrano for lunch and a photo. It was the only photo I would have of the car in its original state, for disaster loomed ahead.

'We were only a few miles from home in San Diego and passed under a freeway. I marveled at the echo of the exhaust in the tunnel and pushed on the throttle to amplify it. In the next instant, an old Ford coming the other way suddenly turned left in front of us. I crashed into the Ford with the brakes locked. The Ford driver took off trying to escape the consequences. Jerry leaped out of my Alfa, flagged down a passing car and took off after the escaping culprit. They caught him a few blocks away and brought him back to the scene. The cops then arrived and promptly gave me a ticket for no registration or plates (contrary to what DMV told me over the phone). The guy who caused the accident had no insurance but promised in writing to pay for my repairs. He never did.

'The Alfa would drive if you didn't turn the steering wheel much, so we limped home. I was more than demoralized. It was hard not to cry in front of my friends.

'The next few months were spent going into debt and watching a craftsman slowly repair the Alfa. Finally, it was done, so I painted it red. After that there were both good times and bad times with the car. I drove it to college and parked it next to my friend Jerry's newly acquired Fiat 8V. Going to school with the top down was a blast on a winding canyon road, and I raced every car I saw. The Alfa even made a trip to the Colton drag strip and won a trophy by beating a VW beetle. I took out a girl on a date in the Alfa but she complained at being stared at because the car had right hand drive. I impressed my hot-rodder friend by taking him for a ride at night and showing him 150 KPH on the speedometer. He thought it was miles per hour.

The Scream of an Engine

'After a while the old engine got water in the oil, the oil pressure was dropping, and it smoked a lot more. I stored it in a rented garage while I saved up enough for an overhaul. A creep broke into the garage and vandalized the car, making my emotions turn to hatred. Luckily it was not too serious.

'I finally overhauled the complex hand-built engine. There should be a law against letting teen agers do such critical things. After a number of errors and corrections the engine finally was running and back in the car. I polished the aluminum, saddle soaped the leather, chromed some parts, and got my upholsterer dad to build a new padded top. The Alfa was looking good.

'But finally, in 1962, the oil pressure was falling again. I am sure it was a mistake I made putting the pressure relief valve back together. In a fit of depression, I traded my beloved Alfa to a guy for an MG TF with a broken rear spring. I never saw my Alfa again.

'In my senior years, nostalgia overwhelmed me. With my wonderful wife's encouragement, I launched a year-long search for the right car. Now an Alfa 6C 2500 SS is mine and I named her 'Sophia.' She shows the scars of a hard life, but there is beauty hiding underneath the surface.

'Once I was infatuated with a curvaceous beauty, with a wonderful mellow sound, and an image that made a boy's wimpy ego feel man-sized. It was a first-love experience and you just don't forget such things. Nostalgia is that feeling that yearns to recapture some of the glorious times with a first love.'

The Scream of an Engine

My old Alfa after I painted it red. Front bumper is not yet assembled, and license plate is attached with baling wire. Fred Puhn

Fred Puhn has also written the story in March 2017 about how his 1935 Maserati V8-RI Grand Prix car came to America. I love this story and the way Fred tells it. The thread is nostalgia, as in the previous story about Sophia, with a touch of the engineer wanting to take this car apart, fix it and make it like it was when new.

'Maserati in a Barn

'It was 1981 and we were selling old parts at the Big 3 Swap Meet in San Diego. A nice man came up to our booth and said he'd just moved in from Minnesota. Our chatting turned to stories about, "I saw an old car in a barn better than anything you ever saw in a barn."

'Naturally such stories are nice to listen to but everyone knows not to take anything too seriously. When my new friend said he found a pre-war Maserati race car in a barn in Minnesota for $1,000 that story topped anything I could ever bring up. He said the car had raced at Indy according to the owner, but he knew nothing else about it.

'At that time, I knew nothing much about pre-war Maseratis, but I did see one at the Monterey Historic races and I was very *impressed. The beautiful workmanship, neat design details, and the serious twin cam supercharged racing engine were impressive. The car was also beautiful, lean and slender with semi-streamlining.*

'Since the incredible story at the swap meet beat mine, I had to call his bluff. I said I really wanted the Maserati, no matter what the condition or the details. I said I would buy it and hang it on the wall if I couldn't restore it. I gave him my name and number and asked him to send me the contact information. I figured that would be the last I would hear about the Maserati in the barn.

'Well, that was wrong. A couple days later I got a note that gave the name and number of the guy with the Maserati in the barn. I quickly made the call expecting the story would unravel. Sure enough, the first comment by the owner was that he talked to a guy in town who owned a Rolls Royce and he said the price was too low. So now he doubled the price to $2000. OK, it is still worth trying to find out about it. I asked the owner if he would send photos if I send him money for the film, and he agreed. That night I ordered a book on Maserati history, so I could get some knowledge about the car.

'About two weeks later the photos arrived along with the book. I stayed up most of the night trying to figure out from the photos what the car was. It was tough because instead of a narrow chassis like the car I saw at Monterey this chassis was wide enough for a sports car with two seats. The car was obviously missing the engine and the body, and there was a small pile of small parts with it. The drive train and suspension looked complete, but a lot different than the little Maserati I saw at Monterey. The suspension was all independent and the car had a transaxle at the rear. I could not find much in the book showing such a car. There was a large Maserati logo cast on the bell housing, so I was 80% sure I was looking at a Maserati.

'One of the problems was a lack of photos in the book I was looking at. By process of elimination, I ruled out almost every Maserati

The Scream of an Engine

described. I did see a photo of a Maserati 750kg car at the Carrousel at the Nürburgring that had a wider body at the frame which might be wide enough to be this car. This car in the photo was a 750KG Grand Prix car driven by Richard Seaman. It was so beautiful with a streamlined body and exhausts out both sides of the hood. It was the rare V8-RI model and the book had very little to say about it. It did have independent rear suspension, so maybe this could be it. I took a chance and ordered the car.

'After me sending payment, the owner put the car in the back of his truck and brought it to my house in National City, near San Diego. Then the work began to find out what I had.

'A little flashback is in order. As a teenager, I fell in love with sports cars and racing cars. I bought a book on the world's fastest cars in 1955 and a short article described what they called the "hottest" car of all time. This was a description of a 1937 Mercedes 750kg Grand Prix car that would go 200 mph and could burn the tires on dry pavement up to 150 mph. In 1955, I was impressed by any car that could chirp the tires taking off from a dead stop, so this sounded unreal. All my life I dreamed about seeing a 750KG Grand Prix car such as the Mercedes, Auto Union, Bugatti, Alfa Romeo or Maserati, but they made so few of them from 1934 through 1937. I never saw one until my Maserati was delivered to my house. Yes, after 3 years of research I found out my car was a Maserati V8-RI 750KG Grand Prix car, chassis number 4502. They made only four of them, and they all still exist.

'Since that time, I have seen all of the other three Maserati V8-RI cars. Luckily, two of them were being restored at the time, so I was able to photograph, measure and sketch all the various missing parts on my car. I discovered my car's engine with one of the other cars and bought it. I found the right people in England to duplicate the original body, restore the frame, and build the exotic parts, such as new engine blocks, supercharger, instruments, etc. I researched the racing history and found that it extended twenty years and included Grand Prix races,

The Scream of an Engine

Vanderbilt Cup, Indy 500, prewar ARCA road races and even postwar SCCA road races. It was driven and owned by some famous people including Nino Farina, Richard Seaman, Count Trossi, Wilbur Shaw, Deacon Litz, George Rand, Enzo Fiermonte, Dick Wharton, Andy Granatelli, Jim Rathmann, Milt Marion and Tommy Hinnershitz.

'Now that I have retired, I can devote my time to finishing the last 10% of the restoration. This would complete my childhood dream, to not only see a 750KG Grand Prix car, but actually drive it. This Maserati was a really wonderful "barn find." But it required decades of work and money to bring it back to its original glory.'

Fred is clearly the quintessential gearhead, far right on the curve plotting all gearheads. Imagine: inventing the bundle-of-snakes exhaust system and re-inventing the wheel, all in one career. Every vintage car, race car and sports car is Fred's oyster, and they all end up better than they were when he found them.

Maserati Serial Number 4502 on display. Fred Puhn

The Scream of an Engine

A beauty! Front view of Maserati S/N 4502. Fred Puhn

Charles 'Chuck' Earl Engberg

I met Chuck Engberg when I decided to change careers, trading in a twenty-eight-year high tech business career, ending as president of a software development company, for high school physics and summer sailing. Especially summer sailing on a Kettenburg K-43 and later, a J/Boats J/133. I had this idea that helping center city kids boot strap themselves out and up would be a noble calling in life. And I love science, especially physics. Always have.

Chuck was Chairman of the Science Department at West Hills High School, Santee, CA, in fall 1996. After a year of theory classes at University of California, San Diego's two-year Teacher's Education Program, I was placed at West Hills for my first year of in-classroom teaching by UCSD.

I was good at the theory.

The Scream of an Engine

The practical side of teaching is tougher than it looks. Because of my early classroom management issues, like corralling up hormone-loaded high school seniors and keeping them on target, Chuck and I got off to a rough start. But with his help, the advice of the other eleven science teachers in the department and UCSD professors who visited my classroom, I was soon up to speed. Chuck and I bonded on science and sports car racing. Those two subjects led us to overcome all adversity.

In his biology classroom at West Hills, Chuck displayed the Lotus 11 door left from the racing accident which totaled his car. The wheel hub on the Lotus broke at speed and Chuck's helmeted head somehow smashed the light-gauge aluminum door panel. You can imagine the contortions this 6'3", 200-pound man went through to achieve that result.

This is how Chuck describes his experiences in racing. He was reluctant to start writing. But the margaritas did the trick.

'With a couple of Margaritas and you prompting me, I think maybe I can recall something about my racing career. And write about it.

'I owned an MGTC and decided to go racing. Trips to Torrey Pines to see the early SCCA races with my buddies fired my imagination. I watched the hot shoes go at it, and knew I could do this, too. I wanted to try racing more than anything I could think of.

'My brother in law Dallas Dickson inspired me to become a racer. Dallas designed and built his own 'Chingazo' 1100cc sports racer which ate Lotuses for breakfast.

'Dallas won the first race he entered with the Chingazo, an SCCA race at San Luis Obispo, CA, the day of the Watts riots, August

11, 1965. He was a University of California, Berkeley civil engineer working for Cal Trans. He was promoted to be chief engineer for the new Interstate 8 between Pine Valley and Descanso. Previously, Dallas' influence started me, Fred Puhn and my brother Bob Engberg into sports cars and racing.

Chuck Engberg's MG TC at Pomona, CA in late 1959. In his first race in May 1959 at Santa Barbara, CA, there were forty-nine cars in SCCA classes D, E, F, G and H. Chuck was the first MG TC to finish and the second MG, behind a newer MG A. Steve McQueen won the race in a Porsche 356 Spyder. Chuck Engberg

'My first race in my MG was in Santa Barbara, CA in 1959. The adventure started just three days after my twenty-first birthday. I borrowed my Dad's flathead Plymouth 6 as our tow car. Fred Puhn, Gerry Sullivan and my brother Bob Engberg and me pretty much filled the tow car along with tools and the minimum of spare parts: a few cans of oil and a spare set of spark plugs.

The Scream of an Engine

'A bumper hitch was rigged up to tie the MG to the Plymouth. In those days, there were no freeways between San Diego and Santa Barbara. We drove up old slow, curving Highway 101 all the way.

'The weekend in Santa Barbara: I remember the clear blue skies, the Entry Fee of $20 and my pit crew each giving me $5 to help cover it, the roar of forty-nine engines on the grid for my race – there were a lot of cars racing in those days – and free gasoline. Steve McQueen won my novice event. To be in this race you had to have had three or less races so it might have been McQueen's first race. (Note: Chuck says there were no SCCA Driver's Schools on the West Coast then, unlike my Dad's experience in SCCA on the East Coast in the mid-Fifties and my experience in the Midwest in the early Seventies.)

'My car was fitted with a stock 1250 cc engine, legally stock, but did have higher compression pistons. My compression ratio was 12:1 and therefore needed Ethyl gasoline to run. I was running 600 x 16" tires on smaller wheels in place of the original 19" x 4.5" tires and taller wheels. This change put a lot more rubber on the road, so much so that in later races, at Del Mar, for example, I snapped off the spindles on both sides. I did spin out on the opening lap at Santa Barbara which was pretty much my general pattern over forty-nine years of racing. Of course, I should mention rolling my first Lotus 11....

'In between my races at Santa Barbara, I studied for my Chemistry Final Exam, which I passed the following week. Without two nickels to rub together, we had to fill the Plymouth up with gas to get home. We'd fill the MG at the track pump, drive it back to our allotted pit space, drain the fuel into the Plymouth, return to the pump and repeat.

'To say that I was hooked on racing after Santa Barbara understates the case. I maintained my SCCA license for forty-nine years, racing everywhere I could in everything I could: the MG, two

The Scream of an Engine

Lotus 11s with Coventry Climax fours, and an RX 7 Mazda coupé. The Mazda was so reliable it finished every race but one over many years: the one DNF was due to a flat tire. My last race was at Fontana, CA, in 2007. It all seemed normal at the time.

'There were very few turns on most tracks where I didn't at least leave the road. I figured you had to push hard to improve.

'The MG TDs I raced against in my MGTC had the same engine but were lower and had Independent front suspension, so the handling, such as it was, was better by far on the TD. In fact, the TC really had no suspension at all except for the twisting of the frame...especially if termites had gotten into it.'

The MG lasted for quite a while. But it was time for a change. Chuck's first of two Lotus 11s was a real beauty, but equipment failure at Phoenix International Raceway put the car into the 'totaled' category. Chuck was in the hospital for five hours. This adventure occurred on December 6, 1968.

Chuck reports that his original Lotus 11 now has three copies out in the world with Chucks' Vehicle Identification Number – VIN – 216. None of the three copies are 'real' because Chuck still has the VIN number plate from his original car. As Chuck says, the purveyors of the copies didn't even have the decency to buy a real part or two off his crashed Lotus 11. Buyers of vintage race cars need to be aware of this issue and do much homework before plunking down cash for fakes.

Chuck drove a BSA 650cc motorcycle for years. In a moment of sheer exasperation, he sold it during the process of cleaning out his garage. One less new grease spot on the garage floor every week, he says.

The Scream of an Engine

Chuck Engberg's 1956 Lotus 11 VIN No. 216 at Phoenix International Raceway, December 1968. Thirty minutes after this photo was taken, the car was a basket case. Chuck Engberg

Chuck and his wife Janet, both Francophiles and teachers, have spent almost every summer in France for over forty years. One stopover they make is at Le Mans. And the HOTEL DE FRANCE, 20 Place de la République, 72340 La Chartre-sur-le-Loir, France, southeast of Le Mans. This is the hotel featured in my novel, *Death by Design*, where Fifties drivers stayed before wending their way over thirty miles – about an hour on the French roads - to the Le Mans course and victory in the 24-Hour race. Like Carroll Shelby and Roy Salvadori for their 1959 win in the Aston Martin DBR1. And Maurice Trintignant and Paul Frère who finished second in another DBR1 that year.

Chuck is a fellow gearhead with tendencies toward Lotus and Mazda cars and jokes about being forced to park Alfas – he owned one, so he's allowed to say this – at the top of the hill, so they can be coasted down to start them. Chuck was hooked on gravity cars in high school

The Scream of an Engine

and inspired by the sights and sounds of real cars when that white BMW 328 came roaring into his life.

Hotel de France, south of Le Loir River, north of La Loire River, stopover for many Le Mans competitors over the years, as it appears in 2017. Thirties cars are often seen here. Chuck Engberg

The Scream of an Engine

Ken Braun

Ken, my sophomore roommate at Cornell, studied astronomy. This was an exciting time in astronomy at Cornell with classmates Bill Nye, who became The Science Guy and head of The Planetary Society, and Jill Tartar, who later joined the Search for Extra-Terrestrial Intelligence. Professor Carl Sagan led the charge.

Rick Finlay, Ken's third roommate, and I rowed crew, so would often return to our fraternity house room late in the evening after training table dinners at Willard Straight Hall. There we'd find Ken doing astronomy homework – stretching into late at night - writing page after page of equations. He was fast but the equations were long and Ken was losing patience with them.

Ken later graduated with a major in another field: Pontiacs. He has a special passion for GTOs to this day.

His present 1965 GTO is startlingly red and show quality. He's won many trophies with this car. Braun is a Founder and President of the Windy City Goats – 'Goats' is the Sixties term for GTOs. Ken's car club resume is much more extensive, though. He's also a member in good standing with the Cruisin' Tigers GTO Club (#151) which he joined in 1991, GR-RRR8'R Wichita GTO Club, GTOAA (#6518), and POCI (#64588). Here's what Ken says about his discovery of GTOs.

'My car passion came a little later in life, and was not inspired so much by a person but rather a song. During Thanksgiving week of my senior year at Cornell (what ended up being year four of six spent at Cornell), a friend and I went to a nightclub in a neighboring town for a little excitement. It was there that I heard, I think for the first time, Ronnie and the Daytonas' 'Little GTO', released in 1964.

The Scream of an Engine

'I told my Dad about the song and car the next day. Much to my surprise, he said let's go take a look. The surprise was because my parents were ridiculously financially conservative. So, on Christmas break, we did. I don't think we actually saw a GTO, since we lived in a small rural community. But we talked to the salesman. I eventually wrote out a list of options I wanted, which was minimal since I would be paying cash for it. And, I still have that scrap of paper.

'My Dad told me that I had earned the money to pay for it and if I wanted it, order it. So, I did want it and I ordered it. My '62 Corvair was chewing up rear tires at a pretty fast clip at the time so this order was a 'smart' thing to do. (Editor's note: There's always a reason for a car move. This is Ken's.) I was told that delivery would be sometime in early March. It was. And, here it is below from a Polaroid my Dad took. How do you like that Cornell Class of '65 blazer I'm sporting with my Mom?

'And it was shortly after this that my shiny, new red GTO showed up in the parking lot at Greentrees – the Phi Kappa Sigma fraternity house. I sure wish I had that car, but that is for the rest of the story. Besides having that car, I more wish I had my Mom and Dad around and my then-physique.

'Time moves on.

'I could also add that I worked a summer job in 1965 in Rochester as a plant engineer at the Rochester Gas and Electric Lakeside power generating station. During the graveyard shift, things were slow, so I decided I should change the oil in my nice new GTO and put it up on the lift. Those were the days of the big hex nut attached to the end of the oil filter to make it easier to remove. I easily found the correct 1 1/4" wrench to remove it, and darn if I didn't twist the nut right off the filter and now the spent oil was going all over the place.

The Scream of an Engine

'I quickly scrambled to clean up that awful mess, trying not to look too conspicuous out there in the middle of the floor with my car on the lift. Then I obtained a filter wrench, you know the kind, that you snap into place which tightens the metal band so that the oil filter could be easily removed. Well, that action only caved in the metal can of the filter so that the wrench was totally loose and useless. Then somebody happened by and said what I really needed was a chain wrench, and he had one I could use right in his truck. I put that on, tightened it up and gave a big tug. And you know, it came right off, or rather broke right off.

'Now I was in a jam as it was about 2:00 AM. I had no idea what to do. The housing was made of pot metal and was virtually unrepairable. Well, just about then a pipe in one of the boilers I was responsible for sprung a major leak and we had to call in the welding crew. They used a bunch of fans to cool the inside of the boiler so that

Ken Braun in Cornell blazer with first 1965 Pontiac GTO and his Mom. Spring 1965

The Scream of an Engine

when the crew came, they could get inside, assess it, and repair it in quite short order. It was about 5:00 AM when the welders wrapped up their work. I asked one of the welders I knew if he had any idea how to weld pot metal. He replied that it would be no big deal. All he had to do was to fire up the heliarc welder that he had just used to fix the boiler pipe and he could mend it easily. He did.

'WOW, so by 6:00 AM with two hours to spare before my shift ended, I was all set to put the oil into my beloved GTO, take her down off the lift, and make my final shift rounds before my foreman would be in.

'After graduating from Cornell and landing a job with Bell Telephone Laboratories in a western Chicago suburb, my shiny red GTO and I moved out to the Land of Lincoln, where I'd been born some twenty-four years earlier. I was thrilled with my GTO and earned a spot on the '100' team by achieving a speed of 100 MPH on one of the approach roads to the parking lots of my place of employment, a very coveted honor to say the least.

'After a bit of time, I noticed all my friends were driving new cars, and here I was, King of the Hill, driving a car that's three years old. So, I did the right thing and ordered a brand new 1969 red GTO in October of 1968, and I ordered lots of bells and whistles this time. I had a job now. But it was most certainly a sad day when I went to pick up my newly delivered '69 GTO and drove it off the dealer's lot. Even with a larger displacement engine and more horses, I could tell as I drove home that it lacked the get-up-and-go and punch of my old trusty '65. And it really did, because that is when all the new anti-pollution stuff was mandated on new cars, which ultimately killed that thriving muscle car era just a few short years later.

'Every time I would drive by the dealership where I traded my original beloved GTO for a shiny new GTO, I would become super sad

The Scream of an Engine

and annoyed. It was simply downright painful to see my beautiful no rust, shiny '65 GTO sitting up on the 'feature' stand for everyone to see in hopes of attracting a new owner. What is really sad is that that new owner should have been me, and I have wished that so many times.

'Now to continue, let me bring you up to the modern era. I guess I can call this the pursuit of my GTO.

'I cannot pinpoint the motivation or moment when around 1989 I developed a great desire to find my first automotive love, my original 1965 GTO. I had preserved the original window sticker and it had the Vehicle Identification Number (VIN) on it, so I had a head start in my search. I started by contacting the Illinois Motor Vehicle Department in Springfield to see if they had any registration records of that VIN. It was a long drawn out process then before the age of computers, email, and searchable data bases. I had no luck there, so I broadened my horizons to the surrounding states of Indiana, Michigan, Wisconsin, Minnesota, Iowa, and Missouri, but I had no luck there either. I posted notices everywhere I could think of, and found nothing. Whenever I saw a red '65 hardtop for sale, I would check the VIN, but with no success.

Ken Braun's current 'new' 1965 Pontiac GTO. May 2017

The Scream of an Engine

'Around that time, my family and I joined a new church, and I joined the choir. I sang in the bass section, and to my utter surprise, the choir member standing next to me in the bass section was the previous owner of the Pontiac dealership where I had traded my '65 in for that brand new '69 GTO. WOW, what a coincidence. With great anticipation I asked him if he still had business records from back some twenty years ago. I thought that I had it made, but he said that all of that was destroyed when he sold his dealership. WOW, what a letdown!

'Now I was feeling frustrated, so started looking everywhere for one that looked like mine, as a replacement. As I recall, Montero Red with a black interior was not that uncommon, but I sure did not see anything where I was looking. Then in the summer of 1991, I looked through Hemmings Motor News, the absolute bible of used muscle cars. I spotted an advertisement for a red '65 GTO, but with an added feature of tri-power (a trio of two-barrel carburetors), a power plant with considerably more horsepower than my original '65. It was located at Classic Muscle Cars, long gone now, in Warsaw Indiana, some one hundred-eighty miles from my Illinois home. I was really excited, so I called the dealer and we discussed the GTO. Everything really looked great, so I made plans to drive there the next Saturday.

'When I got there, I saw the GTO in the front parking lot and it sent chills throughout me. I met the sales guy I had talked to and we discussed the car, its known history, and its price. Then he said, 'Do you want to take it out for a run?' WOW, I could not believe that I was going to actually drive this GTO that looks just like mine! We walked out to the car, and I went to the driver's door. When I grabbed onto the handle, something strange and magical occurred. It felt totally natural; I was getting into 'my' GTO. It was truly a mystical moment that I will never forget.

'We took it out, and it was simply fantastic. What a ride, what acceleration! It was everything I had hoped for and a whole lot more.

The Scream of an Engine

I was so disappointed when our test drive was done. They raised it on the lift and I acted as if I knew what I was doing. I checked the floor boards for rust and saw none. I checked everything I knew to look for under the car. Then the let it down and I then checked all the panels and chrome trim, and all looked well. I saw no signs of 'Bondo' repair. We adjourned to the salesman's office and discussed needed work and a final sales price. We got close, but I wanted to 'think about it'. I left for home, knowing I could return sometime soon.

'Soon ended up being two weeks later, and I returned, with checkbook in hand. We took the 'for sale' GTO for another spin. The thrill and excitement were still there. Back in the office, we negotiated a deal to fix what I didn't like and a final out-the-door price that I'd been hoping for. I signed the purchase agreement, I signed my deposit check, and guess what, that little red GTO was all mine.

'It took a couple weeks and the agreed upon work was done. My family returned with me that following Saturday. I inspected my now finished GTO and wrote a check for the remainder. Then it dawned on me, I would now have to drive this thirty-six-year old car back to Illinois. We set off on this venture. There were absolutely no problems during the return trip home, except for having to manually roll the window down to pay the tolls as we neared Chicagoland, the land of many toll booths.

'The remainder of the story is about my activity with my GTO for its first decade of my ownership. This included GTO Club activities and membership in both the local and National GTO clubs, followed by the first resto-mod of the car. Later, after a side-swipe accident and a second resto-mod of my GTO, I continued my club participation including my forming a new Chicagoland Chapter of the National Club. And continue to be involved to this day.

Ken Braun is an extreme Pontiac GTO fan. Hooked by a song.

The Scream of an Engine

Michelle Lundeen and Rod van Hess

At a Time Machine Car Show in Surprise in March 2017, I met Michelle Lundeen and husband Rod van Hess, car fans with technical credentials. A few weeks later, I met them again at the Sun City Grand Fair and Car Show on April 1, 2017. That's April Fool's Day but this story is no joke.

Michelle's nickname is 'Mike' from when she owned the Hollywood Tavern in Salem, OR. On meeting Mike for the first time, you're impressed with her strength of character and goal-oriented determination. In other words, she can run a bar.

Mike was travelling in Reno, NV when she spotted a jacket with the logo 'Hollywood' displayed prominently on the jacket. She bought it on the spot. Afterward, Mike realized that the car also displayed on her new jacket was one she didn't even know: a bullet-nosed Studebaker. Soon she decided she had to have one. The one she found needed restoration.

She paid up front to have the work done, but that scurrilous individual didn't do the work, took the money and ran. Customers at the Hollywood Bar led by Gary Lane took up a secret collection, found a '52 Studebaker which was then bolted to her '50 front end in a second restoration shop. The work was finished, painted in pink, as a surprise Christmas present to Mike in 1989.

Mike's husband, Rod, a Corvette man and owner of a cherry silver 2005 LS2, talked Mike into a blue printed 355 cubic inch Chevy engine with 450 BHP for the Studebaker. That engine is just gorgeous. The electronic ignition is by MSD and starts every time.

Mike has driven the car for over twenty-seven years now and still talks passionately about it and its connections to her jacket and the old tavern in Salem. Both are strong fans of Studebakers, Corvettes and really hot Chevy motors.

Michelle 'Mike' Lundeen and husband Rod van Hess display their 1950 'bullet nose' Studebaker which Mike has owned and driven for over twenty-seven years. March 2017

James A. Zeivel

Then there is James A. Zeivel, first and fourth owner of the same '66 GTO and member of the Cactus GTO Club in Phoenix. I met Jim at the Sun City Grand Car Show on April 1, 2017.

His business card says *'Land – Whiskey – Manure – Fly Swatters – Racing Forms – Bongos: Bought and Sold.'* The same busy

The Scream of an Engine

card also says he's retired but from the twinkle in his eye, I'm more inclined to believe not, after reading a bit further: *'Wars Fought, Revolutions Started, GTO's Driven, Computers Trashed, Chickens Plucked, Women Seduced, Tigers Tamed, Bars Emptied, Airplanes Flown, Witnesses Rehearsed.'*

I mean, with all that going for him, how could he be retired?

We talked for about a minute and were immediately best friends. Jim says he bought the car new from a Chicago Pontiac dealer when he arrived back from serving in Viet Nam. He'd been riding around in his sister's '62 Chevy convertible when he first spotted the GTO. He bought it on the spot.

Jim became a founder of the Cruising Tigers GTO Club in Chicago with seven friends. He still holds Member Card No. 5 in that club. Close inspection of this GTO shows a car with all parts – or nearly all – new or looking new and the paint job an original color which shows no orange peel. This is one nice car.

Jim Zeivel's first '66 GTO when he lived in Chicago. He's now also the fourth owner of the same car. The in-between photos I've seen show a car that had been run completely down. Jim fixed it up to immaculate once again

Chapter Twenty-Five: The Heart of the Matter

Jim Zeivel shows that streak of nostalgia that powers so many gearheads. He's reliving his first car. No ego here but certainly lots of fine memories. Big sense of humor. Jim is a bona fide gearhead, hooked by the chutzpah of a GTO.

Rob Ludwig

Most have never heard of the English Daimler marque. I spotted one at the Sun City Grand Car Show on April 1, 2017. A friend of mine, Bob Evelyn, raced one out of eastern Connecticut in the mid-Sixties at the Lime Rock Park and Thompson, CT race tracks. This is when I was first introduced to the Daimler in person.

Rob's car is a 1964 English-made Daimler SP 250 – no relationship to the German Daimler company - a vehicle powered by a 2.5-liter V-8 and wrapped in a fiberglass body with tail fins.

In a move just the reverse of GTO gearhead Jim Zeivel, Rob bought a Daimler like this one as his first car when he was twenty. He then sold it to go into the service. When he bought his original Daimler, he'd been looking for an MG TD. His Daimler showed up on a friend's used sports car lot. He immediately fell in love with it and purchased the car. A Daimler is certainly a lot more powerful automobile than a 1950s MG TD. Like a top speed of 124 MPH vs maybe 80.

As we exchanged notes on this story, Rob tells me that in May 2017 he and his wife were driving on the Monaco Formula 1 Grand Prix circuit – on the public streets of Monaco. It's the second time they were there - 1972 and 2017 - and now more than 1972 it's difficult for Rob to imagine driving a Formula 1 car on such a circuit at such speeds.

Rob loves Formula 1 and vintage European sports cars.

The Scream of an Engine

Rob's background is more like mine. He liked imported sports cars from the get-go. At Watkins Glen, NY for a Formula 1 race weekend, he stood in the pits close to Jim Clark, Jackie Stewart and Phil Hill. It may be that Rob and I stood side by side, too, because those are three of the drivers I stood next to during my visit to the Glen in September 1961.

Rob Ludwig's 1964 Daimler SP 250 polished and ready to be seen. The hood is slightly open suggesting a peek to see inside where the V-8 is nestled

This second time around, Rob has owned his 'new' SP 250 for four years. The car is very clean and presents well, daring you to open the door, jump in and drive away. Rob is behind the wheel regularly when not showing it, unlike many Concours cars which rest at home in the garage between shows. Rob's connection to the SP 250, it seems to me, is nostalgia mixed with memories of his youth dreaming about racing and the race drivers of his day. Like me.

Chapter Twenty-Five: The Heart of the Matter

The Scream of an Engine

Rob is an enthusiastic fan of vintage European sports cars, Daimler SP 250s and Formula 1, hooked as a teenager on imported sports cars.

Rhonda Lindsey

Friend Rhonda Lindsey in Surprise, AZ owns a 1990 Camaro with the 350-cubic inch engine and stick shift. She loves the control that stick shifting gives her. The 1978 Camaro owned before buying her present car was her heart's passion for many years. Then the '78 was stolen and dropped into a remote Oregon canyon, not accessible from roads. The insurance company had to cut a road, bring in a crane, and recover the wreck to settle Rhonda's claim.

It's still not clear how the '78 got into the canyon.

It's clear that Rhonda still has a real passion for that original car. But her 'new' Camaro is still her daily driver twenty-seven years later and she says she'll keep it forever. Camaros for her are about the memories from when she raised her kids and drove them to school, their sports games and their concerts. She also loves to drive Camaros. The memories of the early days are precious to her.

Her husband, Dick, supports her in her passion for Camaros. Recently, during the photographic session, Rhonda fired up the Camaro. She looked up at me standing outside the car, a big smile spreading across her face.

'What do you think?' she asked. Terrific sound, I responded. Rhonda is an enthusiastic Camaro fan.

The Scream of an Engine

Rhonda Lindsey and her dark blue, stick shift Camaro, at rest for a change

Bob Peralta

Why and how did Bob Peralta end up with a 1940 Ford Coupé? I met Bob and his gray, perfectly presented Ford at the Sun City Grand Car Fair on April 1, 2017. Bob is president of Phoenix Painting, Inc. which specializes in Graphics Imaging, Wall Coverings and Industrial Coatings. They don't paint cars.

Peralta's first car was a 1940 Ford Coupé, purchased for $400 when he was in high school, and those memories came flooding back when he found another one for sale. He found this second Ford Coupé in Long Beach, CA where it had been undergoing an eight-year restoration. The decision to buy it was mutual: he and wife Dolli's 50th Anniversary was at hand. They both wanted to re-create their high school days driving together in the original car.

The Scream of an Engine

Bob and Dolli lived next door in New Jersey and were sweethearts from third grade.

Bob recalls that the original Ford clock on the dashboard of his second car worked when he bought the car and it still works. But the car itself was still only half done. Bob brought it back to Phoenix where he was born and raised to finish the re-birth of his memories.

What was the biggest issue in bringing this car back to Bob's definition of perfection? Removing and re-installing the new Ford Cobra V-8 engine to get it to fit correctly: eight times.

Let me tell you, this car is cherry. Every detail is immaculate. He's proud of the Halibrand racing wheels which would cost $750 each brand new. But he found four used in good condition for $500 total and restored them to like-new. Adapters were machined to fit the wheels to the Ford running gear. A Lincoln rear end was installed. Disk brakes replace the original drum brakes at all four corners.

Bob calls the result of his work a Street Rod. He's a definite gearhead hooked by nostalgia.

Peralta's immaculate Ford Cobra V-8 engine, chrome everywhere and not a speck of dust or oil

The Scream of an Engine

Marv Blank

Marv grew up in Chicago, his parents grew up in Germany and Marv loves German cars. But his family sedan today is a Lincoln. He thinks the Lincoln indicates why he'd be considered a flag waving, 'Buy American' citizen. But he also owns a beautiful red Mercedes 560 SL roadster with both soft and hard tops. Marv, like me, got gifts like chemistry sets and wood burning kits when he was a kid. We laughed about the smell of burning wood when he told me this story.

The chemistry set probably explains why he ended up running his own dental business for forty years after receiving his Master's Degree in dental technology. Marv likes chemistry – essential when making replacement teeth – and precision technical devices like dental drills and jigs for making teeth, examples of which he still displays in his home garage.

Yet when he ate the crystal candy he made with the chemistry set – which I also recall making - he got sick as a dog. To this day, he can't eat crystal candy.

Marv recalls that his 'Ah, ha' moment came when he walked out of a hobby shop in Chicago. He'd been building a B-25 bomber model airplane and needed lacquer to finish the wings. Right in front of him was a brand new 1953 Corvette, white with red interior and wire mesh covers on the headlights. Marv fell immediately in love with what he calls 'science fiction-looking' sports cars.

A dentist friend of Marv's Dad owned an MG. When Marv turned sixteen, the friend offered to let Marv drive it – the offer accepted with enthusiasm. Two years later, the same friend offered a drive in his new TR 3. Marv recalls reaching inside the car to pull the cord and open the door from the outside.

The Scream of an Engine

Marv read car magazines in his youth and today talks about Gum Out, STP Oil Treatment, transmission fluid additives and issues with changing oil on his 560 SL, but says he was never into the details like how many cubic centimeters' capacity in this engine or that, or other gearhead stuff. But he still opens the hood up every time after returning to the garage. Marv believes this cools the engine faster and increases the life of rubber and plastic components in the engine compartment.

In 1956, Marv was shipped off to Guatemala City by his parents to get him 'out of the way' for the summer, he says. Family members lived there and Marv loved the exotic semi-tropical nature of life there, so this was no form of punishment. That summer the streets were closed, hay bales lined the curbs and a race was run down Boulevard Reformer. Marv stood right beside the track with his Kodak 8mm camera filming the first and second overall wins by a pair of Mercedes 300 SLs. He still has the movies.

Marv fell in love with Mercedes.

Marv Blank, always ready to play tennis, with his red 560 SL in Sun City Grand, AZ

The Scream of an Engine

But from the start, Marv was a Porsche fan. Many of his Chicago friends drove 356s. Mercedes were for wealthier, older folks and parents.

Marv at one point bought a 1963 Corvair Monza, maroon with black interior, where he became aware of Corvair handling anomalies; then later a yellow 1970 Fiat 124 with a real wood dash. This soon morphed into a 1972 350 cubic inch-engine Corvette with removable top and rear window. He loved the Corvette, kept it for eleven years and sold it for slightly more than he paid for it.

Then he set out to buy a Porsche 911 at last. Instead Marv ended up with a 944. But he recalls concerns about the engine not being the traditional air-cooled Porsche. He was ahead of the curve: today, Porsches are all water cooled. Two years later he traded the 944 in on a 944 Turbo, a rocket in its day with 0-60 time of 6.6 seconds. Except for the turbo lag, he loved this car, too.

As kids had arrived on the scene, the Turbo was followed by an Audi coupé. The German theme continues.

Marv reflects there may have been a little bit of ego and self-esteem involved in his passion for German cars. First, exotic because they are foreign; second, only the wealthier, more successful could afford them. I would argue his car culture was influenced by his family's German heritage more than anything else. Mercedes was, of course, at the top of his list of German cars then and probably now. Marv's passion for cars is clear.

We went for a drive in his meticulously clean 1986 560 SL with the top down. Marv purchased the car in 1997 from a Chicago dentist friend who was downsizing his fleet. The skies were blue for our drive and the Arizona temperature a balmy 75^0. Nice car. Everything works except the outside temperature gauge which just quit. But Marv has already talked with his German mechanic Schulte in downtown Phoenix. Fixing this will be no problem.

I'd classify Marv as a passionate Mercedes fan even today, but he says he's spending more time on researching political issues and playing tennis now, and less on the car. He was hooked on cars when he spied a new 1953 Corvette outside a hobby shop and watched 300 SL Mercedes cars race when he was fifteen.

Harry Sandoval

At another Time Machines Car Club show in Surprise on April 28, 2017, I met Harry Sandoval, a Vietnam vet from the end of that war. And his recently acquired Superformance 427 Shelby Cobra Mk III. Harry is a stocky, confident man whose salt and pepper gray hair is neatly cut. And he's enthusiastic about this car which he says was built in 2006 in Port Elizabeth, South Africa. Superformance is authorized by Shelby and headquartered in Irvine, CA to make authentic new build, new part copies of the 1960s Cobra classic.[89]

Sandoval says the attractive dark green car which he bought in May 2016 with 11,000 miles on the clock, sight unseen, was delivered by truck from Indiana to his son's house in Glendale, AZ. His son didn't know what it was until it came off the truck. He exclaimed, 'Dad, I didn't know you had such good taste.' Thanks, son.

---

[89] "Superformance International makes replica Cobras in South Africa and calls the two-seat roadster they build the MKIII. It's not a true Shelby, but I've endorsed and licensed the car for being as close to correct and well-built as possible." Carroll Shelby, Octane, Oct. 2006. From the Superformance website.

The Scream of an Engine

    The workmanship and details of this new replica Cobra appear perfect under my brief inspection. Although the body is fiberglass, without ripples or imperfections, Sandoval says for an additional charge, the original aluminum body can be ordered from Superformance. I'd say fiberglass is more practical for a car that's used on the streets and roads of America, from the standpoint of wear and tear and repair.

    Harry's passion for this car originates from listening to Wolfman Jack's XERB station, the original call sign for the 250,000-watt border blaster located in Rosarita Beach, Mexico. This station was branded as The Mighty 1090 in Hollywood, California. The show was on from midnight to 6 AM in 1964. Harry was eleven. Wolfman, born in Brooklyn, NY, now living in El Segundo, CA, was a fervent, passionate fan of the then new Shelby Cobras.

Harry Sandoval with his 2006 replica 427 Ford Cobra. Harry says he's still getting the knack of safety wiring the knockoffs

Chapter Twenty-Five: The Heart of the Matter

The Scream of an Engine

I asked Harry if his passion extended to all Fords. He said he once owned a 1965 fastback Mustang. But he never put anyone down for being in love with other brands. Then he said, 'My favorite American car is the 1967 Chevy Chevelle.' Could have knocked me over with a feather. Most fans are either/or. He's not the only person I've met that likes the 66-67 Chevelles the best. But most of them are dyed in the wool Chevy fans, too, and would never drive a Ford.

Harry is a passionate fan of both Fords and Chevys – an exception to my rule. He was first hooked by listening on Mighty 1090 radio to Wolfman Jack extolling the virtues of Cobras.

Jack Gilmore

I met Jack Gilmore at the April 28, 2017 Time Machines Car Club show in Surprise, AZ.

Jack's enthusiasm for his '34 Ford Coupé is unparalleled in my local car show experience. He's an encyclopedia of knowledge about the details of the project that took him six and a half years. He's just finished. Jack is seventy-eight years old in July 2017 and a bundle of energy. His motivation for taking this project on at the age of seventy-one? When he was fourteen, he loved hot rods, read about them, drooled over them. He always wanted to build one.

Then the University of Nebraska trained him for a career as a lifelong aerospace engineer. That's where Jack gets his attention for detail.

His other car fetish from early on was Rolls Royce. He wanted to own one of those, too, and ended up owning two at separate times.

But he'd never built the hot rod of his dreams. Now he's done that, too.

The Scream of an Engine

Jack took me through the car from stem to stern, discussing each feature one at a time, followed by showing me his book of detailed construction progress photos. Mind you, Jack did all the work himself at home in his three-car garage.

No detail was too small to lovingly describe: polished stainless steel mufflers; chromed suspension pieces; the chassis Jack made from scratch; Wilwood disk brakes, fiberglass body from a Florida company now out of business; Cragar wheels; DVD/CD/AM/FM; air conditioning; power assisted brakes; rack and pinion steering; 700R4 Chevy four-speed coupled with hopped up Chevy V-8; 9" Ford rear end – had to be a Ford piece in here somewhere; Bob Drake Reproductions, Inc., new old stock running boards for $1100; Drake Reproductions new Taiwan-made '34 Ford chromed grille that required an extension of the fiberglass body to fit at the bottom and trimming at the top; spare tire mounted vertically inside the trunk – covered by a custom panel – Jack says almost no hot rod has a spare; an original, restored Arizona copper metal 1934 Ford license plate; and a fender lip that Jack added so that if you reach up underneath, feels like the original metal fender.

Then there is the fabulous paint job, the color taken from a 1968 Ford Contour Light Pewter Gray that Jack fancied. The result is attractive and from some angles in the late afternoon light, appears somewhat greener than gray.

Jack is a gearhead. With credentials.

The Scream of an Engine

Jack Gilmore's '34 Ford three window coupé – a lifelong dream now complete. This was the car's first show, April 28, 2017

Lynn Hitson

Lynn's charming wife Cheryl greets Mike Cross, Rich Orth and I warmly as we motor into the Hitson front driveway on a sunny Monday morning, May 1, 2017. Cheryl asks Mike, who is friends with the Hitsons for sixty years, to 'park out back.' There's too much going on in the front driveway today.

Lynn and Cheryl were married when they were nineteen.

Lynn wears a bandana while he's wet sandblasting in the shop and chewing Copenhagen snuff. In fact, he chews Copenhagen every day of his life except during meals. He has a twinkle in his clear blue eyes while telling us this over a pizza-with-everything in his favorite local parlor. Lynn owns a collection of bandanas.

Professionally, Lynn was a project manager in construction for over forty years. His father helped build the incredible Arizona road system by driving and repairing the machinery that made this task possible.

It's also clear that he likes to tell stories about his passion for Ford cars from 1934 through a 1970 yellow Mustang fastback. Yet a 1950 Pontiac sedan delivery – car derived van - a production series used to ferry parts between buildings internally at GM; a Chevy 'dually' fire truck chassis with Chevy V-8 engine and a '47 Ford truck body sitting on top; and a '41 Chevy sedan delivery are also to be found sprinkled throughout his considerable vehicle collection. There's a Massey-Ferguson tractor bought new in 1979 outside in the pasture.

Lynn's daughter Faith, now thirty-eight, drove the yellow fastback in high school. Lynn hopes to get this car back on the road soon with a rebuilt, re-blueprinted 351 Cleveland V-8 engine with fancy ported head. We note the Mickey Thompson valve covers. Faith attends yard sales pursuing vintage quilts for her business on Etsy. When she comes across a sign for Dad's garage wall, she buys it and brings it home.

After I'd seen the garages, the cars, the parts, the extensive period signs, the antique gas pumps and the equipment and tools Lynn has accumulated since buying this property in 1970, I'd call Cheryl a good sport. Perhaps even a grand sport.

Lynn is a self-acknowledged gear head, a gentleman, a story teller and a car guy to get to know. Don't miss his garage on your next trip to Phoenix. He's a strong man and has HUGE projects to complete. Watch him pull it off. Here's the rest of his story.

The Scream of an Engine

Lynn's passion for cars and gearhead stuff started with a Cushman Road King scooter when he was fourteen. At the time, a driver's license was available at that age in Arizona for vehicles with less than five horsepower. During the next two years, he lost his license twice.

Entryway to the Hitson garage complex. Best signage I've ever seen in a private collection. Signs are prominently displayed on every available wall surface

Lynn's Dad repaired large road machinery professionally and brought wrecked cars home and fixed them up and sold them. From an early age, Lynn had a top role model for taking vehicles apart and putting them back together.

When Lynn was seventeen in 1964, he bought his first car, a '34 Ford four door sedan he found locally in Phoenix. He and a friend towed it home. But all it needed was a new battery and Lynn was off to the races. Or rather, the lakes. He and his high school buddy Terry would check in at school in the morning, say 'Hi!' to the teachers in the courtyard, then head for the one of the many lakes north and east of Phoenix for a day of swimming and jumping off bridges. He smiles when he describes playing hooky from school.

The Scream of an Engine

Lynn was also fond of water skiing on the Central Arizona Project canals, pulled by a car running along the canals. Strictly forbidden. Lynn says that because of the pulling angle, he had to fight the tow rope to avoid skiing into the canal the bank. Then there was the occasional steel pole along a canal edge that snagged the tow rope....

Lynn Hitson's two and a half-acre 'farm' in Phoenix, AZ, presents many work-in-process vehicles. There are other cars he's storing for friends. For example, a '56 Ford Fairlane two-tone is on display next to the barn, owned by a police officer friend who wants to restore it one day. This Ford may turn out to be like his '55 Harley Davidson motorcycle that a friend asked him to store. Lynn later bought it.

Lynn showed us his cherished '65 Mustang fastback which he found stuck in the mud in a barn in Ohio. After thinking about it, he purchased the vehicle and drove to Ohio to dig it out, put it on the trailer and haul it back to the farm. There were four convertible Mustangs in the same barn also stuck in the same mud, also for sale. Lynn declined to buy those as he favors fastbacks.

Why did he buy this car? Lynn always wanted a '65 Shelby GT 350 fastback replicar, so he's decided to make his own. The cost? Just $1500, plus his towing time and making virtually every single body part from scratch. The only original body part is going to be the hardtop, he says. Plus, he's using a High Output '89 Ford V-8 which he already owns. Now there's 15,000 miles on the fastback's odometer, corroborated by the 15,000 miles listed on the title.

Lynn has two complete Ford flathead V-8s ready to go and parts to build many more. Offenhauser heads ready for flathead V-8s being built are stacked like cordwood. But Lynn farms his engine rebuilds and blueprinting out to a shop in Mesa, AZ. Lynn's expertise is in sheet metal and he does all his own. For him, sheet metal work is like therapy.

He's also a professional sandblaster and is sought for his expertise throughout the Phoenix area. Lynn charges $90/hour which Rich tells me is a bargain for professional work. Lynn is also quick with a wrench and puts all these cars together or takes them apart himself depending on what's required.

Lynn Hitson's Shelby GT350 replicar project. Lynn is making all the exterior sheet metal for the car himself, except the roof panel. May 2017

Lynn owns a fully operational, clean, straight, white and attractive '47 Ford sedan delivery. The car includes a Ford flathead V-8 with four-barrel carburetor and Offenhauser heads. The special front chassis is configured with a 4" drop, solid axle and modern disk brakes. Lynn purchased the vehicle in 1984. The attractive professional sign on the side says, 'Hitson Farms Sandblasting, Maybe Eggs'.

Lynn is selling a second 'country home' in Dewey, AZ, he bought as an investment, and consolidating everything into the Phoenix farm. At seventy, he's also decided to part with his vast supply of metal car parts which he sells to others and focus on finishing his many project cars.

The Scream of an Engine

Lynn is a gearhead in every sense of the word. He does have his work cut out for him and loves that idea. He's ready for the challenge. His Daddy got him hooked on cars.

Escondido Car Show

The next part of my field research took me to Escondido, CA for the famous Cruisin' Grand event held every Friday night from April through September.

There are many car-related events like this one throughout America. This is one of the largest with four to five hundred entries every Friday, and as many as eight hundred on an especially good day, or as few as two hundred in bad weather, according to Steve Waldron, the man who started the whole thing on April 7, 2000, in a rainstorm.

The town of Escondido, CA has rolled out the welcome mat for this unusual car event for the past eighteen years, backing the show with manpower and trucks carrying special street signs and orange marking cones. The event sponsors pay for the town's costs. Streets are blocked off. Signs are posted.

Cruisin' Grand takes place along Grand Avenue with show vehicles parked on both sides of the street. The visual impact is much larger than that, with side streets like Maple Avenue and Broadway packed with additional show vehicles. The cars start arriving about two or three in the afternoon. The last one leaves about nine. There is no formal parade today for all cars. There are special parades scheduled from time to time such as for Packards, or Cadillacs, or dragsters - only.

I sipped a Guinness on draft at O'Sullivan's Bar on Grand preparing for the official 5 PM start. The charming bar tender Jennifer understands how to pour. It was 85^0 F and humid out along the parade route but that didn't faze early birds and owners and their families who

The Scream of an Engine

set up folding chairs along Grand Avenue to hold favorable viewing spots.

Grand Avenue, Escondido, at 2:30 PM before the arrival of most of the cars for Cruisin' Grand

The cars on display tend toward hot rods and pickup trucks, but there are a fair mix of sedans and coupés. None are permitted to be more recent than 1974 in this year's version of Cruisin'. The cars are American, but I spotted a Jaguar sedan, a Porsche Speedster and two Datsun 510s.

What a mix of fans and gearheads show up for this view into the past.

Randy Clark

I met Randy, his exuberant and charming wife Patricia, also known as Peaches, and their '32 Ford hot rod as it got closer to show time. Randy, now with sparkling blue eyes and thick gray hair, started building cars in 1964. Much later, he converted this passion into his

The Scream of an Engine

own business, *Hot Rods and Custom Stuff*, in 1989, and now all these twenty-eight years later the business thrives with forty employees, 40,000 square feet and a general manager. Randy no longer appears every day to manage the place, but does so every morning anyway to stay in touch.

Randy Clark's immaculate 1932 Ford Coupé

He built this latest hot rod for Peaches who takes the grandkids for rides. All ten of them, but not all at once. He and Peaches drove the '32 Ford to Vancouver, British Columbia and back last summer. He used the custom luggage rack he built on the back of the car to carry everything they needed for this twenty-two-hour, nearly fourteen-hundred-mile trip each way - without a roof rack.

The '32 Ford ran flawlessly.

Randy is an entrepreneurial gearhead. And a very successful one at that.

The Scream of an Engine

Patsy Hamlin

Patsy and her husband Tom have an unusual story to tell. They met when Tom was in the Armed Forces in the Sixties and dated in a 1929 Ford which they still own. That's when they were first hooked on cars. But this story is about their 'new' Ford.

Patsy rebuilt their 1946 Ford Convertible herself. This car is the second one she built. The tasks included the entire restoration of the Ford flathead V8 engine. Her first engine rebuild was a 428 Ford. Tom showed me the photos of Patsy, wrenches in hand, taken during the restoration as proof. The photos were extensive, demonstrating Patsy's multiple talents.

Patsy Hamlin re-building a Ford V-8

Tom is a career Ford man, working for U-Haul for ten years over forty years ago as the Ford engine rebuilding specialist. Tom knew that as soon as he finished torqueing the last head bolt on an engine

The Scream of an Engine

rebuild the car might be on a cross country journey the next day. Tom had to get it right the first time.

So Patsy has a good backup man for her foray into the mechanical arts. And I'd say, the best teacher a girl could have.

But the Hamlin's are also modest. They showed a '41 Cadillac they also own on Friday, July 28 at Cruisin' Grand. And won one of the five prizes awarded that day for best in category. They never mentioned this car in our discussions until after they won.

Both are true gearheads and regular participants in the Cruisin' Grand. And they're the only husband and wife gearheads I've met during this research.

Louis Garcia

Louie's Dad purchased the used 1948 Chevy truck from his employer, C.C. Graber Co., in 1956. His Dad used this truck to drive his whole family - Dad, Mom three boys including Louie and a girl - to Mexico every August for ten years to visit their grandparents' ranch. The truck sported a canvas cover shaped like an old covered wagon at that time. Dad then purchased another car to drive and retired the old Chevy truck to hauling debris to the dump.

Louie's Dad gave Louie the pickup truck in 1970, fourteen years later. Louie drove the truck to high school, every kid's dream. Louie dated his future wife, squiring her around town, in this truck. Louie decided to restore the truck in 1978 when retired from his full-time job. He dis-assembled the truck and kept the parts he wanted to re-use and sold or gave away the parts he wasn't going to use for the restoration. Thirty-nine years from the 1978 start of restoration, the Chevy truck looks like the photo below. Not one defect that I could detect.

The Scream of an Engine

Louie did all the restoration work himself except the painting which a friend did for him. The reason the job took so long, he says, involves raising two girls, working several jobs and moving several times after the truck was entirely in pieces. Each move required boxing up all the parts, labelling everything and not losing anything in the process.

All the body parts on this very attractive truck were painted separately. The glass is new. The rubber molding Louie says was no trouble: new molding he found readily available. The interior is simple with all the original parts cleaned, painted or chromed, like the seat, seat frame, stainless steel window moldings, dash components and knobs. The only upgrades were electric windows and locks, new gauges, steering wheel and column to add turn signals and an updated brake switch. Louie's goal was to make his truck look like when he first received it from his Dad, to the extent possible.

Louie Garcia's splendid 1946 Chevy truck

The chassis is new and was built for the truck. The steering system and suspension are Mustang II. The new transmission is a TREMEC six-speed manual with a Hurst shifter from a 1957 Chevy

The Scream of an Engine

Belair. The rear end is a Posi-traction 9-inch Ford with 4.11 gears. Louie added the new, freshly stained and varnished Maple truck bed wood to finish the job.

Brake drums were upgraded all around with Wilwood disc brakes and calipers. The original drum brakes scared him silly many times. He and his buddies liked to drive up to the mountains near Ontario and swim in the lakes during the summer months. Coming back down the mountain, the original brakes would smoke, smell and eventually not even slow the truck down much.

The engine in Louie's truck is a late model Chevrolet 383 cubic inch crate engine with new air conditioner, power steering, aluminum radiator and electric fans which he installed himself. He raised the hood to show me. It's a beaut!

Louie gained his basic knowledge of cars by working on the original truck brakes and conducting all the repairs to keep the old truck on the road himself. He even changed the oil in the engine, transmission and rear end.

Louie is a knowledgeable gearhead. His love of this truck is passed down from his Dad.

Gene Huffman

I spot a red Chevrolet across the street, standout color on an immaculate car. I approach a man sitting with his wife alongside the car and ask if it's OK if I take photos. They seem pleased that I want to. We talk and I discover this is a '38 Chevrolet chopped 4 ½" that Gene and Sandy Huffman bought in 2000, already a finished hot rod. Gene liked the looks of this car he spotted at the Del Mar Car Show from the start. But he says if it hadn't been chopped, he'd have walked right on by.

The Scream of an Engine

Gene does 100% of the maintenance himself. He's had the car painted twice. He fixes anything on the 350-cubic inch Chevy V-8 that needs attention, changes the oil and lubes where required.

I ask Gene why he participates in Cruisin' Grand almost every Friday night. He likes meeting other hot rodders like himself, he avers. He and Sandy like buying lunch along Grand, and often add dinner at the end of the day when they feel like it. He and Sandy live in Vista, which is not a long drive away, but they eat here anyway.

Gene also mentions Nitro Night. Dragsters, some with serious recent credentials, are trailered up and down Grand. The drive shafts are disconnected for this event, but the engines run up to full song, on nitro – nitromethane for increasing horsepower in alcohol-powered dragster motors. Gene says there's a rumor that one of the dragsters broke glass windows on Grand it was so loud. So the cars were towed further away from the windows, toward the middle of Grand, afterward.

Later, Steve Waldron, founder of Cruisin' Grand, tells me that never happened, but it came close, with large panels of glass unsupported except by the frames flexing too much in the center. One of Steve's assistants pipes up and says, yeah, we almost taped those windows to keep them from breaking.

Gene owns a Sanger flat bottom drag racing boat with a 390 Ford Interceptor V-8 bored out to 427. He keeps it at the lake in Parker, AZ, where his sons run it on the lake on weekends. I find that hot rod gearheads often participate in multiple venues with multiple brands – in this case, a Chevy hot rod owner builds a Ford hot rod and owns a Ford-powered drag racing boat.

Gene Huffman is a certified gearhead, hooked on hot rods at the Del Mar Car Show.

The Scream of an Engine

Steve Waldron

Steve started Cruisin' Grand eighteen years ago and still runs it. Steve proposed to the City Council that the event would be self-funding, and the Council wholeheartedly endorsed his plan. Everyone I spoke with said Steve is a terrific guy who has done an excellent job with this popular show. And his Daddy owned a hot rod. I think that's how he got hooked.

A renaissance of downtown Escondido has occurred over the last eighteen or twenty years. This largely deserted, blighted area of Escondido, with boarded up buildings, has become teaming with upmarket and popular restaurants and stores. I've tested several, like Vincent's French restaurant, Swami's and O'Sullivan's Bar.

Steve also owns a popular T-shirt store on Grand.

Cruisin' Grand gets credit for much of the change to the downtown area.

Steve says there's no charge to enter a car in Cruisin' Grand. Escondido businesses provide the support for the event every year. In turn, the businesses get lots of traffic from the car crowd. The town puts up barricades to block off streets and provides other services for which Cruisin' Grand is billed and pays. Steve says Cruisin' Grand has been written up as being the largest car show of its kind in the U.S.

Many towns and cities throughout the U.S. support 'Car Cruises' on their streets. La Mesa, CA offers one on Thursday nights, the Bob Stall Chevrolet-sponsored La Mesa Classic Car Show, from June 1 – August 31, 5 - 8 PM. Encinitas, CA offers another Thursday night cruise.

The Scream of an Engine

Woodward Avenue Dream Cruise

The nationally famous Woodward Avenue Dream Cruise in Detroit, MI has been an official attraction for enthusiasts since 1995. But the roots go back to the 1800s when young men raced horses and buggies along the route, or much later, drag racing cars down the Avenue. Now we have the Dream Cruise.

What is it? Just the world's largest one-day automotive event, drawing about 1.5 million people and forty thousand classic cars each year from around the globe. This is a different category of record breakers: the Escondido Cruisin' Grand happens every Friday night over several months each year. Not just once a year.

No question that this once a year Woodward Avenue event is record setting. Spectators see muscle cars, street rods, custom, collector and special interest vehicles dating across several decades, mostly from the Fifties, Sixties and early Seventies.[90] The route runs from Pontiac, MI through Ferndale in Detroit to the State Fairgrounds, a distance of over fifteen miles.

Specialty Car Shows

Then there are the local specialty shows. Like the *Concorso Italiano* held every August at Black Horse Golf Course In Monterrey Bay, CA. At this one, part of a weeklong celebration, over eight hundred Italian cars from around the world are gathered to be judged and win prizes. For years, I entered my '69 Alfa Spider in the San Diego equivalent, held in Little Italy, with thirty or forty entrants, mostly local.

Now let's wrap up the research.

---

[90] Wikipedia, May 2017

Chapter Twenty-Six: Epilogue

What have I learned about distinguishing car enthusiasts from those who care less?

Enthusiasts – fans and gearheads - start and finish with passion. Gearheads are extreme fans favored with extreme passion.

The passion of a fan comes from romantic notions of exotic vehicles from far-away places, the beauty of a physical object, perfection in the details, visceral responses to the sights and sounds of motoring, loving to wash and clean a car, a remembered song when a car is first spotted, racing and other memorable times and places where a car figured into the picture.

The passion of a gearhead, in addition to the features of a fan, comes from loving to play with gadgets, especially taking them apart to see how they work or to repair them, and getting to know all their measurements. Restoring them to like new condition. Those inclined to be engineers.

The Scream of an Engine

Those engineers without passion for cars, those who read, for example, *Consumer Reports,* and follow the advice so freely offered there, where reliability and cost effectiveness overrule sound, feel, handling and excitement, will never be gearheads. They're too practical. Like most people, they're not car enthusiasts: neither gearheads nor fans.

They're just good people who think cars are made for efficient transportation.

Culture is all-important in defining enthusiasts, especially when car culture comes early in the first ten years or so of life: a vision of mobility, a small sports car appears one day, a parent buys one, a young nose first smells leather seats, the scream of an engine is experienced for the first time.

There must be cultural triggers in the early days that cause excitement in a small boy or girl's life, most likely coming from enthusiastic parents or friends. That excitement must be nourished by the culture surrounding the budding enthusiast, with magazines, family vehicles, race reports, trips in cars to car places, and especially now, the Internet for news.

Loyalty to brands, as in my case, is a major defining characteristic of car enthusiasts. Loyalty is a human trait appearing everywhere in sports as well as clothing, food and appliances in homes. Loyalty to people, processes, places and lifestyles is part of the package. Developing a skill set, like racing in Steve McQueen's case, or rebuilding an Austin 850 engine and building slot cars as I did, or designing a part for a car or an entire car, as in Fred Puhn's case, is a solid basis for being categorized a gearhead.

Nostalgia for the 'old days' is an important ingredient for enthusiasts. Memories are a big component, an aching sense of wanting to recover what's past and gone, like Ken Braun wanting his Mom and Dad back to share his new successes in life with his GTO, or ask details about the early years in the Braun family. Like me, Ken no longer has a way to call home.

Memories of how an earlier vehicle looked, the color, the shape, the size, the sound - big factors - and what was happening when this budding enthusiast first saw this earlier vehicle: part of the enthusiast package.

The danger inherent in racing is a draw for enthusiasts like I'm sure it was for Steve McQueen, or much later, Paul Newman. Newman was forty-four and McQueen thirty-one when the racing bug bit. The movie *Winning*, which debuted on Thursday, May 22, 1969, required Newman and costar Robert Wagner to attend the Bob Bondurant Racing School for a week to prepare themselves. They were the program's fifth and sixth-ever students.[91]

For me, it's never the focus on accidents. I prefer thinking about wheel-to-wheel dicing in my favorite car against an enemy car and driver combination, like a James Dean or Steve McQueen Porsche, and of course eking out the win. As I like to say, my pulse after a race never returned to normal until Wednesday the following week. Part of the danger and excitement component, I guess.

A competitive streak is important in a gearhead. James Dean won his first novice race in a Porsche 356 in March 1955 and McQueen his first novice race in a Porsche 356 in 1959. Dean traded his 356 in on a 550 later in 1955. McQueen later raced a 550. Both actors were competitive in car racing. What was going on here?

---

[91] http://www.roadandtrack.com/car-culture/news/a29277/paul-newmans-racing-career-began-with-this-1969-movie/

In the early days, McQueen saw Dean as his competitor in becoming the top actor in Hollywood. To my knowledge, they never met on a race course, but if it happened, my money would be on McQueen who was more aggressive about his pursuits than anyone. But both were intense.

Ego is part of a car enthusiast. A need arises to drive faster than anyone else, or become more attractive to the opposite sex, or own something that has the allure of being from far away, unattainable for most. First kid on the block syndrome. A fan who likes having a rare car, perhaps a foreign car or maybe even an expensive domestic one, is partly motivated by ego. A gearhead who rebuilds an engine or another major system in a car is proud of the result and of what he can do himself: another aspect of ego.

When my first wife Brooke found out I'd bought a Jaguar after being placed in charge of transportation for our daughter's wedding, my old car worn out, she exclaimed that I was on an ego trip. That couldn't have been further from the truth: I was connecting with Jaguar's Fifties Le Mans wins, with the drivers, the childhood memories and passions. I was on a nostalgia trip, not an ego trip.

There seems to me to be differences between gearhead groups. Hot rodders and sports car owners, for example, fall into different camps: hot rodders want their vehicles to be unique to them, like no other on the planet; sports car owners, especially in the 1950s, relished being part of a like-minded group with identical cars. MG owners liked being a TC, TD, TF or A owner and getting together with other owners of those cars, to reinforce the idea that they'd made the right choice in the first place, and were inspired by being part of this unique group of identical vehicles and colorful owners.

Yet sports car enthusiasts like to modify their cars to gain an edge, too. Increased compression ratios, ported and polished heads, low back pressure mufflers, new free-flow headers, better tires. But appearing street stock so competitors experience a complete shock when nailed at a stoplight.

Music is a draw for enthusiasts. It's a component of many memories: hear the tune, be transported to that day and time. A song drew Ken Braun into his first GTO. The music for the 1966 epic movie *Grand Prix* with James Garner, Graham Hill, Francoise Hardy, Phil Hill and Eva Marie Saint stirs my memories of so many other car experiences, as well as the time and place I saw the movie, and especially the scream of the engine at the beginning of the movie.

Those enjoying working on a car in the garage until midnight, risking the ire of their significant others, have discovered an important part of being a gearhead.

Fans love their cars, usually obsess about keeping them clean and visually perfect – no dings or paint chips - and mechanically tip top. Like Marv Blank and Roy Disney, fans with passion enlist the help of expert mechanics to achieve perfection in their cars. And if a part is missing, like the center of a hubcap in Marv's case, no stone is left unturned to find the replacement part, hopefully New Old Stock, and the fan won't rest until its properly installed. And all is well again.

When you boil it all down, though, we humans love to be part of something bigger than ourselves: a car club, a sports team, a church, a dance group – members in a collective that shares a passion, in which ideas can be tested, members can connect with innovative suggestions and ideas, and the group reinforces underlying beliefs that what the group does and thinks is the very best, and certainly better than beliefs in any other group.

Say, Porsche Club of America members thinking about how they stack up against the BMW Car Club of America.

The Scream of an Engine

That's true of all car enthusiasts. Car clubs and racing groups meet the need to belong. The group reinforces decisions about a marque, a race series like Formula 1 or a professional rally series.

A baseball, basketball or football enthusiast may be no different from a car enthusiast. He or she likes the sport, goes to games and if serious, can quote numbers and statistics from players and teams all the way back to childhood – just like a gearhead does with cars. And may have played or still play that sport.

The baseball, basketball or football fan remembers epic games that come down to the last minute of play, like I remember Gary Wood driving the Cornell football team the length of the field in the last minutes, scoring the touchdown, coming from behind to beat heavily favored Princeton, 35-34. In 1962, but the memory is like it happened yesterday.

Favorite players, stadiums, championships. Meeting the stars of the game and securing autographs like my seven-year-old daughter Elizabeth obtaining San Diego Padres Steve Garvey's autograph during the Padres 1984 World Series run, or buying signed memorabilia, like bats or balls, which I've done during Major League Baseball Spring Training games in Surprise, AZ.

Then the only difference between enthusiasts for cars and enthusiasts for sports or the theater or the movies or any other human endeavor is what they got hooked on at an early age. I argue that the process for gaining the passion for each is the same.

When I stand back and think about those I've interviewed for these pages, I'm concerned that when these present generations of enthusiasts pass away, new ones to fill their shoes may not be coming along. Hot rod fans, as we know them today and watch them in car

The Scream of an Engine

shows in Surprise, AZ, Escondido, CA and throughout America are a period statement.

I met no young hot rodders at the car shows I attended. One hot-rodder, Gene Huffman, age seventy-one, sitting on folding chairs with his wife on the sidewalk near his parked hot rod, told me he thought hot rods were from a period that's past, mostly coming together in the Fifties and Sixties. The Fifties were a time, he said, when you could buy a Thirties Ford or Chevy for $100 and an engine for $20. And work to make them your own, different from anyone else's.

Those days, he argues, are gone.

Like hot rodders who got their start in the Fifties, Fifties sports car enthusiasts like me may also fade away as a group.

But enthusiasts are being replaced. Car enthusiasts today get started in Go Karts at age six, or as teens hankering for the keys to Dad's fire breathing sedan, or in their early twenties. In their teens and early twenties, they advance the passion by securing a stream of monthly payments to buy what are called 'pocket rockets' – small cars with small engines and huge power, decorated with stickers or not, usually in garish colors. Cars like the Ford Focus RS with a 2.3-liter turbo four and 350 BHP, 0-60 in 4.6 seconds, with 19"X8" wheels and electric blue paint. Or the steel gray Honda Civic Type R with 2-liters and 306 BHP, 170 MPH and the wild look that can only inspire today's youth to become enthusiasts.

Teenagers who follow in Dad's Chrysler-loyal footsteps might wangle a showroom stock Dodge Demon sedan hemi V-8 with over 800 BHP. I'd of course go for the 2017 Ford GT with 0-60 in 3.2 seconds, 216 MPH top speed, and race car-like handling for just $453,750. But I'm not a teenager and so am ineligible for this paragraph.

The Scream of an Engine

These cars are not hot rods or sports cars in the Fifties sense. That model's going away. These new cars are comfortable, relatively affordable cars capable of sustained drifting on suitable race tracks. The Fifties car enthusiast's choices are dead, long live the Fifties enthusiast.

Cars for enthusiasts today are different in another way: they work. When can you remember a new car that wouldn't start or run, mostly carefree, for the first 100,000 miles? No need to learn how to fix them. Cars are now computers tied to a large number of sensors, anyway. Even tubeless modern tires get many fewer flats than the old tube type tires. No need to go to a service department as often – service stations are history - or learn the repair tricks yourself.

As a result, young enthusiasts are different. Some will still want to go racing. But that game has changed, too, and rather than start off from scratch by buying a prepared race car as I did, and work up the ladder, today kids race Go Karts and special small off-road trucks to gain a toe hold. These vehicles are better engineered and require less driver involvement in fixing them. The best drivers at this young age go up the ladder by driving someone else's car.

Technology has advanced tremendously since the Fifties. The bottom line? In a 2017 test on the Spring Mountain Motor Sports, Parumph, NV, 2.2-mile race track, my favorite 3.8-liter D-Type Jaguar was bested by…a 3.0-liter all-wheel-drive Jaguar F-Pace S. An SUV! By over three seconds a lap![92] Takes the wind right out of my sails. I immediately counter with defensive arguments: the owner insisted the D-Type be limited to 5000 RPM; who was driving the D-Type?; was the D-Type tuned?; was the rear axle ratio right for a short course? After

---

[92] *Road & Track's* 70th Anniversary issue, July 2017, page. The BMW X5 and Porsche Macan GTS SUVs were even quicker.

all, D-Types were never designed for short courses without significantly long straights where streamlining counted.

But I'm missing the point. What was quick in 1955 isn't in 2017. Technology has advanced. Which is why 2-liter Honda Civic R's might be more attractive to today's teenagers than a Fifties race car.

And the cars today look much more alike than before, designed by computers to offer minimal drag. Manufacturing defects on all brands have become nearly non-existent.

I pause and reflect that as the internal combustion engine is legislated out of existence, designed-alike hydrogen or electric powered cars won't inspire the same passions of old. Especially when autonomous cars are ubiquitous. The Chairman of Toyota Motor Corp. also reflects on this issue.

How do you differentiate batteries under the hood of an electric car? Oh, I know, my battery is better than yours.

Thirty years from now, I'll miss the scream of an engine when we're all driving hydrogen or electric cars which make no sound at all.

But what happy, emotional, memorable fun it is to be an automobile enthusiast today – fan or gearhead - while the internal combustion engine still prevails and screams!

A suitable passion.

In the future? 'Nevermore' quoth the raven.[93]

---

[93] Edgar Allen Poe's *The Raven*, 1845

The Scream of an Engine

The Scream of an Engine

Appendix I. Automotive Revolution

The New Model

The car culture we've come to know, understand and love is changing. By 2020, many believe that a new automotive industry model will have replaced the old.

Consider the potential impact of Uber, Lyft, Gig and other ride hailing services which provide transportation on demand almost instantaneously. Call and a few minutes later the ride shows up. Many of these services are planning to employ driverless autonomous vehicles: eliminating the human driver offers a major transportation cost reduction. Uber is testing this driverless solution as this is written with Volvos in Pittsburgh, PA and Phoenix, AZ, admittedly with a driver along for the present to see that everything works.

Waymo is offering test rides in driverless cars in Phoenix today.

It's not just cars: forecasters say the F-35 now being deployed is the last manned U.S. fighter plane; the next generation of Navy warships will be autonomous, and of course, drones are already here and to some extent 'self-driving' today as are most of the major planes in airline use today. The latest bomber to make its debut over Iraq has four engines, no cockpit, and a flight time limited by the length of its battery: ISIS is using drones to bomb Syria, Iraq and the Allies as this is written.

Uber has contracted to provide *flying* cars in Dallas and Dubai in 2020. The third dimension gives autonomous vehicles more room to maneuver. Uber has just contracted to buy *ground* cars from Volvo: 24,000 of them. Uber will convert the XC 90s to autonomous.[94]

---

[94] Ad Age, November 21, 2017

The Scream of an Engine

Autonomous vehicles are a new idea and a newer reality. The first autonomous vehicles competed in an obstacle course/race in the desert on March 13, 2004. Why? The U.S. government through the Defense Research Projects Agency – DARPA – put a million-dollar prize on finishing first.

In 2001, Congress set a target of 2015 for one-third of all military ground combat vehicles being unmanned. DARPA had been trying to develop these kinds of vehicles for doing the dirty work in war and not risking human lives. DARPA used defense contractors to reduce human involvement, not eliminate it. Two yards and a cloud of dust was the result.

Internal DARPA development wasn't cutting it. Tony Tether, Director of DARPA, announced a 142-mile race in February 2003 with the big prize money. A kick-off event was staged at the Peterson Museum in Los Angeles for prospective racers.

Fourteen vehicles and one motorcycle, surrounded by teams of geeks, computer professionals, academics, skilled mechanics – yes, gearheads - arrived to begin the race. The start was in Barstow, CA, the course running through the Mojave Desert and finishing in Primm, NV. These vehicles brought lidar sensors, GPS and software to the line, plus the inexhaustible energy of the designers and builders. One observer said they looked like they came from the movie, *Mad Max*. A preliminary round had already eliminated ten competitors deemed 'not yet ready.'

The result? The fourteen-ton Oshkosh truck got stuck between two tumbleweeds, going back and forth. Palos Verdes High School's Acura called the Doom Buggy forgot how to turn. The Carnegie Mellon 'Sandstorm' Humvee left the starting line at 40 MPH and was leading, but hit a rough road shoulder due to faulty sensor alignment and got stuck: with smoke coming off the tires, the decision was made to hit the kill switch. The Jeep Cherokee made it twenty feet, did a U-turn and came back. The motorcycle's stabilizer was inadvertently not switched on and the motorcycle fell over at the starting line.

None finished.

But DARPA doubled the prize and the second event was staged a year later.[95] And now we see the entire automotive industry about to be turned on its ear.

Barely a decade after DARPA's humble beginnings with autonomous vehicles in 2004, this new automotive vector is threatening to take over the landscape. Soon.

A major advantage of autonomous cars is that we'll eventually avoid 35,000 or more automotive crash-related deaths a year in the U.S. and thereby reduce damage and repair costs on new Vehicles in Operation. Older cars with human drivers will continue to crash and be repaired. Since there were over 40,000 deaths on American highways reported in 2016, an increase from 2015's 35,000 due to 'more miles driven,' the pressure for reduction in deaths may be even more telling by the time autonomous cars become popular.

A side effect of autonomous vehicles taking over our roads is that the giant automotive insurance industry will be restructured and significantly changed from what we know today. There will be major downward pressure on insurance premiums.

---

[95] Alex Davies, *Wired*, August 2017

The Scream of an Engine

A recent report says that by 2030, 95% of miles driven will be in robo-taxis. The incredibly rapid transition to an entirely new transportation system – when it will be so much cheaper and easier *not* to own a car - will force selling the family car as soon as possible. A delay will return a lower sale price.

Self-driving cars, the report predicts, will make ride hailing so cheap that the market will quickly transform. Because electric cars can last longer with heavy use than internal combustion powered cars, it will make economic sense for those cars to be electric, as well. By 2030, passenger miles traveled in the U.S. could be in on-demand, autonomous electric cars owned by fleets rather than individuals. The average family could be saving $5,600 a year on transportation. Also, the oil industry as we know it could collapse.[96]

With the peaking and flattening new car market in 2017, comes the news that used car values are falling faster. Is this caused by anticipation of the changes about to sweep the industry? In my case, the answer is yes. I'm leasing until this change shakes out. My 2014 leased SUV was worth $3K less than my guaranteed purchase price when I turned it in.

Purchased vehicles are experiencing the same thing. Negative-equity levels are at record highs as lengthening loan terms, rising transaction prices and falling used-vehicle values combine to take a toll on consumers and the industry. More is owned on the finance agreement than the car is worth.

In the first quarter of 2017, the percentage of vehicle trade-ins on new vehicles that had negative equity reached a record 32.8 percent.

---

[96] Adele Peters for *Fast Company* writing about the new *ReThinkX Report* at: https://www.rethinkx.com/transportation, May 31, 2017

The average amount of negative equity, at $5,195, was also a high, Edmunds data show.[97]

My mere $3K hit was lucky. On the surface, the price drop also eliminated the option of buying the lease out, although the dealer would negotiate on behalf of Ford Credit, I'm sure.

Uber, despite the recent negative press, may now have the largest market capitalization of any private company in the world: nearly $52B in December 2015, based on that year's $2.1B round of private equity fund raising by Uber.[98] This is approaching the capitalization of Ford or General Motors which are publicly traded. Someone out there thinks there is enormous potential in the Uber idea.

In 2017, estimates run as high as $70B for Uber's value.

Innovative ideas get huge market premiums; mature industries, like car manufacturing, get low premiums. Regardless of their current profitability.

Uber is anything but profitable today.

In Europe and the Far East tests of autonomous vehicles are at least as far along. Paris has banned older cars within city limits to reduce congestion and pollution and has partially banned all cars starting September 2016 on a trial basis: *"Cars will be outlawed from four hundred miles of Paris streets on Sunday as the French capital joins the likes of Brussels, Bogotá, Jakarta and Copenhagen in marking World Car-Free Day."*[99]

---

[97] Autoweek Daily Drive, June 13, 2017, from Car News
[98] Forbes, Liyan Chen, December 4, 2015
[99] The Guardian, U.S. Edition, September 22, 2016

The Scream of an Engine

While taxis fill the gap today, the Ubers of the world will certainly replace them: lower cost, more efficient solutions will win out in the marketplace. Uber and other ride on demand services may partner with large automobile manufacturers by contracts or through merger. Uber has announced a contractual alliance with Mercedes-Benz.

Traditional auto manufacturers are already anticipating this new market opportunity. BMW and Volvo are early entrants into the fray.

"Ride-hailing is nothing more than manual autonomous driving," Tony Douglas, head of strategy for BMW's mobility services said. "Once you dispense with the driver you have a license to print money. The popular press likes to call these vehicles 'robotaxis.'

"BMW has already made significant progress expanding into the market for car-sharing by introducing pay-by-the-minute services like ReachNow in Seattle," Douglas said.

"We had 14,000 people sign up in four days, in a market already served by Zipcar, Uber, Lyft and Car2go.

"Someone else spent the money to educate the market and then we came in with a cool product. We will not be the largest, but we can be the coolest," according to Douglas.[100]

Ford Motor Company's efforts to stay relevant in the changing automotive landscape include the purchase of a crowdsourced ride sharing company in 2016 for $65 million. The business called Chariot is now operating in San Francisco, Austin and Seattle and is expanding to New York City in 2017. The business employs Ford Transit vans of multiple sizes, giving Ford a vertically integrated business opportunity

---

[100] Automotive News Europe, December 6, 2016

to provide rides for an average of $4 one way that are not well served by public transportation systems.[101]

These Transit vans will soon also become autonomous. In my opinion.

But China may become the earliest adopter of autonomous vehicles per this report:

"Within a decade, Wu Hu, about 200 miles west of Shanghai, aims to become the first city in the world to ban human drivers and go fully autonomous. Baidu – China's equivalent of Google - hopes to use the city to showcase the increased safety and decreased congestion and emissions that come with letting the AI – artificial intelligence - drive."[102]

Google, based in Mountain View, CA, has been testing autonomous vehicles on America's streets and roads since 2009 racking up over one and half million miles on Toyota Prius cars, Lexis SUVs and since 2014 with an all-Google car without steering wheel or pedals. They've had only one accident. In addition, they've simulated an additional billion miles on computers. If Google partners with a major manufacturer, instant fleets of autonomous vehicles will soon appear.

In 2016, Google focused autonomous vehicle design and testing in a new Google company called, appropriately, Waymo. I like the new name. Not everyone does. Google, to confuse the issue further, is now known as Alphabet, Inc. since October 2015. The Google we've known in the past is now one of Alphabet's companies, like Waymo. Over 99%

---

[101] https://www.cnbc.com/2017/07/27/

[102] Wired, Inside China's Plan to Beat America to the Self-Driving Car, Jack Stewart, June 15, 2016

of Alphabet's revenue comes from Google. This restructuring seems fitting for a corporation with projected revenues of more than $80B in 2016. New technology bets, like Waymo, can now be watched and managed separately.

Imagine for a moment that Wu Hu, China IS the first city in the world to go 100% autonomous.... with the Waymo vehicle. What results?

Waymo in Wu Hu.

Ford Motor Company, second largest US car maker in 2016 and fifth largest in the world, has now weighed heavily into the burgeoning new market.

Ford is investing a billion dollars in the autonomous car startup, Argo AI, over the next five years. Argo AI is headquartered in Pittsburgh, PA, with offices in Michigan and California. Argo was co-founded a few months ago by Google car project veteran Bryan Salesky and Uber engineer Peter Rander.

Mark Fields, recent past Ford Chief Executive Officer, told USA Today, "The reason for the investment is not only to drive the delivery of our own autonomous vehicle by 2021 but also to deliver value to our shareholders by creating a software platform that can be licensed to others. This move gets us the agility and speed of a startup combined with Ford's global scale."[103]

Today, not everything is resolved in the world of autonomous vehicles.

---

[103] USA Today, February 11, 2017

Autonomous vehicle software is faced with ethical questions which must be addressed and decided. For example, if a car is about to hit a bicycle rider who suddenly appears ahead, should the bicycle rider be killed, or should the car take evasive action which will kill the five occupants of the car? I suspect everyone knows what the bicycle rider thinks.

Insurance rates may balance the many possible ethical risks: the car owner selects the 'fewest killed' option in the software, covers the remaining death risk through insurance, the rate adjusted for number killed. Or the 'save my skin first' option. Frankly, I can't imagine anyone not selecting 'save my skin first.' But you never know.

Even with autonomous vehicles, the death rate cannot be zero because of situations like the bicycle rider. Nonetheless, it will approach zero as all vehicles become autonomous. This will take many decades especially as automakers will continue to offer people-controlled vehicles while there is demand.

The many issues remaining to be resolved on the autonomous vehicle technology curve include: continued public road testing; reliability of software and hardware testing, and issuance of Federal and State validation and approval certificates for each vendor of autonomous vehicles or services; cyber-threat testing and 'anti-virus' issues; legislation changes to assure public safety issues are addressed; manufacturers like General Motors pushing legislation to bar non-manufacturers from testing autonomous vehicles.

In another indication how fast this technology is moving, Waymo has signed an agreement with Lyft, the ride-hailing startup. The agreement calls for the companies to work together to bring autonomous vehicles into the mainstream through pilot projects and product development efforts. General Motors is a major investor in Lyft. GM also bought Cruise Automation in 2016 for more than one billion dollars in cash and stock. Cruise is testing GM vehicles autonomously on the roads of California.[104]

How fast these changes are moving toward us is brought home by a February 2017 trip to the local Ford dealer to exchange our 2014 Escape for a 2017 model: end of lease. The 2017s are changed immensely over the 2014s in three years. Autonomous features now show up on the 2017 cars: parks itself without operator intervention; can be started via the Internet at a distance; and shakes the steering wheel if the driver drifts out of lane, a feature ensuring the driver stays awake late at night on open roads. For starters.

These changes are accelerating and will be immense over the next decade as cars become more sensors and computers than traditional cars.

Fuels of the Future

Another major change is roiling the automotive marketplace: fuels.

In 1862, Congress passed the Internal Revenue Act to fund the Civil War, signed by President Abraham Lincoln on July 1, which placed a two dollar a gallon tax on alcohol, part of the 'sin' tax package of taxes which included tobacco, yachts and other non-essentials. This accelerated revenue for the war effort.

Gasoline was around before the invention of the internal combustion engine but for many years was considered a useless

---

[104] The San Diego Union-Tribune, Monday May 15, 2017, page A10

byproduct of the refining of crude oil to make kerosene, the standard fuel for lamps through much of the 19th century.

In the 1862 Act, alcohol was taxed disproportionately to oil, $2.00/gallon vs. $.10/gallon. The disparity had the effect of discouraging the drinking of alcohol in a society in which it was popular. The unanticipated side effect was to eliminate alcohol as a fuel. Two dollars was a lot of money in 1862.

By 1906, oil and the derivative gasoline was dominant as a transportation fuel.[105]

Now fracking – hydraulic fracturing of deep shale rocks – which commenced in the U.S. in 1949 is threatening to extend the leadership of oil. Fracking gained serious momentum by 2006 when the U.S. was still a huge net petroleum importer.

The U.S. faces environmental issues with petroleum fueled vehicles – transportation accounts for 28% of total U.S. energy consumption, and gasoline and diesel fuels account for 88% of petroleum used in transportation, natural gas and biofuels only 8%.[106] The U.S. has also been dependent for supply from overseas sources – principally Canada, Saudi Arabia and Venezuela - with the potential to hold our economy hostage with price increases or supply decreases.

In 2015, the United States imported approximately 9.4 million barrels per day (MMb/d) of petroleum from about eighty-eight countries. This increased to 10.1 MMb/d in 2016, a change of 6.9% due

---

[105] *Right Fuel for the Future*, Bud Suiter, 2013
[106] U.S. Energy Information Administration, https://www.eia.gov/dnav/pet/hist/LeafHandler.ashx?n=PET&s=MTTIMUS1&f=M, May 2017

The Scream of an Engine

to continuing market shift toward thirsty SUVs and pickup trucks, and increased mileage driven.[107]

Petroleum includes crude oil, natural gas plant liquids, liquefied refinery gases, refined products such as gasoline and diesel fuel, and biofuels like ethanol mixed in gasoline and biodiesel. About 78% of U.S. gross petroleum imports are crude oil which is refined here.

In 2016, the United States exported about 5.2 MMb/d of petroleum products to one hundred forty-seven countries. The resulting net imports of petroleum - imports minus exports - were about 4.9 MMb/d, up about 4.3% from 2015.

Net imports of petroleum are down from roughly 12.6 MMb/day in 2005-2006 to 4.9 MMb/day in 2016, a huge decrease of nearly two thirds in ten years. Fracking has made a difference.[108]

Fracking has also introduced environmental protection issues.

Despite this dramatically lower dependence on imported petroleum fuels by nearly two thirds in just a few years, further change is coming in transportation fuels. In October 2017, Phil Ting, D-San Francisco, has proposed banning gasoline powered vehicles in CA by 2040. He says this is necessary to meet California's 2050 carbon goals.[109]

---

[107] Ibid.
[108] Ibid.
[109] San Diego Union, 10-27-17

Appendix I: Automotive Revolution

Hydrogen Next

I must admit upfront that my high school science project senior year was a hydrogen-oxygen fuel cell. Just eight years later, NASA used hydrogen-oxygen fuel cells for the mission that landed men on the moon on July 20, 1969. I rode in a Ford Contour quietly powered by a hydrogen-oxygen fuel cell stack in January 2001 at the San Diego Auto Show.

Spencer Abrams, head of the Department of Energy in the George W. Bush Administration, announced in January 2002, that hydrogen would be the U.S. fuel of the future. I personally lobbied for this idea with the new administration the fall of 2001 and was rewarded with a long and thoughtful letter back from Christie Whitman, then head of the environmental Protection Agency. I didn't hear back from President Bush or Spencer Abrams.

Because of my positive firsthand experiences with fuel cells, I espoused these energy converting devices as the next big technology shift in the world. One friend labelled me a 'hydrogen bigot.'

I must admit that not everyone agrees with my views on hydrogen, the simplest and most abundant element in the universe. In engineering and physics, simplicity of new concepts and their design and engineering is a virtue. Fuel cells are simple, hydrogen is simple. That's why I figure that in the end, whenever that is, hydrogen fuel cells will prevail.

A billion dollars of Federal funds was invested in hydrogen fuel cell development over the six years 2002-2008 before the Obama Administration changed course and backed battery electric vehicle research and development.

The Scream of an Engine

In a hydrogen-oxygen fuel cell stack for vehicles, hydrogen combines with oxygen to produce pure water out the exhaust pipe. Zero emissions except heat. Electricity is the by-product which drives electric motors which can then propel cars or be used in other applications. Hydrogen suffers infrastructure and distribution issues that push general acceptance of hydrogen-powered vehicles out a decade or two from now.

Electric vehicles can be built now, reducing dependence on oil and cleaning up the air in the cities of the world, or so the thinking went when the Obama administration shifted gears. After all the hoopla, less than one percent of cars sold in 2017 are electric.

But once the electric vehicle platform is in place, it's an easy transition to hydrogen: fuel cells in cars of the future merely replace the heavy, slow to charge battery packs in electric vehicles. The rest of the design is in place.

Looking toward a hydrogen future, Hyundai of South Korea and Honda and Toyota of Japan offer hydrogen powered vehicles today. They're for lease and in two cases, purchase, in Los Angeles and San Francisco.

After returning from living in Spain for two years in 2014 – we lived there from late 2012 through mid-2014 - I inquired and was awarded a production Hyundai Tucson SUV hydrogen fuel cell powered vehicle. If I lived in Los Angeles. The $499/month three-year lease included fuel and maintenance. These cars have longer ranges and quicker fill-up times than electric vehicles. I so wanted one, but ended up living near Phoenix where this Hyundai model wasn't yet available.

A new Hyundai hydrogen model is planned to replace the Tucson in 2018 at half the price with a 45% increase in range, from 258 miles to 373 miles per tank. Hyundai's goal is to place 10,000 of these

Appendix I: Automotive Revolution

on the roads of South Korea by 2020. As the third largest producer of cars in the world, Hyundai has the resources to pull that off.

Honda offers the 2017 Clarity Fuel Cell four door-sedan at $369/month with a range of 366 miles today. Fuel is included in the lease. Honda has been leasing earlier fuel cell cars on a limited basis in Los Angeles for several years now. Actress Jamie Lee Curtis leased one of the earlier ones.

Toyota offers the Mirai four door-sedan at $349/month with a range of 312 miles on a tank. Fuel is included with the lease and refueling takes just five minutes. Purchase is also offered at $57,500 before Federal and State rebates. At the end of 2016, only eight California dealerships were selling the Mirai: four in the San Francisco area and four in Los Angeles.

Toyota expects to deliver 3,000 fuel cell cars to the U.S. in 2017.

Many new developments in fuel cell technology and production are underway, most behind the scenes. General Motors and Honda announced jointly in early 2017 a mass production facility at GM's Brownstown Township, MI, plant south of Detroit. High volume production of next-generation turnkey fuel cell stacks will begin there by 2020. Both companies will share the fuel cell stack production output using common part numbers for components to reduce costs.

GM and Honda can differentiate their individually unique stack performance by changing power output. This is done by adding or subtracting more layers or cells to the stack.

The size of the GM-Honda fuel cell stack shown to reporters in January 2017 in Detroit is about the same as today's 1.5-liter four-cylinder engine.

"With the next-generation fuel cell system, GM and Honda are making a dramatic step toward lower cost, higher-volume fuel cell systems," said Charlie Freese, GM executive director of global fuel cell activities.

"Precious metals have been reduced dramatically and a fully cross-functional team is developing advanced manufacturing processes simultaneously with advances in the design. The result is a lower-cost system that is a fraction of the size and mass."[110]

These car makers are serious about the next steps being taken in alternative fuel vehicles.

Electric Vehicles

Battery electric vehicles have been around since the early 1900s. They fell by the wayside due to heavy and expensive battery packs with limited range. All-electric vehicles have leaped back onto the automotive stage over the last few years. Battery technology has advanced as the Federal government and states like California establish the need for zero-emission vehicles to meet environmental goals.

I view all-electric vehicles as a step in the direction of hydrogen fuel cell powered cars, as do Honda, Hyundai and Toyota. Electric vehicle fans like Elon Musk of Tesla disagree.

The entrepreneurial Elon Musk of PayPal, SpaceX, Solar City, Boring and Neuralink fame is leading the 'charge' with very high-

---

[110] http://autoweek.com/article/technology/gm-honda-partner-build-hydrogen-fuel-cells-2020

performance Tesla, Inc. totally electric vehicles. These cars perform on the road in the super car category: 0-60 MPH in the sub-three second range on some models. Electric car motors generate maximum torque at zero RPM, meaning these vehicles can be real rockets off a standing start. Especially when the electric motors are large and the batteries immense. 'Refueling' is still the Achilles heel with all-electric cars. Although charging stations are available, the time to charge is an issue. 'Jumping' charging stations has become a challenge, too: the plug is prematurely pulled on one car to start charging another. This forces the owner of the first vehicle to stay and watch during the charging process which can take hours.

Battery research may turn around this idea that batteries are stepping stones to hydrogen fuel cells. Several companies are working on solid state batteries that reduce charging time to minutes. Production is targeted for 2023. Supplying hydrogen everywhere for fuel cell cars then begins to look like an unnecessary challenge.

But with present battery technology, there are key negative issues with electric vehicles: range anxiety, waiting two hours or longer for a complete charge; followed by short driving range. Longer driving range costs money as Tesla's high-end cars demonstrate.

At the other end of the price point spectrum from Tesla, the Nissan Leaf EPA rating is one hundred seven miles and the 2017 Focus Electric will be over one hundred miles. But at freeway speeds, these cars get much less range than the EPA figures suggest. They're good for short roundtrip commutes on local streets and roads.[111]

---

[111] Caranddriver.com 1-17

The Scream of an Engine

The Toyota Prius, the pioneer electric hybrid vehicle, the Ford Fusion Energi hybrid and the Toyota Camry hybrid, among many others, are not 100% electric. They also carry small to medium-sized gasoline motors to recharge batteries on the go and prevent a driver being stranded. Battery depletion/range anxiety fears are eliminated when you can switch to gasoline. Of course, the hybrids bear the cost and complexity of having two independent propulsion systems aboard.

Yet, battery electric cars are proliferating. Volvo is going all-or-partially electric by 2019. The automaker has long been known for its focus on safety, but it has been putting increasing emphasis on the environment in recent years.

Either way Volvo is moving in the right direction. If hydrogen wins in the long run, Volvo will have the platforms to exchange battery packs for fuel cells and quickly catch up with Honda, Toyota and Hyundai and the rest of the industry presently investing in fuel cells.

Several countries have announced banning gasoline and diesel-powered vehicles to meet their commitments to carbon neutrality under the Paris Agreement. The Paris Agreement is structured under the United Nations Framework Convention on Climate Change – UNFCCC – dealing with greenhouse gas emissions mitigation, adaptation and finance starting in the year 2020. Representatives from 196 countries have adopted the agreement on December 12, 2015, and by June 2017, 153 countries have ratified the document.

France has just signaled the intention to ban gasoline and diesel-powered vehicles by 2040, while the Netherlands and Norway previously said they wanted to get rid of petrol and diesel vehicles by

The Scream of an Engine

2025 and Germany and India announced similar plans by 2030.[112] This signals the end of the internal combustion engine.

Donald Trump has withdrawn the U.S. from the Paris Agreement in 2017, a change that may or may not slow the U.S. on its trajectory toward more fuel efficient, lower carbon footprint vehicles.

As soon as cars appear, races appear. Battery powered open wheel cars are racing in the Formula E series, now three years old. Governing body for the series is the Fédération Internationale de L'Automobile (FIA), so this is serious stuff. The French car maker Renault is on top at the moment, but newcomers like Jaguar are joining the fray.

The design of the electric race cars is aggressive and snarly. Watching these cars compete reminds spectators of slot car racing. Fast and quiet. But without the slot. Recently, the first Formula E race on New York City streets was held in Red Hook, Brooklyn. Perhaps a better description is that these are grown up electric Go-Karts. Formula E cars are fast, hitting 150 MPH, and the races short, forty-five minutes to an hour. Races are close and exciting.

Luxury automakers in general have been announcing major electric-vehicle plans in recent months. BMW will reveal an all-electric version of its 3-Series sedan at the upcoming Frankfurt Motor Show. Mercedes-Benz is planning a new battery-car brand, Mercedes-EQ; and its parent, Daimler AG, in 2017 announced plans to invest more than $700 million to build battery cars in China.

---

[112]http://www.independent.co.uk/environment/france-petrol-diesel-ban-vehicles-cars-2040-a7826831.html

The Scream of an Engine

Gasoline

Gasoline won the battle with alcohol as a vehicle fuel soon after the beginning of the twentieth century. Additives such as lead, which helped gasoline win by allowing increased compression ratios and power, have been removed. Higher octane fuels, good for more power and engine efficiency, have been dummied down to three available octanes in the U.S.: 87, 89 and 91.

Demand for gasoline will peak around the mid-2030s as the new battery electric/hydrogen model takes the place of the internal combustion engine. Perhaps sooner.

Now that top performance engines like the Dodge Challenger SRT Demon deliver over 800 BHP out of the factory, there is sense in bringing back higher-octane fuels which may improve fuel economy and efficiency of large capacity, powerful V-8 or V-12 engines.

I'd say, given our global situation, this is a good example of too little, too late.

As automakers ramped up the horsepower wars of the 1960s, oil companies stepped up to the plate to produce fuel that could keep high-compression engines from blowing up pistons. Eventually, the big-engine fun stopped and the Clean Air Act, outlandish insurance premiums and an oil crisis killed the demand for 100-plus octane fuel at local pumps. This forced performance enthusiasts to either hunt for 100-plus octane race gas or detune their cars to run on 91-octane.

I splashed a little 100+-octane gasoline into my Focus SVT at Ford's SVT Owner's Association races at Buttonwillow, CA in 2004. Couldn't detect much difference. Car went well no matter what I did.

The *Detroit Free Press* reports automakers are working with oil companies to bring back super premium fuels. This will enable automakers to introduce engines with higher turbo and supercharger boost pressures and compression ratios. Higher compression ratios and more boost will make engines more efficient, limited by the fuel's resistance to detonation. For enthusiasts who get to own Dodge's new Demon, they would be able to generate 840 BHP on 100-plus octane gas compared with today's 808 BHP on 91-octane.[113]

Now that difference might be detectable.

Alcohol

Last, but not least in the way of changes, is ethanol. Ethanol, from corn or other biomass like sugar cane, is added to gasoline to reduce emissions of carbon dioxide.

It works, but not so well on sixty-year old and older cars, which have gasoline line seals that aren't compatible with alcohol and degrade quickly. On older cars, there are other issues as well.

An ethanol mixture of 10% with gasoline at 90%, E10, is widely available today. In 2017, the EPA has mandated more total alcohol in transportation fuels, so E15 to E85 are increasingly available to purchase.

Approved by the Environmental Protection Agency in June 2012, E15 is now available in about five hundred gas stations in the United States, largely in the upper Midwest, according to the Department of Energy's Alternative Fuels Data Center. About 3,200

---

[113]http://autoweek.com/article/technology/rejoice-good-gas-might-be-coming-back#ixzz4gF1cTdsf, May 1, 2017

The Scream of an Engine

stations sell E85 over a wider geographic distribution. In its final numbers for 2017, the EPA mandated 19.28 billion gallons of ethanol be blended into the nation's fuel supply, making up about 10.7 percent of the total vehicle fuel supply.[114]

Diesels

Rudolf Christian Karl Diesel was a German inventor, born in Paris from where his family was exiled to London during the 1870 Franco-German war.

His training in mechanical engineering led to invention of the diesel engine which he patented in 1892. He later published a book on the engine and by 1897, with funding from Krupp and Maschinenfabrik in Augsburg, built a single cylinder, 25 BHP working model. Diesel disappeared off the deck of a mail ship crossing to London in 1913, presumably drowning, but a mystery to this day.

European gearheads, fans and practical owners who value economy favor diesels. The diesel offers more torque at lower speeds and greater fuel economy compared with gasoline powered engines.

Automotive diesels have never significantly caught on in the U.S. They're favored here in heavy trucks. Now diesels have suffered two more blows: Volkswagen's 'Dieselgate' points out the difficulty of meeting present emission standards with diesels. In addition, recent tests have confirmed that fine particulate matter in diesel exhaust contributes to lung cancer.[115]

---

[114] Hemings.com, March 23, 2017
[115] Wikipedia, Concerns Regarding Particulates, 1-17

The Scream of an Engine

Diesel is not the only carcinogenic vehicle fuel: ethanol, the key ingredient in wine, rum and scotch is also listed as a Group 1 carcinogen by the IARC and the also the FDA.[116] Of course, this requires that you, not your car, drink the ethanol.

By 2030, less than a decade and a half away, the internal combustion engine we know so well today will be a greatly diminished commodity in new cars, SUVs and light trucks.

As will, sadly, the scream of an engine.

With these major shifts in automotive culture occurring globally, I believe there is one part of car culture that will not change: ownership of at least one classic car, kept in the garage at home, insured, and driven on weekends or for special occasions, if no longer to work.

That's certainly the case for me. The passion for these earlier internal combustion vehicles will never be extinguished in gearheads' hearts.

Automakers are concerned about this issue. These changes are radical. Which one or ones should they pursue? Toyota's President, Akio Toyoda, is recently dealing with falling profits in addition to all the industry changes predicted.

After driving an electrified version of a 1986 model he is credited with designing originally, Toyoda didn't like it. The most recent two fiscal quarters for Toyota resulted in the first back-to-back net profit decline in more than twenty years for the company founded by Toyoda's grandfather.

---

[116] International Agency for Research on Cancer, Wikipedia, 1-17

Toyota Motor Corp. and all automobile manufacturers find themselves struggling to mold conventional ideas about what a car should be into the new reality of zero emissions, autonomous driving and on-the-go connectivity.

After expressing negative feelings about driving the electric '86 Toyota, he added, 'What I meant was, for an OEM manufacturer, you're choking yourself. It is commoditizing your vehicle,' Toyoda said of the proposition of next-generation battery-powered cars.

'I feel a strong sense of crisis' he said, 'about whether or not we're actually executing car-making from the perspective of the customer in all Toyota workplaces, from development, production, procurement and sales, all the way to administrative divisions.[117]

Ford feels the same sense of crisis, as they've replaced President and Chief Executive Officer Mark Fields with Jim Hackett in May 2017, amid falling stock price and lower earnings, just like Toyota. Jim Hackett, who has overseen Ford's efforts on autonomous vehicles as chairman of Ford Smart Mobility, replaces Fields.

Don't feel bad for Mark: Detroit Free Press says Bloomberg estimates his termination package at $57.5 million after Field's thirty-year career at Ford ends.[118]

---

[117] Autoweek.com, May 15, 2017
[118] Detroit Free Press, May 25, 2017

Appendix II. Museums

While museums have the potential to fire the imagination of youngsters, turning them into wild, gearhead-like things, I missed that phase growing up. Museums have advanced mightily since I was a ten-year old. They can be found everywhere today. They do have a significant mission in educating the public as well as next generation gearheads about the past successes and failures of the automotive industry.

These are stories about my favorites. The first two are in San Diego, CA where I lived for thirty-eight years.

San Diego Automotive Museum

Many visits over the years convinced me that the San Diego Automotive Museum – SDAM - in Balboa Park was a diamond in the rough. I could do something to help.

I met the Director, Bob Swanson, and asked him to consider me for a position on the Board of Directors. I would help raise funds to spruce up the Museum. He backed my candidacy and in 2006 I was elected to the Board.

In an open Board meeting, one of the long-time directors, also Board Treasurer, said there was no money in San Diego for SDAM. That hole had been dug and the well was dry.

We openly disagreed.

As we approached the 20th Anniversary of the Museum in 2008, I suggested that a full time Development Director would improve our chances of making this a banner year for fund raising. The Board asked me to take the job for a year.

The Scream of an Engine

I said I would but with the condition that a fund-raising consultant be hired to assist and guide the efforts. We interviewed several firms and the Board hired Cliff Underwood & Associates, an experienced San Diego firm. I'd worked with Cliff previously raising a million dollars to renovate the St. James Hall for my church, St. James by the Sea in La Jolla. This enabled a complete renovation of the landmark building once operated for the USO during World War II, now owned by St. James.

San Diego Automotive Museum, Balboa Park, San Diego, CA, greeting by Luigi, the yellow Fiat 500. 2008

The San Diego Automotive Museum had raised $150K in 2007.

In 2008, we raised $300K, a nice increase but falling far short of our aggressive goals. The Board abandoned the effort for 2009 considering the catastrophic recession that gripped the nation which threatened every fund-raising campaign in America.

No amount of pushing or pulling in 2009 would make a difference, in my opinion. Also, it's clear that fund raising is a long-term process, developing and cultivating donor lists, building programs, building relationships, expanding programs. And attracting large donors. The Peterson Museum in Los Angeles has been sustained by large gifts from Margie Peterson and the Margie and Robert E. Peterson Foundation, including a founding gift of $25 million and another $100 million through 2011.[119]

I was right. The big bucks are out there.

The San Diego Automotive Museum has an eclectic collection of vehicles, the most famous of which is Louie Mattar's 1947 Cadillac. Mattar built this car to be a recreational vehicle allowing him to tour the entire U.S., which he did. In 1952, he and two other men established a cross-country endurance record by driving the Cadillac from San Diego to New York and back without stopping. Their trip totaled 6,320 miles and required refueling from a moving gas truck three times.

To achieve this feat, Mattar added a refrigerator, a chemical toilet, an ironing board, a medicine cabinet, and a kitchen sink. These appliances are stored under the backseat cushions. Up front, in addition to the many switches and dials surrounding the dashboard, are a nationwide mobile telephone, a tape recorder, a bar and a public-address system for communicating with those on the outside of the car. On the

---

[119] https://www.philanthropy.com/article/100-Million-Donation-Made-to/158527

The Scream of an Engine

right running board is a shower and at the rear taillight is a drinking fountain. Mattar developed a unique flat tire changing system that allowed a flat tire to be changed while the car was being driven at 30 MPH down the highway.

That's how he made it non-stop across the U.S. and back.

But the collection is far more than this Cadillac.

It also includes special shows that emphasize interesting historical events, like the Plank Road exhibit of the early 20th century showing how roads were built across the sands of southwestern deserts, especially Imperial County, CA, when Col. Ed Fletcher encouraged San Diego investors to beat Los Angeles in making a road to Phoenix, AZ. The San Diego-Phoenix plank road started in Holtville, CA in February 1915.

Other special shows at the San Diego Automotive Museum have included a nearly all-Ferrari show for the 20th Anniversary celebration in 2008, a Low Rider show and motorcycle shows on multiple occasions.

The permanent collection of vehicles on display include a 1909 International Harvester, a 1914 Model T Ford shown in the Plank Road exhibit, a 1922 Mack Water Truck located in front of the Museum, a 1928 barn find Studebaker Coupé, a 1929 L-29 Cord Brougham, and more recently, a 1953 Jaguar XK 120, a 1960 Alfa Romeo coupé and a unique 1966 Bizzarrini P538 with a 4-liter V-12 engine and a five-speed transaxle. Only a handful of these striking Bizzarrini Italian cars were built, with both V-8 and V-12 engines, before bankruptcy claimed the company.

The Scream of an Engine

In the library, volunteers organize and present an impressive collection of artifacts including early automotive magazines and newspapers, model cars, photographs, design documents and other automobilia.

As a result, this Museum exceeds 100,000 visitors every year in beautiful Balboa Park, San Diego, CA.

Evans Garage

The Evans family started a museum of objects that they've collected over the years. This includes automobiles. Friend Bill Evans, Cornell Hotel School '83, inherited responsibility for the Museum from his Dad, William Evans, Sr. who assembled the original collection.[120]

I arranged to take the Alfa Romeo Owners Clubs of San Diego and Southern California for a tour of the Evans Garage. Groups are scheduled and reserved well in advance. Our October 17, 2009 visit to the facility at 4953 Pacific Highway, San Diego, CA 92110 was set for from 11 AM to 2 PM. The cost was $35/person including a luncheon catered by the Evans hotels.

The Evans Garage was created in 1983 by William Evans, Sr., a San Diego hotelier whose properties now include the Bahia and Catamaran Hotels on Mission Bay, and Torrey Pines Lodge by the famous golf course which overlooks the Pacific Ocean.

Bill Evans mentioned to me recently that the family collection offers automobiles from 1886 through 1962, an early fire engine, as well as antique clothing, furniture, stained glass windows, and Persian

---

[120] This story originally appeared in *Romeo and Giulietta*

The Scream of an Engine

carpets gathered by the family over many years. Bill's favorites for our visit are the blue 1911 Bianchi of which only nine were built, the white 1911 Blitzen Benz which the Evans Garage built from new old stock with the blessing of the Mercedes Benz factory, and the red 1913 Isotta Fraschini which raced at the Indianapolis 500 and is in excellent but unrestored condition. Red, white and blue: don't miss these gems.

The Blitzen Benz has since been sold to another museum and replaced with an Alfa Romeo 6C 2500 SS.

The Bianchi on display was built for an Italian Army general. On first sight, this car leaps out as a work of art. The lines of the body, the brass headlamps, and the detailed restoration on this car are exceptional. Bianchi was founded in 1885 as a bicycle manufacturer. Automobile design was started in 1899. The car brand went through many evolutions but finally ended in 1995 while part of the Fiat group. But the bicycle group still thrives: everything from the Bianchi Oltre XR.4 CV extreme racing bike to the Impulso S-Sport 105 sport/fitness bike. With hundreds of models in between.

The Isotta Fraschini also comes with a pedigree. The company was formed by two men, Isotta and Fraschini, in 1900 in Milan, Italy. The innovative company is credited with the first eight-cylinder engine. The cars were raced by such notables as Enzo Ferrari and Alfieri Maserati. The splendid example on display for our tour raced at Indy. The last Isotta Fraschini rolled off the factory floor in 1949.

During our visit to the Evans Garage, Bill Evans was in Elba, Italy driving the supercharged Alfa Romeo 8C 2300 that won Le Mans in 1934. Alfas won at Le Mans in 1931, 1932, 1933, and 1934, finishing a close second in 1935.

The Scream of an Engine

The tour of a private collection like this attracted non-Alfa Club members, including past Commodore of the San Diego Yacht Club, Whitey Cable, who drives a Porsche, and other friends of Alfa club members.

This was one memorable day.

Nethercutt Museum

The San Diego Automotive Museum arranged a bus trip to the Nethercutt, a beautiful museum with hours of cars and other memorabilia to soak up. We travelled there on November 11, 2007, Armistice Day, which celebrates the end of World War I.

During the journey, I read the poem *In Flanders Fields* at 11 AM sharp. Later, two Canadians on the trip with us said they found the reading very emotional, remembering how they celebrate the formal ending of hostilities on the 11th hour of the 11th day of the 11th month in Canada and throughout the Commonwealth every year.

In Flanders Fields was written by Canadian Lieutenant Colonel John McRae on the death of a soldier, a friend, in May 1915. The poem was first published by *Punch* in December that year. McCrae contracted pneumonia and died at the hospital in Wimereux, Belgium, in January 1918, where he's buried. The Armistice ending World War I was signed that November 1918.

The Nethercutt Museum is built from the Merle Nethercutt Norman Cosmetics Co. fortune. I can't think of a better way to spend money.

The cars on display at the Museum aren't all automobiles: there is a marvelously restored 1912 green and maroon Pullman railroad car

The Scream of an Engine

on display outside, 'pulled' by a 1937 Canadian Pacific Royal Hudson Locomotive, crisp in its royal maroon colors with brushed stainless steel and black accents.

We assembled in the Lower Salon inside to start our guided tour. This salon is a microcosm of the collection. There are twenty-five automobiles dating from the early 1900's up till the late 1940's. Also on display are nickelodeons, music boxes, David Winter Cottages, dolls, coins, and crystal figurines.

The Grand Salon offers marble floors and columns, crystal chandeliers and ornately painted ceilings. Unusual in my experience is that many of vehicles are displayed on attractive plush carpeting. On display were thirty automobiles from before World War I and through the War to much more recent dates. Just a few of the cars: the 1909 Gobron-Brille Tourer with huge brass lamps out front; several Duesenbergs including a 1936 Roadster, first car in the collection, purchased in 1956 by J.B. Nethercutt, Merle's nephew and business partner; and Cadillac, Isotta-Fraschini, Delahaye, Minerva, Renault and Maybach cars. The elegance of the Duesenbergs and the flowing lines of the Delahaye stood out for me.

On the mezzanine, there's a huge display of radiator ornaments and strangely, eighteenth and nineteenth century French furniture. All in all, this is a dazzling way to spend a few hours and I highly recommend a visit to these Sylmar, CA facilities outside Los Angeles.

Peterson Museum

The Peterson has the reputation for being one of the best museums in the country, with reason. I've visited many times. This is a huge museum with over 100,000 square feet of space, but is so much more than a collection of vehicles: it's about art, organization of

The Scream of an Engine

automotive themes, and money spent on maintaining exhibits and their contents in superior condition.

The Museum is relatively new, founded by Robert Peterson, the magazine publisher, in 1994. Large gifts from the Margie and Robert E. Peterson Foundation totaled $125 million through 2015 which have contributed to upgraded and improved facilities and exhibits. I've yet to see all the effects of these major capital infusions.

As you'd expect in a Los Angeles museum, a display of cars from noteworthy movies are featured. There's a Batmobile, the Ferrari 308 from Magnum P.I., a DeLorean from *Back to the Future* and the Thunderbird featured in *Thelma and Louise*.

Among recent exhibits was *Jaguar's Pursuit of Speed: 100 to 220*, in the Chuck Wegner Family Gallery. Featured were Steve McQueen's 1956 XKSS, a 1937 SS100 and the 1992 XJ 220 Supercar.

The *Eagles Have Landed* exhibit displays eleven of Dan Gurney's All American Racers' beautiful race car projects, from the first Eagle in 1966 through a Can Am winner to the 1999 CART Champ Car competitor.

The Peterson has established a partnership with Disney/Pixar called The *Cars* Mechanical Institute, inspired by the animated film. Visitors learn through interactive stations the mechanical systems that make cars work. They can also paint and personalize virtual cars as well as trace and color their own movie cars. Though an iPad app called *CARSpad*, a virtual race car can be built to compete with Lightning McQueen's lap times.

There is so much to do in this Museum that those interested should plan on coming early and often.

The Scream of an Engine

BMW Automotive Museum

I traveled to Munich, Germany on business for years, bringing back Hümmel figurines for my wife, Dirndls and Lederhosen for the kids and the unique Bavarian wax candles and intricate and tiny Z-gauge train sets, the latter ostensibly for my two-year old son. Never bought a Porsche. Weekends in Germany provided downhill and cross-country ski breaks in the German Alps and especially in Leutasch, Austria, where my business partners and I skied between each Gasthaus, often stopping along the way for another large Pils and more apple strudel.

And trips to museums. Unlike a later visit to the Alfa Romeo Museum in Arese, north of Milan, Italy, the BMW Museum was open when I arrived.

The BMW Museum, opened to the public in 1973 just five years before my first visit to Munich, is a gem known as 'the salad bowl.' Located close to the Olympic Park, its unique design by Austrian architect Karl Swanzer offers a circular white building with a ramp on the outside wall to walk between floors. The structure is largest at the top and smallest at the bottom and looks like a salad bowl from outside. An elevator whisks visitors to the top floor for viewing down into the Museum. One of the exhibits was an authentic-looking battle scene from World War II detailing BMW's contribution to the war effort. The views through the museum are futuristic with swooping curves and lots of light.

And the history of BMW's wonderful machines and automobiles, my personal favorite the BMW 507. The 507 was an artistic but not commercial success due to high manufacturing costs and marketing price which resulted in limited sales volumes. Only two hundred and fifty-two were built from 1956-1959. But with the 3.2-liter 150 BHP V-8, ZF four speed transmission, Alfin brakes on the early

The Scream of an Engine

models and the aluminum body, these were fine pieces of work. Elvis Presley bought two of them.

The Museum is located next to the BMW administration building which was developed from 1968 to 1972. The admin building looks like four towers joined in the middle. The futuristic structure consists of twenty-two occupied floors. The building can be seen from miles around and suggests BMW is one advanced car company.

Jaguar Heritage Trust Museum

I've visited this Museum twice while it was at Browns Lane in Coventry, England, and under the Jaguar Daimler name. However, the need for more space and other factors caused Jaguar to move this treasure trove of classic Jaguars to two locations, neither of which I've had the chance to visit yet: the Coventry Transport Museum in the center of Coventry, and the British Motor Museum at Gaydon, Warwickshire.

The trick today is to know where the cars you want to see are located. This issue is compounded because the vehicles are often out on display throughout England and elsewhere, especially in the summer. Check the website or call before going.

I visited in the 1970s and again in the late 1990s. This was a time when a tour of the nearby Jaguar factory included talking with craftsmen assembling by hand, for example, the leather boot for the gearshift lever. On one trip to the factory I was offered and accepted leftover cuttings from the leather seats and walnut veneer for the dashboard, anticipating I too would soon own one of these cars. These pieces gave me an idea of what was available to order when choosing a car's interior. I doubt that this personal touch for visitors continues.

The Scream of an Engine

At the time of my visits, just standing beside the Austin Seven Swallow, the SS 100, the XK 120, C-Type and D-Type, the XK 180 – a one off sports car design - and later cars was a genuine thrill. Enough to make me want to go back again. And again.

Beaulieu Museum

Several visits to the Beaulieu Museum in New Forest, Hampshire, England, have impressed me with English ingenuity. Beaulieu means 'beautiful area' or 'friend you know' in English: both apply to this museum.

The Brits have built lots of fine machinery which is on display here. Even the displays are ingenious, with exhibit floors angled at thirty degrees, the cars secured properly so they don't fall off.

Like the Petersen in Los Angeles does for Hollywood, one exhibit at Beaulieu features vehicles that have been in English movies like the Mini in the comedy *Mr. Bean*, Del Boy's Reliant Van from the comedy series *Fools and Horses,* the Jaguar XKR from the James Bond film *Die Another Day* and the `flying` Ford Anglia from *Harry Potter and the Chamber of Secrets.*

There are over two hundred and eighty vehicles at Beaulieu, many restored, all well maintained. Especially impressive to me are the Formula 1 and sports racing cars on steeply angled floor displays, but there is much more, like period 'petrol' stations with back room workshops. The 4.5-liter 1930 supercharged Bentley is here, as is an American 1935 Auburn 851 supercharged Boattail Speedster. The latter offered the 320 BHP straight eight engine that could push 125 MPH.

The Thirties, Fifties and Sixties offered such exciting motor vehicles.

The Scream of an Engine

The Montagu Mansion shows how the Montagu family, owners of the properties, have lived in this beautiful part of the world in grace and elegance. On the grounds, what's left of the eight-hundred-year old monastery, Beaulieu Abbey – founded by King John in 1203 CE and then known as The Abbey Church of St Mary - can be toured. Parliament in 1534 granted King Henry VIII the position of Supreme Head of the Church of England, severing the relationship to the Roman Catholic Church. Henry then ordered all two hundred sixty English monasteries, including Beaulieu, be dissolved, their assets and income accruing to the King thereafter. Stories abound that this monastery is haunted.[121]

An example of Beaulieu's angled display expertise: Silk Cut Jaguar XJR-9LM, 7.0-Liter V-12, raced to wins at Le Mans in 1988 and again in 1990 updated as an XJR-12, by Tom Walkinshaw's independent racing team, TWR

Every time I get close to Beaulieu, in southern England east of coastal Bournemouth, I find a reason to return, as I did in September 2017. To be honest, the entry fees have become too expensive – 23.75 pounds Sterling purchased on day of entry for seniors - and the emphasis here is on showmanship as much as on the cars. But the place was once

---

[121] Wikipedia, July 2017

again packed, the elevated train and beautiful grounds drawing like no other museum.

Brooklands Museum

Great Britain has just allocated funds to restore portions of the Brooklands race track, the oldest closed paved circuit in the world, dating to 1907. Fred Puhn's research indicates the Lakeside Speedway east of San Diego, CA, was completed a few months earlier, but was a dirt oval. But Brooklands is as much about airplanes as cars. Over 18,600 new airplanes were built from 1908 through 1987 at Brooklands. The grounds today are far broader than just a race track overgrown with weeds, a banked cement roadway decaying.

There's also an important museum and the Concorde.

The Concorde supersonic airliner was a joint venture between Great Britain and France. The first UK meeting took place at Brooklands Museum. This amazing supersonic passenger jet craft took the resources of two nations to design, build and fly. In her twenty-seven years of passenger service, over 2.5 million people flew on Concorde. A flight from London Heathrow to New York City took three hours compared with the usual eight hours by subsonic commercial jet liner. Cost a lot more, too.

Brooklands offers her own Concorde on display and a Concorde flight simulator. There's also a Formula 1 simulator for playing, and a simulated trip around the Le Mans, France race track in a D-Type Jaguar, Mike Hawthorn driving.

The photos of the Museum below were taken in September 2017.

The Scream of an Engine

Looking west into the famous Brooklands thirty-degree banking, north side of the 1907 race track

Brooklands Members House. One of many buildings restored or partially restored on site. On this day, a 1930 Bentley 4 1/2-liter 'daily driver' is parked by the front door, like ones raced at Brooklands

Beautifully restored Concorde from beneath the droop nose cockpit that swivels down 12.5 degrees for visibility during landing. The plane flew over Mach 2 – 1335 MPH – on commercial flights and cost $7,995 a ticket for flying from London to New York

The Brooklands Concorde is the first plane to fly one hundred passengers at Mach 2. She was active as a development airplane and sales promotional plane from February 13, 1974 through Christmas Eve 1981. Brooklands obtained this aircraft in 2004 and put her through a two-year renovation to bring her back to her former glory. She was opened to the public on July 26, 2006.

But that's only one of many reasons to visit Brooklands, located about an hour and a half's drive southwest of London.

Brooklands was heavily bombed by the Luftwaffe in 1940 and is the site from which the famous Dam Busters flew their 'bouncing bombs' mission over Germany in May 1943.

The Scream of an Engine

Surprisingly, the Museum didn't open regularly until 1991. It occupies thirty acres of the Brooklands original automobile racing site. The Museum encompasses the London Bus Museum, aircraft like the replica Sopwith Camel and cars like the 24-liter Napier-Railton shown below. The Napier-Railton was built at Brooklands for John Cobb in 1933. It still holds the Brooklands lap record at 143.33 MPH. The cars are mostly unrestored but well maintained. Racers like Malcolm Campbell maintained garages at Brooklands where they worked on their racing projects. Campbell, who held many land speed records, also raced at Brooklands over three hundred times, more than anyone else.

24-liter 1933 silver Napier-Railton is the Brooklands lap record holder at 143.44 MPH since 1935. The Napier Lion W 12 airplane engine makes 580 BHP which pushes the car to 168 MPH

The Scream of an Engine

John Cobb commented on the steep banking at the Brooklands track, 'This was like trying to see how far I could lean out of a ninth-floor window without falling out.'[122]

This museum, unpretentious as it is, should be a must on anyone's bucket list.

Musee Automobile de la Sarthe, Musee Des 24 Heures

Although I visited the Le Mans Museum in 1994, located within the famous Sarthe, France circuit, I was not as impressed as I expected to be, partly because the emphasis was on French cars which I didn't know much about. I do now. The Deutsch-Bonnet and Panhard cars on display were actually very successful racing at Le Mans in the Index of Performance classification, which gave the benefit to small engined cars.

The Panhard & Levassor entry won the Index of Performance at Le Mans in 1953 running in the 750cc class. Deutsch-Bonnet won the Index of Performance in 1954 and 1956 running in the 750cc class. Small engines, high efficiency. These cars are on display in the Museum.

The Matra-Simca French cars won overall at Le Mans in 1972, 1973 and 1974. The Renault Alpines on display were even more impressive and often much faster on the track than the competition. The Renault Alpine A442B won overall at Le Mans in 1978. The Group 6 car employed a 2-liter V-6. Lately, the French Peugeot has surged to the front of the grid at Le Mans and has won in 1992, 1993 and again in

---

[122]http://www.motorsportmagazine.com/archive/article/july-1997/50/napier-railton which says first-floor in the quote. Thrust SSC – Mach 1 Club on the web says ninth-floor. I use ninth. Scarier.

2009. Other French automobile overall winners include Delahaye, Bugatti and Talbot-Lago. A storied lot to say the least.

Can't blame the French museums for emphasizing the home team. Today you can see Nissan race cars, Ferraris, Corvettes, Lotus 11 and Porsche on display.

Now I arrive at several museums on my bucket list that I've not yet visited.

REVS Institute

The REVS Institute commenced operations in 2009. Prior to that, C. Miles Collier was active in SCCA road racing in a Porsche Speedster and had commenced his own car collection. The prior generation Colliers, Sam and Miles who were both Yale University graduates, helped establish sports car racing in the U.S. in the 1930s and later helped found the Sports Car Club of America.

The Collier family were close friends with Briggs Cunningham. In 1986, this-generation Miles Collier purchased the Cunningham collection in Costa Mesa, CA and combined it with the Collier Museum in Naples, FL. I would feel right at home since I visited the Cunningham portion of the collection in the late Seventies and loved it.

But the current Miles Collier feels there is a bigger mission than just collecting the hardware at the Institute: *'Our job as conservators of the past is to present historic objects in a way that maximizes their*

The Scream of an Engine

documentary value, that is, as exemplars of their most representative configuration in period.'[123]

The REVS Institutes' academic mission was bolstered in 2011 by the acquisition of the Ludvigsen Library. Karl Ludvigsen, a former General Motors consultant and past editor of *Car and Driver* and *Motor Trend* magazines, had assembled a vast library with over 7,000 automotive books, 300,000 photographs and hundreds of research files.

Also in 2011, the Institute began an affiliation with Stanford University known as The Revs Program. This established a new transdisciplinary field connecting the past, present and future of the automobile. The Revs Program at Stanford fosters a wide ranging academic focus on the automobile.

Hearst Publishing Corporation transferred its entire archive of *Road & Track* magazine to The Revs Program which will preserve and digitize the collection for future research and make its information available to the public.[124]

The Collier Collection at the REVS Institute in Naples, FL includes an 1896 Panhard & Levassor automobile, a 1912 Hispano Suiza T 15, a comprehensive collection of Porsche racing cars from the Fifties, Sixties and Seventies, a 1955 Lancia D50 Formula 1 car, a 1958 Vanwall Formula 1 car – one of the prettiest race cars ever made in my opinion, and in all, over one hundred magnificent cars on display.

A collection worth visiting.

---

[123] REVS Institute Website, https://revsinstitute.org/about-the-institute/history/
[124] Ibid.

The Scream of an Engine

Simeone Foundation Automotive Museum

This Philadelphia, PA collection of racing automobiles was started by Dr. Frederick Simeone over fifty years ago, but the Museum itself didn't open until 2008. The Museum is guided by the theme, "The Spirit of Competition." The Museum contains over sixty-five historically significant cars including Ferrari, Alfa Romeo, Bugatti, Mercedes, Jaguar, Bentley, Porsche, Aston Martin, Corvette and Ford.

A section of the Museum's Archives contains personal correspondence between Briggs Cunningham and Miles Collier, one of which contains the quote, "Why can't we race in America like they do over in Europe?" The pair did by forming the Automobile Racing Club of America – ARCA - and racing primarily European sports cars on roads around their country estates. Two of the cars that competed in ARCA races and included in the collection and are largely unrestored.

Le Mans race competitors are featured in the collection. Looking down the row of these Le Mans contestants, including Alfa Romeo from the Thirties, Ferrari from the Fifties and Porsche from the Seventies, it becomes obvious that technology change has driven the design of the race cars.

Two Alfa Romeos on display competed at the famed Brooklands banked race track in England, a 1925 Alfa Romeo RLSS and a 1933 Alfa Romeo 8C 2300 Mille Miglia Spyder. Two Sebring, FL competitors, a 1952 Jaguar XK 120 C and a 1956 D-Type are on display. Two Le Mans competitors are on display, a 1966 Ford GT 40 Mark II and a 1967 Ford Mark IV. Visitors learn about the famous tracks and see the specific cars that raced on those venues.

This would be a fun museum for me.

The Scream of an Engine

Henry Ford Museum/Henry Ford Museum of American Innovation

Since Ford cars are a significant part of my culture, I simply must visit this Museum, started in 1929 and opened to the public in 1933. In 2017, the Museum announced a change in name from Henry Ford Museum to Henry Ford Museum of American Innovation.

The Museum, including the Greenfield Village and the Ford Rouge Factory, contains a collection of three hundred years of American innovation, including the beginning of the modern automobile industry inspired by Henry Ford's own manufacturing innovations.

This Museum is not all about cars. Not many of us were around when Ford built the 6,000th B-24 Bomber at the Willow Run Plant on September 9, 1944. Now that part of the history of Ford would be worth seeing.

But it is also about cars. When the Ford V-8 went into production in 1932, Henry Ford revolutionized the automobile market. The engine was the first V-8 light enough and cheap enough to power an inexpensive car like a Ford. The secret was casting the cylinder block in one-piece, widespread practice today. I'd like to see that V-8 Engine No.1, 221 cubic inches, 65 BHP at 3400 RPM.

And of course, there is an immense collection of Ford cars. And an education section among the best in the country. In 2012, I was fortunate to be able to introduce the educational staff at the National Sailing Hall of Fame, Annapolis, MD, to the Ford educational system for Science, Technology, Engineering and Mathematics - STEM. In my opinion, Ford had developed the best lesson plans to introduce these ideas to high school students. The same techniques could now be applied to teaching STEM courses through use of sailing principles.

The Scream of an Engine

Suggested Reading

The following books are from my personal library. It's a partial list, all favorites, used to help research *The Scream of an Engine*.

1. *Jaguar, The Sporting Heritage*, Paul Skilleter in association with the Jaguar Daimler Heritage Trust, Virgin Publishing Ltd., London, 2000. Strong on detail, excellent photos
2. *Jaguars in Competition*, Chris Harvey, Osprey Publishing, Ltd., London, 1971. Most exciting, many excellent photos I missed at the time
3. *Road & Track Jaguar Road Tests*, can be purchased as a package from R & T
4. *Alfa Romeo-Milano*, Michael Frostick, Dalton Watson, Ltd., London, 1976
5. *Road & Track on Alfa Romeo, 1964-1970*, Brooklands Books, Hong Kong, 1970
6. *Automobile Quarterly* - Ralph Stein: *Alfa Remembered*; Cullen Thomas: *The Collector's Alfa Romeo*; Pat Braden: *Viva Alfa!*; Eric Nielssen: Briggs Cunningham and the Cars He Built, Volume III, No. 4, New York, 1965
7. *GT 40, An Individual History and Race Record*, Ronnie Spain, Motorbooks International, St. Paul, MN, 2003
8. *Powered by SVT, Celebrating a Decade of Ford Performance*, Jim Campisano, Worzalla, USA, 2003. For anyone who's ever driven an SVT
9. *Dan Gurney's Eagle Racing Cars*, John Zimmerman, David Bull Publishing, Phoenix, AZ, 2007. This story about an American icon is well told. Photos excellent, too
10. *Maserati*, Bruno Alfieri, Editor, Two Volumes, Automobilia Societa, Milano, Italia, 1984. Substantial detail, many early photos, excellent reference

The Scream of an Engine

11. *Murray Walker's Formula One Heroes*, Murray Walker and Simon Taylor, Virgin Publishing, Ltd., London, 2000. Best photos, ever. This guy knows. He was there
12. *100 Years of Grand Prix*, Trevor Legate, Touchstone Books Ltd., Sutton Valence, Kent, UK, 2006. Details from the past
13. *The Last Open Road*, Burt S. Levy, Think Fast Ink, Oak Park, ILL, 1994. The excitement of post-World War II sports cars and racing arriving in the U.S., a fictional must-read for Fifties fans and gearheads
14. *The Technique of Motor Racing*, Piero Taruffi, Robert Bentley, Inc., Cambridge, MA, 1971. Essential for budding race car drivers
15. *Driving in Competition*, Alan Johnson, 1973, 1976 and earlier editions. Essential reading from a four-time SCCA National Champion who has much to say about racing and learning to do it well
16. *The Jaguar E-Type*, Paul Skilleter, Motor Racing Publications, Ltd., London, 1979. About one of the many cars I almost bought
17. *Great Marques: Jaguar*, Chris Harvey, Octopus Books, Ltd., London, 1982
18. *Great British Marques, Jaguar: The Complete Story*, Octane Magazine, 2008. Well done, facts in abundance
19. *Alfa Romeo Argentina,* Christián Bertschi and Estanislao Iacona, Whitefly, Buenos Aires, Argentina, 2005. The rich history of racing and older Alfa Romeo cars in Argentina through the 1970s with serial number detail. Solid photos

Made in the USA
Middletown, DE
29 September 2019